The Biblical Survival Manual

Scriptural References for Victorious Living

Compiled by
Carolyn J. Baker

The Biblical Survival Manual
by Carolyn J. Baker

Printed in the United States of America

ISBN 1-591609-38-0

Previously distributed as "The Biblical Survival Manual for the Last Day Believer."

Cover Design by Tony L. Russ

Xulon Press
www.XulonPress.com

Xulon Press books are available in bookstores everywhere, and on the Web at www.XulonPress.com.

Table of Contents

III. Our Daily Walk as Believers

Part I

Spiritual Food For Believers

Chapter 1

Faith in God & His Word

A. References to Faith in Scripture

II Chronicles 20:20

. . . Believe in the Lord your God, so shall ye be established; believe in His prophets, so shall ye prosper.

Habakkuk 2:4

Behold, his soul which is lifted up is not upright in him: **but the just shall live by his faith.**

Matthew 17:20

. . . If ye have **faith as a grain of mustard seed**, ye shall say unto this mountain, **Remove hence to yonder place; and it shall remove; and nothing shall be impossible unto you.**

Matthew 21:21-22

Jesus answered and said unto them, Verily I say unto you, **If you have faith, and doubt not**, ye shall not only do this which is done to the fig tree, **but also if ye shall say** unto this mountain, Be thou removed, and be thou cast into the sea; **it shall be done. And all things, whatsoever ye shall ask in prayer, believing, ye shall receive.**

Mark 5:36

As soon as Jesus heard the word that was spoken, He saith unto the ruler of the synagogue, **Be not afraid, only believe.**

Mark 11:22-24

And Jesus answering saith unto them, **Have faith in God.**

For verily I say unto you, **That whosoever shall say** unto this mountain, Be thou removed, and be thou cast into the sea; **and shall not doubt in his heart, but shall believe that those things which he saith shall come to pass; he shall have whatsoever he saith.**

Therefore I say unto you, **What things soever ye desire, when ye pray, believe that ye receive them, and ye shall have them.**

Luke 1:45

And **blessed is she that believed**: for there shall be a performance of those things which were told her from the Lord.

Luke 12:29

And seek not ye what ye shall eat, or what ye shall drink, **neither be ye of doubtful mind.**

Luke 17:5-6

And the apostles said unto the Lord, **Increase our faith.**

And the Lord said, If ye had faith as a grain of mustard seed, ye might say unto this sycamine tree, **Be thou plucked up by the root, and be thou planted in the sea; and it should obey you.**

John 6:28-29

Then said they unto Him, What shall we do, that we might work the works of God?

Jesus answered and said unto them, **This is the work of God, that ye believe on Him Whom He hath sent.**

Romans 1:17

For therein is the righteousness of God revealed from faith to faith: as it is written, **The just shall live by faith.**

Romans 5:1

Therefore being justified by faith, we have peace with God through our Lord Jesus Christ:

Romans 10:8

But what saith it? The word is nigh thee, even in thy mouth, and in thy heart: **that is, the word of faith,** which we preach;

Romans 10:17

So then faith cometh by hearing, and hearing by the word of God.

Romans 14:23

. . . for whatsoever is not of faith is sin.

I Corinthians 2:5

That your faith should not stand in the wisdom of men, **but in the power of God**.

I Corinthians 13:13

And so faith, hope, love abide ***[faith - conviction and belief respecting man's relation to God and divine things;*** *hope - joyful and confident expectation of eternal salvation; love - true affection for God and man, growing out of God's love for and in us], these three; but the greatest of these is love. [AMP]*

II Corinthians 1:24

. . . for by faith ye stand.

II Corinthians 5:7

(For we walk by faith, not by sight:)

Galatians 2:20

I am crucified with Christ: nevertheless I live; yet not I, but Christ liveth in me: **and the life which I now live in the flesh I live by the faith of the Son of God, Who loved me, and gave Himself for me.**

Galatians 3:6

Even as Abraham believed God, and it was accounted to him for righteousness.

Galatians 5:6

For in Jesus Christ neither circumcision availeth any thing, nor uncircumcision; **but faith which worketh by love.**

For [if we are] in Christ Jesus, neither circumcision nor uncircumcision counts for anything, ***but only faith activated and energized and expressed and working through love.*** *[AMP]*

Ephesians 6:16

Above all, taking **the shield of faith,** wherewith ye shall be able to quench all the fiery darts of the wicked.

Philippians 3:9

And be found in Him, not having mine own righteousness, which is of the law, **but that which is through the faith of Christ, the righteousness which is of God by faith:**

Hebrews 6:12

That ye be not slothful, **but followers of them who through faith and patience inherit the promises.**

Hebrew 10:23

Let us hold fast the profession of our faith without wavering; (for He is faithful that promised;)

Hebrews 10:35-36

Cast not away therefore your confidence, which hath great recompence of reward.

For ye have need of patience, that, **after ye have done the will of God, ye might receive the promise.**

Hebrews 10:38

But the just shall live by faith *[My righteous servant shall live by his conviction respecting man's relationship to God and divine things, and holy fervor born of faith and conjoined with it]; and if he draws back and shrinks in fear, My soul has no delight or pleasure in him. [AMP]*

Hebrews 11:1-2

Now **faith** is **the substance** of things hoped for, **the evidence** of things not seen.

For by it the elders obtained a good report.

Now faith is the assurance (the confirmation, the title deed) of the things [we] hope for, being the proof of things [we] do not see and the conviction of their reality [faith perceiving as real fact what is not revealed to the senses].

For by ***[faith - trust and holy fervor born of faith]*** *the men of old had divine testimony borne to them and obtained a good report. [AMP]*

Hebrews 11:3

Through faith we understand that the worlds were framed by the word of God, so that things which are seen were not made of things which do appear.

Hebrews 11:6

But without faith it is impossible to please Him: for he that cometh to God must believe that He is, and that He is a rewarder of them that diligently seek Him.

James 1:5-8

If any of you lack wisdom, let him ask of God, that giveth to all men liberally, and upbraideth not; and it shall be given him.

But let him ask in faith, nothing wavering. For he that wavereth is like a wave of the sea driven with the wind and tossed.

For let not that man think that he shall receive any thing of the Lord.

A double minded man is unstable in all his ways.

James 2:17

Even so faith, if it hath not works, is dead, being alone.

I John 5:4

For whatsoever is born of God overcometh the world: **and this is the victory that overcometh the world, even our faith.**

Jude 20

But ye, beloved, **building up yourselves on your most holy faith, praying in the Holy Ghost,**

B. Examples of Faith

Genesis 22:8 *(Abraham)*

And Abraham said, **My son, God will provide Himself a lamb for a burnt offering:** so they went both of them together.

Joshua 14:12 *(Caleb)*

Now therefore give me this mountain, whereof the Lord spake in that day; for thou heardest in that day how the Anakims were there, and that the cities were great and fenced: **if so be the Lord will be with me, then I shall be able to drive them out, as the Lord said.**

I Samuel 14:6 *(Jonathan)*

And Jonathan said to the young man that bare his armour, Come, and let us go over unto the garrison of these uncircumcised: **it may be that the Lord will work for us: for there is no restraint to the Lord to save by many or by few.**

I Samuel 17:37 *(David)*

David said moreover, **The Lord that delivered me out of the paw of the lion, and out of the paw of the bear, He will deliver me out of the hand of this Philistine.** And Saul said unto David, Go, and the Lord be with thee.

II Chronicles 20:12 *(Jehoshaphat)*

O our God, wilt Thou not judge them? for we have no might against this great company that cometh against us; neither know we what to do: **but our eyes are upon Thee.**

Daniel 3:17 *(the three Hebrew children)*

If it be so, **our God Whom we serve is able to deliver us from the burning fiery furnace, and He will deliver us out of thine hand, O king.**

Matthew 8:8-10,13 *(The centurion)*

The centurion answered and said, Lord, I am not worthy that Thou shouldest come under my roof: **but speak the word only, and my servant shall be healed.**

For I am a man under authority, having soldiers under me: and I say to this man, Go, and he goeth; and to another, Come and he cometh; and to my servant, Do this, and he doeth it.

When Jesus heard it, He marvelled, and said to them that followed, **Verily I say unto you, I have not found so great faith, no, not in Israel.**

And Jesus said unto the centurion, **Go thy way; and as thou hast believed, so be it done unto thee**. And his servant was healed in the selfsame hour.

Matthew 9:20-22 *(the woman with the issue of blood)*

And, behold, a woman, which was diseased with an issue of blood twelve years, came behind Him, and touched the hem of His garment:

For she said within herself, If I may but touch His garment, I shall be whole.

But Jesus turned Him about, and when He saw her, He said, Daughter, be of good comfort; **thy faith hath made thee whole.** And the woman was made whole from that hour.

Matthew 9:28-30 *(the blind men)*

And when He was come into the house, the blind men came to Him: and Jesus saith unto them, Believe ye that I am able to do this? They said unto Him, Yea, Lord.

Then touched He their eyes, saying, **According to your faith be it unto you.**

And their eyes were opened; . . .

Matthew 15:28 *(the Syrophoenician woman)*

Then Jesus answered and said unto her, **O woman, great is thy faith: be it unto thee even as thou wilt.** And her daughter was made whole from that very hour.

Acts 27:25 *(Apostle Paul)*

Wherefore, sirs, be of good cheer: **for I believe God, that it shall be even as it was told me.**

Romans 4:17-22 *(Abraham)*

(As it is written, I have made thee a father of many nations,) before Him Whom he believed, even God, Who quickeneth the dead, **and calleth those things which be not as though they were.**

Who against hope believed in hope, that he might become the father of many nations, according to that which was spoken, So shall thy seed be.

And being not weak in faith, he considered not his own body now dead, when he was about an hundred years old, **neither yet** the deadness of Sarah's womb:

He staggered not at the promise of God through unbelief; but was strong in faith, giving glory to God;

And being fully persuaded that, what He had promised, He was able also to perform.

And therefore it was imputed to him for righteousness.

Hebrews 11:4 *(Abel)*

[Prompted, actuated] by faith Abel brought God a better and more acceptable sacrifice than Cain, because of which it was testified of him that he was righteous [that he was upright and in right standing with God], and God bore witness by accepting and acknowledging his gifts. And though he died, yet [through the incident] he is still speaking. [AMP]

Hebrews 11:5 *(Enoch)*

By faith Enoch was translated that he should not see death; and was not found, because God had translated him: for before his translation he had this testimony, that he pleased God.

<u>**Hebrews 11:7**</u> *(Noah)*

[Prompted] by faith Noah, being forewarned by God concerning events of which as yet there was no visible sign, took heed and diligently and reverently constructed and prepared an ark for the deliverance of his own family. By this ***[his faith which relied on God]*** *he passed judgment and sentence on the world's unbelief and became an heir and possessor of righteousness* ***(that relation of being right into which God puts the person who has faith).*** *[AMP]*

<u>**Hebrews 11:8**</u> *(Abraham)*

[Urged on] by faith Abraham, when he was called, ***obeyed*** *and went forth to a place which he was destined to receive as an inheritance;* ***and he went, although he did not know or trouble his mind about where he was to go.*** *[AMP]*

<u>**Hebrews 11:11**</u> *(Sarah)*

Through faith also Sara herself received strength to conceive seed, and was delivered of a child when she was past age, because **she judged Him faithful Who had promised**.

<u>**Hebrews 11:17-19**</u> *(Abraham)*

By faith Abraham, **when he was tried,** offered up Isaac: **and he that had received the promises offered up his only begotten son,**

Of whom it was said, That in Isaac shall thy seed be called:

Accounting that God was able to raise him up, even from the dead; from whence also he received him in a figure.

<u>**Hebrews 11:20**</u> *(Isaac)*

[With eyes of] faith Isaac, looking far into the future, invoked blessings upon Jacob and Esau. [AMP]

<u>**Hebrews 11:21**</u> *(Jacob)*

By faith Jacob, when he was a dying, blessed both the sons of Joseph; and worshipped, leaning upon the top of his staff.

<u>**Hebrews 11:22**</u> *(Joseph)*

[Actuated] by faith Joseph, when nearing the end of his life, referred to [the promise of God for] the departure of the Israelites out of Egypt and gave instructions concerning the burial of his own bones. [AMP]

<u>**Hebrews 11:23**</u> *(Moses' parents)*

By faith Moses, when he was born, was hid three months of his parents, because they saw he was a proper child; **and they were not afraid of the king's commandment.**

<u>**Hebrews 11:24-28**</u> *(Moses)*

By faith Moses, when he was come to years, **refused** to be called the son of Pharaoh's daughter;

Choosing rather to suffer affliction with the people of God, than to enjoy the pleasures of sin for a season;

Esteeming the reproach of Christ greater riches than the treasures in Egypt: **for he had respect unto the recompence of the reward.**

By faith he forsook Egypt, not fearing the wrath of the king: **for he endured, as seeing Him Who is invisible.**

Through faith he kept the passover, and the sprinkling of blood, lest he that destroyed the firstborn should touch them.

Hebrews 11:29 *(the children of Israel)*

By faith they passed through the Red sea as by dry land: which the Egyptians assaying to do were drowned.

Hebrews 11:30 *(Joshua)*

By faith the walls of Jericho fell down, after they were compassed about seven days.

Hebrews 11:31 *(Rahab the harlot)*

By faith the harlot Rahab perished not with them that believed not, when she had received the spies with peace.

Hebrews 11:33-34 *(the ancient heroes)*

Who **through faith** subdued kingdoms, wrought righteousness, obtained promises, stopped the mouths of lions,

Quenched the violence of fire, escaped the edge of the sword, out of weakness were made strong, waxed valiant in fight, turned to flight the armies of the aliens.

C. God Does Not Lie

I Samuel 15:29

And also the Strength of Israel will not lie nor repent: for He is not a man, that He should repent.

Numbers 23:19

God is not a man, that He should lie; neither the son of man, that He should repent: hath He said, and shall He not do it? or hath He spoken, and shall He not make it good?

Romans 3:4

. . . yea, **let God be true,** but every man a liar; . . .

Titus 1:2

In hope of eternal life, **which God, that cannot lie**, promised before the world began;

Hebrews 6:18

That by two immutable things, **in which it was impossible for God to lie**, we might have a strong consolation, who have fled for refuge to lay hold upon the hope set before us:

D. Nothing is Impossible with God

Genesis 18:14

Is anything too hard or too wonderful for the Lord? . . . [AMP]

Jeremiah 32:17

Ah Lord God! behold, Thou hast made the heaven and the earth by Thy great power and stretched out arm, and **there is nothing too hard for Thee:**

Jeremiah 32:27

Behold, I am the Lord, the God of all flesh: **is there any thing too hard for Me?**

Matthew 17:20

. . . If ye have faith as a grain of mustard seed, ye shall say unto this mountain,
Remove hence to yonder place; and it shall remove; **and nothing shall be impossible unto you.**

Mark 9:23

Jesus said unto him, **If thou canst believe, all things are possible to him that believeth.**

Mark 10:27

And Jesus looking upon them saith, With men it is impossible, but not with God: **for with God all things are possible.**

Luke 1:37

For with God nothing shall be impossible.

For with God nothing is ever impossible, and no word from God shall be without power or impossible of fulfillment. [AMP]

E. God Will Perform His Word

Genesis 28:15

And behold, I am with thee, and will keep thee in all places whither thou goest, and will bring thee again into this land; **for I will not leave thee, until I have done that which I have spoken to thee of.**

Numbers 23:19

God is not a man, that He should lie; neither the son of man, that He should repent **hath He said, and shall He not do it? or hath He spoken, and shall He not make it good?**

Deuteronomy 9:5

Not for thy righteousness, or for the uprightness of thine heart, dost thou go to possess their land: but for the wickedness of these nations the Lord thy God doth drive them out from before thee, and **that He may perform the word which the Lord sware unto thy fathers, Abraham, Isaac, and Jacob.**

Joshua 23:14

And, behold, this day I am going the way of all the earth: and ye know in all your hearts and in all your souls, **that not one thing hath failed of all the good things which the Lord your God spake concerning you;** all are come to pass unto you, and not one thing hath failed thereof.

I Kings 8:56

Blessed be the Lord, that hath given rest unto His people Israel, according to all that He promised: **there hath not failed one word of all His good promise**, which He pro ised by the hand of Moses His servant.

Psalm 89:34

My covenant will I not break, nor alter the thing that is gone out of My lips.

Isaiah 14:24

The Lord of Hosts hath sworn, saying, **Surely as I have thought, so shall it come to pass; and as I have purposed, so shall it stand:**

Isaiah 46:9-11

Remember the former things of old: for I am God, and there is none else; I am God, and there is none like Me,

Declaring the end from the beginning, and from ancient times the things that are not yet done, saying, **My counsel shall stand, and I will do all My pleasure:**

Calling a ravenous bird from the east, the man that executeth My counsel from a far country: **yea, I have spoken it, I will also bring it to pass; I have purposed it, I will also do it.**

Isaiah 55:11

So shall My word be that goeth forth out of My mouth: **it shall not return unto Me void, but it shall accomplish that which I please, and it shall prosper in the thing whereto I sent it.**

Jeremiah 1:12

Then said the Lord unto me, Thou hast well seen: **for I will hasten My word to perform it.**

*Then said the Lord to me, You have seen well, **for I am alert and active, watching over***

My word to perform it. *[AMP]*

Ezekiel 24:14

I the Lord have spoken it: it shall come to pass, and I will do it; I will not go back, neither will I spare, neither will I repent; . . .

Habakkuk 2:3

For the vision is yet for an appointed time, but at the end it shall speak, and not lie: though it tarry, wait for it; **because it will surely come,** it will not tarry.

Romans 4:20-21

He staggered not at the promise of God through unbelief; but was strong in faith, giving glory to God;

And being fully persuaded that, **what He had promised, He was able also to perform.**

II Peter 3:9

The Lord is not slack concerning His promise, . . .

Chapter 2

The Power of Prayer

A. General References in Scripture

Exodus 25:22

And there **I will meet with thee, and I will commune with thee** from above the mercy seat, from between the two cherubims which are upon the ark of the testimony, . . .

Psalm 65:4

Blessed is the man whom Thou choosest, and causest to approach unto Thee, that he may dwell in Thy courts: we shall be satisfied with the goodness of Thy house, even of Thy holy temple.

Psalm 141:2

Let my prayer be set forth before Thee as incense; and the lifting up of my hands as the evening sacrifice.

I Timothy 2:8

I will therefore that men pray every where, lifting up holy hands, without wrath and doubting.

Revelation 5:8

And when He had taken the book, the four beasts and four and twenty elders fell down before the Lamb, having every one of them harps, **and golden vials full of odours, which are the prayers of saints.**

Revelation 8:3-4

And another angel came and stood at the altar, having a golden censer; and there was given unto him much incense, that he should offer it with the prayers of all saints upon the golden altar which was before the throne.

And the smoke of the incense, which came with the prayers of the saints, ascended up before God out of the angel's hand.

B. Prayer That God Hears

II Chronicles 7:14

If My people, which are called by My name, shall humble themselves, and pray, and seek My face, and turn from their wicked ways; then will I hear from heaven, and will forgive their sin, and will heal their land.

Psalm 66:17-20

I cried unto Him with my mouth, and He was extolled with my tongue.

If I regard iniquity in my heart, the Lord will not hear me:

But verily God hath heard me; He hath attended to the voice of my prayer.

Blessed be God, which hath not turned away my prayer, nor His mercy from me.

Psalm 102:17

He will regard the prayer of the destitute, and not despise their prayer.

Psalm 145:18-19

The Lord is nigh unto all them that call upon Him, **to all that call upon Him in truth.**

He will fulfil the desire of them that fear Him: He also will hear their cry, and will save them.

Proverbs 15:29

The Lord is far from the wicked: **but He heareth the prayer of the righteous.**

Luke 18:10-14

Two men went up into the temple to pray; the one a Pharisee, and the other a publican.

The Pharisee stood and prayed thus with himself, God, I thank Thee, that I am not as other men are, extortioners, unjust, adulterers, or even as this publican.

I fast twice in the week, I give tithes of all that I possess.

And the publican, standing afar off, would not lift up so much as his eyes unto heaven, but smote upon his breast, saying, **God be merciful to me a sinner.**

I tell you, this man went down to his house justified rather than the other: for every one that exalteth himself shall be abased; and he that humbleth himself shall be exalted.

I Peter 3:12

For the eyes of the Lord are over the righteous, and His ears are open unto their prayers: but the face of the Lord is against them that do evil.

C. Calling Upon The Lord

Genesis 4:26

And to Seth, to him also there was born a son; and he called his name Enos: **then began men to call upon the name of the Lord.**

Psalm 4:3

But know that the Lord hath set apart him that is godly for Himself: **the Lord will hear when I call unto Him.**

Psalm 5:1-3

Give ear to my words, O Lord, consider my meditation.

Hearken unto the voice of my cry, my King, and my God: for unto Thee will I pray.

My voice shalt Thou hear in the morning, O Lord; in the morning will I direct my prayer unto Thee, and will look up.

Psalm 55:17

Evening, and morning, and at noon, will I pray, and cry aloud: and He shall hear my voice.

Psalm 91:15

He shall call upon Me, and I will answer him: I will be with him in trouble; I will deliver him, and honour him.

Psalm 145:18-19

The Lord is nigh unto all them that call upon Him, to all that call upon Him in truth.

He will fulfil the desire of them that fear Him: He also will hear their cry, and will save them.

Isaiah 26:9

With my soul have I desired Thee in the night; yea, with my spirit within me will I seek Thee early: for when Thy judgments are in the earth, the inhabitants of the world will learn righteousness.

Isaiah 55:6

Seek ye the Lord while He may be found, **call ye upon Him while He is near:**

Isaiah 58:9

Then shalt thou call, and the Lord shall answer; thou shalt cry, and He shall say, Here I am. . .

Isaiah 65:24

And it shall come to pass, that before they call, I will answer; and while they are yet speaking, I will hear.

<u>**Jeremiah 29:12-14**</u>

Then shall ye call upon Me, and ye shall go and pray unto Me, and I will hearken unto you.

And ye shall seek Me, and find Me, when ye shall search for Me with all your heart.

And I will be found of you, saith the Lord: and I will turn away your captivity, and I will gather you from all the nations, and from all the places whither I have driven you, saith the Lord; and I will bring you again into the place whence I caused you to be carried away captive.

<u>**Jeremiah 33:3**</u>

Call unto Me, and I will answer thee, and shew thee great and mighty things, which thou knowest not.

<u>**Zechariah 13:9**</u>

And I will bring the third part through the fire, and will refine them as silver is refined, and will try them as gold is tried: **they shall call on My name, and I will hear them: I will say, It is My people: and they shall say, The Lord is my God.**

D. Asking Specific Requests

<u>**Exodus 33:17**</u>

And the Lord said unto Moses, **I will do this thing also that thou hast spoken**: for thou hast found grace in My sight, and I know thee by name.

<u>**I Kings 13:6**</u>

And the king answered and said unto the man of God, Intreat now the face of the Lord thy God, and pray for me, that my hand may be restored me again. **And the man of God besought the Lord, and the king's hand was restored him again, and became as it was before.**

<u>**II Kings 20:5**</u>

Turn again, and tell Hezekiah the captain of My people, Thus saith the Lord, the God of David thy father, **I have heard thy prayer, I have seen thy tears: behold, I will heal thee...**

<u>**Psalm 2:8**</u>

Ask of Me, and I shall give thee the heathen for thine inheritance, and the uttermost parts of the earth for thy possession.

<u>**Psalm 20:5**</u>

We will rejoice in Thy salvation, and in the name of our God we will set up our banners: **the Lord fulfil all thy petitions.**

Isaiah 7:11

Ask thee a sign of the Lord thy God; ask it either in the depth, or in the height above.

Isaiah 45:11

Thus saith the Lord, the Holy One of Israel, and his Maker, **Ask Me of things to come concerning My sons,** and concerning the work of My hands command ye Me.

Matthew 6:5-8

And when thou prayest, thou shalt not be as the hypocrites are: for they love to pray standing in the synagogues and in the corners of the streets, that they may be seen of men. Verily I say unto you, They have their reward.

But thou, when thou prayest, enter into thy closet, and when thou hast shut thy door, **pray to thy Father which is in secret; and thy Father which seeth in secret shall reward thee openly.**

But when ye pray, use not vain repetitions, as the heathen do: for they think that they shall be heard for their much speaking.

Be not ye therefore like unto them: **for your Father knoweth what things ye have need of, before ye ask Him.**

Matthew 6:9-13

Pray, therefore, like this: Our Father Who is in heaven, hallowed (kept holy) be Your name.

Your kingdom come, Your will be done on earth as it is in heaven.

Give us this day our daily bread.

And forgive us our debts, as we also have forgiven (left, remitted, and let go of the debts, and have given up resentment against) our debtors.

And lead (bring) us not into temptation, but deliver us from the evil one. For Yours is the kingdom and the power and the glory forever. Amen. [AMP]

Matthew 7:7-8

Ask, and it shall be given you; seek, and ye shall find; knock, and it shall be opened unto you:

For every one that asketh receiveth; and he that seeketh findeth; and to him that knocketh it shall be opened.

Matthew 7:7-11

Keep on asking and it will be given you; keep on seeking and you will find; keep on knocking [reverently] and [the door] will be opened to you.

For everyone who keeps on asking receives; and he who keeps on seeking finds; and to him who keeps on knocking, [the door] will be opened.

Or what man is there of you, if his son asks him for a loaf of bread, will hand him a stone?

Or if he asks for a fish, will hand him a serpent?

If you then, evil as you are, know how to give good and advantageous gifts to your children, ***how much more will your Father Who is in heaven [perfect as He is] give good and advantageous things to those who keep on asking Him!*** *[AMP]*

Matthew 21:22

And **all things**, whatsoever ye shall ask in prayer, **believing**, ye shall receive.

Mark 11:24

Therefore I say unto you, **What things soever ye desire, when ye pray, believe that ye receive them, and ye shall have them.**

John 14:12-14

Verily, verily, I say unto you, He that believeth on Me, the works that I do shall he do also; and greater works than these shall he do; because I go unto My Father.

And whatsoever ye shall ask in My name, that will I do, that the Father may be glorified in the Son.

If ye shall ask any thing in My name, I will do it.

John 15:7

If ye abide in Me, and My words abide in you, ye shall ask what ye will, and it shall be done unto you.

John 15:16

You have not chosen Me, but I have chosen you and I have appointed you [I have planted you], that you might go and bear fruit and keep on bearing, and that your fruit may be lasting [that it may remain, abide], ***so that whatever you ask the Father in My Name [as presenting all that I AM], He may give it to you.*** *[AMP]*

John 16:23-24

And in that day ye shall ask Me nothing. Verily, verily, I say unto you, **Whatsoever ye shall ask the Father in My name, He will give it you.**

Hitherto have ye asked nothing in My name: **ask, and ye shall receive, that your joy may be full.**

Ephesians 3:20

Now unto Him that is able to do exceeding abundantly above all that we ask or think, according to the power that worketh in us,

Philippians 4:6-7

Do not fret or have any anxiety about anything, ***but in every circumstance and in everything, by prayer and petition (definite requests), with thanksgiving, continue to make your wants known to God.***

And God's peace [shall be yours, that tranquil state of a soul assured of its salvation through Christ, and so fearing nothing from God and being content with its earthly lot of whatever sort that is, that peace] which transcends all understanding shall garrison and mount guard over your hearts and minds in Christ Jesus. [AMP]

I Timothy 2:1-4,8

First of all, then, I admonish and urge that petitions, prayers, intercessions, and thanks-

givings be offered on behalf of all men,

For kings and all who are in positions of authority or high responsibility, that [outwardly] we may pass a quiet and undisturbed life [and inwardly] a peaceable one in all godliness and reverence and seriousness in every way.

For such [praying] is good and right, and [it is] pleasing and acceptable to God our Savior,

Who wishes all men to be saved and [increasingly] to perceive and recognize and discern and know precisely and correctly the [divine] Truth.

I desire therefore that ***in every place men should pray,*** *without anger or quarreling or resentment or doubt [in their minds],* ***lifting up holy hands.*** *[AMP]*

Hebrews 4:16

Let us therefore come boldly unto the throne of grace, that we may obtain mercy, and find grace to help in time of need.

Let us then fearlessly and confidently and boldly draw near to the throne of grace (the throne of God's unmerited favor to us sinners), that we may receive mercy [for our failures] and find grace to help in good time for every need [appropriate help and well-timed help, coming just when we need it]. *[AMP]*

James 1:5-7

If any of you lack wisdom, **let him ask of God, that giveth to all men liberally, and upbraideth not**; and it shall be given him.

But let him ask in faith, nothing wavering. For he that wavereth is like a wave of the sea driven with the wind and tossed.

For let not that man think that he shall receive any thing of the Lord.

James 4:2-3

Ye lust, and have not: ye kill, and desire to have, and cannot obtain: ye fight and war, **yet ye have not, because ye ask not.**

Ye ask, and receive not, because ye ask amiss, that ye may consume it upon your lusts.

James 5:13-18

Is anyone among you afflicted (ill-treated, suffering evil)? He should pray. *Is anyone glad at heart? He should sing praise [to God].*

Is anyone among you sick? He should call in the church elders (the spiritual guides). And they should pray over him, anointing him with oil in the Lord's name.

And the prayer [that is] of faith will save him who is sick, and the Lord will restore him; and if he has committed sins, he will be forgiven.

Confess to one another therefore your faults (your slips, your false steps, your offenses, your sins) and pray [also] for one another, that you may be healed and restored [to a spiritual tone of mind and heart]. ***The earnest (heartfelt, continued) prayer of a righteous man makes tremendous power available [dynamic in its working].***

Elijah was a human being with a nature such as we have [with feelings, affections, and a constitution like ours]; and he prayed earnestly for it not to rain, and no rain fell on the earth for three years and six months.

And [then] he prayed again and the heavens supplied rain and the land produced its crops [as usual]. [AMP]

I John 3:22

And whatsoever we ask, we receive of Him, because we keep His commandments, and do those things that are pleasing in His sight.

And we receive from Him whatever we ask, *because we [watchfully] obey His orders [observe His suggestions and injunctions, follow His plan for us] and [habitually] practice what is pleasing to Him. [AMP]*

I John 5:14-15

And this is the confidence that we have in Him, that, **if we ask any thing according to His will, He heareth us:**

And if we know that He hear us, whatsoever we ask, we know that we have the petitions that we desired of Him.

And this is the confidence (the assurance, the privilege of boldness) which we have in Him: [we are sure] that if we ask anything (make any request) according to His will (in agreement with His own plan), He listens to and hears us.

And if (since) we [positively] know that He listens to us in whatever we ask, we also know [with settled and absolute knowledge] ***that we have [granted us as our present possessions] the requests made of Him.*** *[AMP]*

I John 5:16

If any man see his brother sin a sin which is not unto death, he shall ask, and He shall give him life for them that sin not unto death. . . .

E. Corporate Agreement

Matthew 18:19-20

Again I say unto you, **That if two of you shall agree on earth as touching any thing that they shall ask, it shall be done for them of My Father which is in heaven.**

For where two or three are gathered together in My name, there am I in the midst of them.

Again I tell you, ***if two of you on earth agree (harmonize together, make a symphony together) about whatever [anything and everything] they may ask, it will come to pass and be done for them by My Father in heaven.***

For wherever two or three are gathered (drawn together as My followers) in (into) My name, there I AM in the midst of them. [AMP]

Luke 1:10

And the whole multitude of the people were praying without at the time of incense.

Acts 1:14

These all continued with one accord in prayer and supplication, with the women, and Mary the mother of Jesus, and with His brethren.

Acts 4:24

And when they heard that, **they lifted up their voice to God with one accord**, and said, Lord, Thou art God, which hast made heaven, and earth, and the sea, and all that in them is:

Acts 4:31

And when they had prayed, the place was shaken where they were assembled together; and they were all filled with the Holy Ghost, and they spake the word of God with boldness.

Acts 12:5

Peter therefore was kept in prison: **but prayer was made without ceasing of the church unto God for him.**

Acts 12:12

And when he had considered the thing, he came to the house of Mary the mother of John, whose surname was Mark; **where many were gathered together praying.**

F. References to Binding and Loosing

Psalm 149:6-9

Let the high praises of God be in their mouth, and a twoedged sword in their hand;
To execute vengeance upon the heathen, and punishments upon the people;
To bind their kings with chains, and their nobles with fetters of iron;
To execute upon them the judgment written: this honour have all His saints. Praise ye the Lord.

Matthew 16:19

And I will give unto thee the keys of the kingdom of heaven: **and whatsoever thou shalt bind on earth shall be bound in heaven: and whatsoever thou shalt loose on earth shall be loosed in heaven.**

I will give you the keys of the kingdom of heaven; ***and whatever you bind (declare to be improper and unlawful) on earth must be what is already bound in heaven; and whatever you loose (declare lawful) on earth must be what is already loosed in heaven. [AMP]***

Matthew 18:18

Verily I say unto you, Whatsoever ye shall bind on earth shall be bound in heaven: and whatsoever ye shall loose on earth shall be loosed in heaven.

Truly I tell you, whatever you forbid and declare to be improper and unlawful on earth must be what is already forbidden in heaven, and whatever you permit and declare proper and lawful on earth must be what is already permitted in heaven. [AMP]

Mark 3:27

No man can enter into a strong man's house, and spoil his goods, **except he will first bind the strong man;** and then he will spoil his house.

G. Intercessory Prayer

I Samuel 12:23

Moreover as for me, **God forbid that I should sin against the Lord in ceasing to pray for you**: but I will teach you the good and the right way:

Job 16:21

Oh, that there were one who might plead for a man with God and that he might maintain his right with Him, as a son of man pleads with or for his neighbor! [AMP]

Job 22:30

He will even deliver the one [for whom you intercede] who is not innocent; yes, he will be delivered through the cleanness of your hands. *[AMP]*

Psalm 30:5

For His anger endureth but a moment; in His favour is life: **weeping may endure for a night, but joy cometh in the morning.**

Psalm 126:5-6

They that sow in tears shall reap in joy.

He that goeth forth and weepeth, bearing precious seed, shall doubtless come again with rejoicing, **bring his sheaves with him.**

Isaiah 64:7

And there is none that called upon Thy name, **that stirreth up himself to take hold of Thee:** for Thou hast hid Thy face from us, and hast consumed us, because of our iniquities.

Isaiah 66:8-9

Who hath heard such a thing? who hath seen such things? Shall the earth be made to bring forth in one day? or shall a nation be born at once? **for as soon as Zion travailed, she brought forth her children.**

Shall I bring to the birth, and not cause to bring forth? saith the Lord: shall I cause to bring forth, and shut the womb? saith thy God.

Ezekiel 22:30

And I sought for a man among them, **that should make up the hedge, and stand in the gap before Me for the land,** that I should not destroy it: . . .

Romans 8:26-27

Likewise **the Spirit also helpeth our infirmities**: for we know not what we should pray for as we ought: but the Spirit Itself maketh intercession for us with groanings which cannot be uttered.

And He that searcheth the hearts knoweth what is the mind of the Spirit, **because He maketh intercession for the saints according to the will of God.**

So too the [Holy] Spirit comes to our aid and bears us up in our weakness; for we do not know what prayer to offer nor how to offer it worthily as we ought, ***but the Spirit Himself goes to meet our supplication and pleads in our behalf with unspeakable yearnings and groanings too deep for utterance.***

And He Who searches the hearts of men knows what is the mind of the [Holy] Spirit [what His intent is], ***because the Spirit intercedes and pleads [before God] in behalf of the saints according to and in harmony with God's will.*** *[AMP]*

Ephesians 6:18

Pray at all times (on every occasion, in every season) in the Spirit, with all [manner of] prayer and entreaty. ***To that end keep alert and watch with strong purpose and perseverance, interceding in behalf of all the saints (God's consecrated people).*** *[AMP]*

H. Examples of Intercessory Prayer

Genesis 18:23-26 *(Abraham for Sodom & Gomorrah)*

And Abraham drew near, and said, **Wilt Thou also destroy the righteous with the wicked?**

Peradventure there be fifty righteous within the city: wilt Thou also destroy and not spare the place for the fifty righteous that are therein?

That be far from Thee to do after this manner, to slay the righteous with the wicked: and that the righteous should be as the wicked, that be far from Thee: Shall not the Judge of all the earth do right?

And the Lord said, If I find in Sodom fifty righteous within the city, then I will spare all the place for their sakes.

Exodus 32:31-32 *(Moses for Israel)*

And Moses returned unto the Lord, and said, Oh, this people have sinned a great sin, and have made them gods of gold.

Yet now, if Thou wilt forgive their sin—-; **and if not, blot me, I pray Thee, out of Thy book which Thou hast written.**

<u>Numbers 12:13</u> *(Moses for Miriam)*

And Moses cried unto the Lord, saying, **Heal her now, O God,** I beseech Thee.

<u>Numbers 14:17-19</u> *(Moses for Israel)*

And now, **I beseech Thee, let the power of my Lord be great, according as Thou hast spoken,** saying,

The Lord is longsuffering, and of great mercy, forgiving iniquity and transgression, and by no means clearing the guilty, visiting the iniquity of the fathers upon the children unto the third and fourth generation.

Pardon, I beseech Thee, the iniquity of this people according unto the greatness of Thy mercy, and as Thou hast forgiven this people, from Egypt even until now.

<u>Deuteronomy 9:18-20</u> *(Moses for Israel & Aaron)*

And I fell down before the Lord, as at the first, forty days and forty nights: I did neither eat bread, nor drink water, because of all your sins which ye sinned, in doing wickedly in the sight of the Lord, to provoke Him to anger.

For I was afraid of the anger and hot displeasure, wherewith the Lord was wroth against you to destroy you. But the Lord hearkened unto me at that time also.

And the Lord was very angry with Aaron to have destroyed him: and I prayed for Aaron also the same time.

<u>Deuteronomy 9:25-26</u> *(Moses for Israel)*

Thus I fell down before the Lord forty days and forty nights, as I fell down at the first; because the Lord had said He would destroy you.

I prayed therefore unto the Lord, and said, O Lord God, destroy not Thy people and Thine inheritance, which Thou hast redeemed through Thy greatness, which Thou hast brought forth out of Egypt with a mighty hand.

<u>I Samuel 7:8-9</u> *(Samuel for Israel)*

And the children of Israel said to Samuel, **Cease not to cry unto the Lord our God for us, that He will save us out of the hand of the Philistines.**

And Samuel took a sucking lamb, and offered it for a burnt offering wholly unto the Lord: and Samuel cried unto the Lord for Israel; and the Lord heard him.

<u>I Samuel 15:11</u> *(Samuel for Saul)*

It repenteth Me that I have set up Saul to be king: for he is turned back from following Me, and hath not performed My commandments. **And it grieved Samuel; and he cried unto the Lord all night.**

<u>I Kings 13:6</u> *(the man of God for Jeroboam)*

And the king answered and said unto the man of God, Intreat now the face of the Lord thy God, and pray for me, that my hand may be restored me again. **And the man of God**

besought the Lord, and the king's hand was restored him again, and became as it was before.

I Kings 17:19-22 *(Elijah for the widow's dead son)*

And he said unto her, Give me thy son. And he took him out of her bosom, and carried him up into a loft, where he abode, and laid him upon his own bed.

And he cried unto the Lord, and said, **O Lord my God, hast thou also brought evil upon the widow with whom I sojourn, by slaying her son?**

And he stretched himself upon the child three times, and cried unto the Lord, and said, **O Lord my God, I pray thee, let this child's soul come into him again.**

And the Lord heard the voice of Elijah; and the soul of the child came into him again, and he revived.

I Chronicles 21:17 *(David for Israel)*

And David said unto God, **Is it not I that commanded the people to be numbered? even I it is that have sinned and done evil indeed; but as for these sheep, what have they done? let Thine hand, I pray Thee, O Lord my God, be on me, and on my father's house; but not on Thy people, that they should be plagued.**

II Chronicles 30:18-20 *(Hezekiah for the people)*

For a multitude of the people, even many of Ephraim, and Manasseh, Issachar, and Zebulun, had not cleansed themselves, yet did they eat the passover otherwise than it was written. But Hezekiah prayed for them, saying, **The good Lord pardon every one**

That prepareth his heart to seek God, the Lord God of his fathers, though he be not cleansed according to the purification of the sanctuary.

And the Lord hearkened to Hezekiah, and healed the people.

Job 42:10 *(Job for his friends)*

And the Lord turned the captivity of Job, when he prayed for his friends: also the Lord gave Job twice as much as he had before.

Psalm 106:23 *(Moses for Israel)*

Therefore He said that He would destroy them, **had not Moses His chosen stood before Him in the breach, to turn away His wrath,** lest He should destroy them.

Isaiah 53:12 *(Jesus for us)*

Therefore will I divide Him a portion with the great, and He shall divide the spoil with the strong; because He hath poured out His soul unto death: and He was numbered with the transgressors; and He bare the sin of many, **and made intercession for the transgressors.**

Luke 19:41 *(Jesus for Jerusalem)*

And when He was come near, **He beheld the city, and wept over it,**

Luke 22:31-32 *(Jesus for Simon Peter)*

And the Lord said, **Simon, Simon, behold, Satan hath desired to have you, that he may**

sift you as wheat:

But I have prayed for thee, that thy faith fail not: and when thou art converted, strengthen thy brethren.

Luke 23:34 *(Jesus for those crucifying Him)*

Then said Jesus, **Father, forgive them; for they know not what they do.** And they parted His raiment, and cast lots.

John 11:33-36 *(Jesus for Lazarus)*

When Jesus therefore saw her weeping, and the Jews also weeping which came with her, **He groaned in the spirit, and was troubled,**

And said, Where have ye laid him? They said unto Him, Lord, come and see.

Jesus wept.

Then said the Jews, Behold how He loved him!

Romans 8:34 *(Jesus for us)*

Who is he that condemneth? It is Christ that died, yea rather, that is risen again, **Who is even at the right hand of God, Who also maketh intercession for us.**

Galatians 4:19 *(Apostle Paul for the church at Galatia)*

My little children, **of whom I travail in birth again until Christ be formed in you,**

Ephesians 1:16 *(Apostle Paul for the church at Ephesus)*

Cease not to give thanks for you, **making mention of you in my prayers;**

Hebrews 7:24-25 *(Jesus for us)*

But He holds His priesthood unchangeably, because He lives on forever.

Therefore He is able also to save to the uttermost (completely, perfectly, finally, and for all time and eternity) those who come to God through Him, since ***He is always living to make petition to God and intercede with Him and intervene for them****. [AMP]*

I. Watching In Prayer

Matthew 26:40-41

And He cometh unto the disciples, and findeth them asleep, and saith unto Peter, **What, could ye not watch with Me one hour?**

Watch and pray, that ye enter not into temptation: the spirit indeed is willing, but the flesh is weak.

Luke 6:12

And it came to pass in those days, that He went out into a mountain to pray, and **continued all night in prayer to God.**

<u>Luke 12:37-38</u>

Blessed are those servants, whom the Lord when He cometh shall find watching: verily I say unto you, that He shall gird Himself, and make them to sit down to meat, and will come forth and serve them.

And if He shall come in the second watch, or come in the third watch, and find them so, blessed are those servants.

<u>Luke 21:36</u>

Watch ye therefore, and pray always, that ye may be accounted worthy to escape all these things that shall come to pass, and to stand before the Son of man.

<u>Colossians 4:2</u>

Continue in prayer, and **watch in the same with thanksgiving;**

<u>I Peter 4:7</u>

But the end of all things is at hand: **be ye therefore sober, and watch unto prayer.**

J. Persistence & Importunity

<u>Genesis 18:23-25,32</u> *(Abraham)*

And Abraham drew near, and said, **Wilt Thou also destroy the righteous with the wicked?**

Peradventure there be fifty righteous within the city: wilt Thou also destroy and not spare the place for the fifty righteous that are therein?

That be far from Thee to do after this manner, to slay the righteous with the wicked: and that the righteous should be as the wicked, that be far from Thee: Shall not the Judge of all the earth do right?

And he said, Oh let not the Lord be angry, and I will speak yet but this once: Peradventure ten shall be found there. And He said, I will not destroy it for ten's sake.

<u>Genesis 32:24-26</u> *(Jacob)*

And Jacob was left alone; and there wrestled a Man with him until the breaking of the day.

And when He saw that He prevailed not against him, He touched the hollow of his thigh; and the hollow of Jacob's thigh was out of joint, as he wrestled with Him.

And He said, Let Me go, for the day breaketh. And he said, **I will not let Thee go, except Thou bless me.**

<u>Deuteronomy 9:18-19</u> *(Moses)*

And I fell down before the Lord, as at the first, forty days and forty nights: I did neither eat bread, nor drink water, because of all your sins which ye sinned, in doing wickedly in the sight of the Lord, to provoke Him to anger.

For I was afraid of the anger and hot displeasure, wherewith the Lord was wroth against you to destroy you. But the Lord hearkened unto me at that time also.

<u>**I Kings 18:42-45**</u> *(Elijah)*

So Ahab went up to eat and to drink. And Elijah went up to the top of Carmel; and he cast himself down upon the earth, and put his face between his knees,

And said to his servant, Go up now, look toward the sea. And he went up, and looked, and said, There is nothing. And he said, Go again seven times.

And it came to pass at the seventh time, that he said, **Behold, there ariseth a little cloud out of the sea, like a man's hand.** And he said, Go up, say unto Ahab, Prepare thy chariot, and get thee down, that the rain stop thee not.

And it came to pass in the mean while, **that the heaven was black with clouds and wind, and there was a great rain.** And Ahab rode, and went to Jezreel.

<u>**Isaiah 62:6-7**</u>

I have set watchmen upon thy walls, O Jerusalem, which shall never hold their peace day nor night: ye that make mention of the Lord, keep not silence,

And give Him no rest, till He establish, and till He make Jerusalem a praise in the earth.

<u>**Matthew 15:22-28**</u> *(the Syrophenician woman)*

And, behold, a woman of Canaan came out of the same coasts, and cried unto Him, saying, Have mercy on me, O Lord, Thou Son of David; my daughter is grievously vexed with a devil.

But He answered her not a word. And His disciples came and besought Him, saying, Send her away; for she crieth after us.

But He answered and said, I am not sent but unto the lost sheep of the house of Israel.

Then came she and worshipped Him, saying, Lord, help me.

But He answered and said, It is not meet to take the children's bread, and to cast it to dogs.

And she said, **Truth, Lord: yet the dogs eat of the crumbs which fall from their master's table.**

Then Jesus answered and said unto her, **O woman, great is thy faith: be it unto thee even as thou wilt.** And her daughter was made whole from that very hour.

<u>**Luke 11:5-10**</u> *(the importunate neighbor)*

And He said unto them, Which of you shall have a friend, and shall go unto him at midnight, and say unto him, Friend, lend me three loaves;

For a friend of mine in his journey is come to me, and I have nothing to set before him?

And he from within shall answer and say, Trouble me not: the door is now shut, and my children are with me in bed; I cannot rise and give thee.

I say unto you, **Though he will not rise and give him, because he is his friend, yet because of his importunity he will rise and give him as many as he needeth.**

And I say unto you, Ask, and it shall be given you; seek, and ye shall find; knock, and it shall be opened unto you.

For every one that asketh receiveth; and he that seeketh findeth; and to him that knocketh it shall be opened.

<u>Luke 18:1-7</u> *(the widow & the unjust judge)*

And He spake a parable unto them to this end, that men ought always to pray, and not to faint;

Saying, There was in a city a judge, which feared not God, neither regarded man:

And there was a widow in that city; and she came unto him, saying, Avenge me of mine adversary.

And he would not for a while: but afterward he said within himself, **Though I fear not God, nor regard man;**

Yet because this widow troubleth me, I will avenge her, lest by her continual coming she weary me.

And the Lord said, **Hear what the unjust judge saith.**

And shall not God avenge His own elect, which cry day and night unto Him, though He bear long with them?

<u>Luke 22:44</u> *(Jesus)*

And being in an agony He prayed more earnestly: and His sweat was as it were great drops of blood falling down to the ground.

<u>Acts 12:5</u> *(the early Church)*

Peter therefore was kept in prison: **but prayer was made without ceasing of the church unto God for him.**

<u>Ephesians 6:12</u> *(the Christian)*

For we wrestle not against flesh and blood, but against principalities, against powers, against the rulers of the darkness of this world, against spiritual wickedness in high places.

<u>Ephesians 6:18</u>

Praying always with all prayer and supplication in the Spirit, and watching thereunto with all **perseverance** and supplication for all saints;

<u>Colossians 1:9</u>

For this cause we also, since the day we heard it, **do not cease to pray for you,** and to desire that ye might be filled with the knowledge of His will in all wisdom and spiritual understanding;

<u>I Thessalonians 3:10</u>

Night and day praying exceedingly that we might see your face, and might perfect that which is lacking in your faith?

<u>I Thessalonians 5:17</u>

Be unceasing in prayer [praying perseveringly]; [AMP]

<u>James 5:17</u> *(Elijah)*

Elias was a man subject to like passions as we are, and he prayed earnestly that it might not rain: and it rained not on the earth by the space of three years and six months.

K. Ministering Unto The Lord

II Chronicles 20:18

And Jehoshaphat bowed his head with his face to the ground: and all Judah and the inhabitants of Jerusalem fell before the Lord, **worshipping the Lord.**

II Chronicles 31:2

And Hezekiah appointed the courses of the priests and the Levites after their courses, every man according to his service, the priests and Levites for burnt offerings and for peace offerings, **to minister, and to give thanks, and to praise in the gates of the tents of the Lord.**

Psalm 72:15

And He shall live, and to Him shall be given of the gold of Sheba: **prayer also shall be made for Him continually; and daily shall He be praised.**

Ezekiel 44:15-16

But the priests the Levites, the sons of Zadok, that kept the charge of My sanctuary when the children of Israel went astray from Me, **they shall come near to Me to minister unto Me,** and they shall stand before Me to offer unto Me the fat and the blood, saith the Lord God:

They shall enter into My sanctuary, and they shall come near to My table, to minister unto Me, and they shall keep My charge.

Luke 24:52-53

And they worshipped Him, and returned to Jerusalem with great joy:

And were continually in the temple, praising and blessing God. Amen.

Acts 2:46-47

And they, continuing daily with one accord in the temple, and breaking bread from house to house, did eat their meat with gladness and singleness of heart,

Praising God, and having favour with all the people. And the Lord added to the church daily such as should be saved.

Acts 13:2

As they ministered to the Lord, and fasted, the Holy Ghost said, Separate Me Barnabas and Saul for the work whereunto I have called them.

Acts 16:25

And at midnight Paul and Silas prayed, and sang praises unto God: and the prisoners heard them.

L. Sample Prayers from Scripture

Matthew 6:9-13

After this manner therefore pray ye: Our Father which art in heaven, Hallowed be Thy name.

Thy kingdom come. Thy will be done in earth, as it is in heaven.

Give us this day our daily bread.

And forgive us our debts, as we forgive our debtors.

And lead us not into temptation, but deliver us from evil: For Thine is the kingdom, and the power, and the glory, for ever. A-men.

Ephesians 1:15-19

Wherefore I also, after I heard of your faith in the Lord Jesus, and love unto all the saints,

Cease not to give thanks for you, making mention of you in my prayers;

That the God of our Lord Jesus Christ, the Father of glory, may give unto you the spirit of wisdom and revelation in the knowledge of Him:

The eyes of your understanding being enlightened; that ye may know what is the hope of His calling, and what the riches of the glory of His inheritance in the saints,

And what is the exceeding greatness of His power to us-ward who believe, according to the working of His mighty power,

Ephesians 3:14-19

For this cause I bow my knees unto the Father of our Lord Jesus Christ,

Of Whom the whole family in heaven and earth is named,

That He would grant you, according to the riches of His glory, to be strengthened with might by His Spirit in the inner man;

That Christ may dwell in your hearts by faith; that ye, being rooted and grounded in love,

May be able to comprehend with all saints what is the breadth, and length, and depth, and height;

And to know the love of Christ, which passeth knowledge, that ye might be filled with all the fulness of God.

Philippians 1:9-11

And this I pray, that your love may abound yet more and more in knowledge and in all judgment;

That ye may approve things that are excellent; that ye may be sincere and without offence till the day of Christ;

Being filled with the fruits of righteousness, which are by Jesus Christ, unto the glory and praise of God.

Colossians 1:9-11

For this cause we also, since the day we heard it, do not cease to pray for you, and to desire that ye might be filled with the knowledge of His will in all wisdom and spiritual understanding;

That ye might walk worthy of the Lord unto all pleasing, being fruitful in every good work, and increasing in the knowledge of God;

Strengthened with all might, according to His glorious power, unto all patience and longsuffering with joyfulness;

II Thessalonians 1:11-12

Wherefore also we pray always for you, that our God would count you worthy of this calling, and fulfil all the good pleasure of His goodness, and the work of faith with power:

That the name of our Lord Jesus Christ may be glorified in you, and ye in Him, according to the grace of our God and the Lord Jesus Christ.

Chapter 3

Foundations of Spiritual Warfare

A. General References in Scripture

<u>**Exodus 14:14**</u>

The Lord shall fight for you, and ye shall hold your peace.

<u>**Exodus 15:3**</u>

The Lord is a Man of War: the Lord is His name.

<u>**Exodus 15:6**</u>

Thy right hand, O Lord, is become glorious in power: Thy right hand, O Lord, hath dashed in pieces the enemy.

<u>**Exodus 23:22**</u>

But if thou shalt indeed obey His voice, and do all that I speak; **then I will be an enemy unto thine enemies, and an adversary unto thine adversaries.**

<u>**Exodus 23:27**</u>

. . . I will make all thine enemies turn their backs unto thee.

<u>**Leviticus 26:8**</u>

And five of you shall chase an hundred, and an hundred of you shall put ten thousand to flight: and your enemies shall fall before you by the sword.

<u>**Deuteronomy 1:30**</u>

The Lord your God Which goeth before you, **He shall fight for you**, according to all that He did for you in Egypt before your eyes;

<u>**Deuteronomy 11:22-25**</u>

For if ye shall diligently keep all these commandments which I command you, to do them, to love the Lord your God, to walk in all His ways, and to cleave unto Him;

Then will the Lord drive out all these nations from before you, and ye shall possess greater nations and mightier than yourselves.

Every place whereon the soles of your feet shall tread shall be your's: from the wilderness and Lebanon, from the river, the river Euphrates, even unto the uttermost sea shall your coast be.

There shall no man be able to stand before you: for the Lord your God shall lay the fear of you and the dread of you upon all the land that ye shall tread upon, as He hath said unto you.

<u>**Deuteronomy 20:1**</u>

When thou goest out to battle against thine enemies, and seest horses, and chariots, and a people more than thou, be not afraid of them: **for the Lord thy God is with thee, which brought thee up out of the land of Egypt.**

<u>**Deuteronomy 28:7**</u>

The Lord shall cause thine enemies that rise up against thee to be smitten before thy face: **they shall come out against thee one way, and flee before thee seven ways.**

<u>**Deuteronomy 33:27**</u>

The eternal God is thy refuge, and underneath are the everlasting arms: and **He shall thrust out the enemy from before thee; and shall say, Destroy them**.

<u>**Joshua 23:10**</u>

One man of you shall chase a thousand: for the Lord your God, He it is that fighteth for you, as He hath promised you.

<u>**Judges 3:1-2**</u>

Now these are the nations which the Lord left, **to prove Israel by them**, even as many of Israel as had not known all the wars of Canaan;

Only that the generations of the children of Israel might know, **to teach them war,** at the least such as before knew nothing thereof;

<u>**I Samuel 14:6**</u>

And Jonathan said to the young man that bare his armour, Come, and let us go over unto the garrison of these uncircumcised: **it may be that the Lord will work for us: for there is no restraint to the Lord to save by many or by few.**

<u>**II Chronicles 32:7-8**</u>

Be strong and courageous, be not afraid nor dismayed for the king of Assyria, nor for all the multitude that is with him: for there be more with us than with him:

With him is an arm of flesh; **but with us is the Lord our God to help us, and to fight our battles . . .**

Psalm 3:3

But Thou, O Lord, art a shield for me; my glory, and the lifter up of mine head.

Psalm 8:2 *(compare with Matt. 21:6)*

Out of the mouth of babes and sucklings hast Thou ordained strength because of Thine enemies, **that Thou mightest still the enemy and the avenger**.

Psalm 18:1-3

I will love thee, O Lord, my Strength.

The Lord is my Rock, and my Fortress, and my Deliverer; my God, my Strength, in Whom I will trust; my Buckler, and the Horn of my salvation, and my High Tower.

I will call upon the Lord, Who is worthy to be praised: **so shall I be saved from mine enemies.**

Psalm 20:1

The Lord hear thee in the day of trouble; **the name of the God of Jacob defend thee;**

Psalm 20:5-9

We will rejoice in thy salvation, **and in the name of our God we will set up our banners:** the Lord fulfil all thy petitions.

Now know I that the Lord saveth His anointed; He will hear him from His holy heaven with the saving strength of His right hand.

Some trust in chariots, and some in horses: but we will remember the name of the Lord our God.

They are brought down and fallen: but we are risen, and stand upright.

Save, Lord: let the King hear us when we call.

Psalm 31:7-8

I will be glad and rejoice in Thy mercy: for Thou hast considered my trouble; **Thou hast known my soul in adversities;**

And hast not shut me up into the hand of the enemy: Thou hast set my feet in a large room.

Psalm 44:5

Through Thee will we push down our enemies: through Thy name will we tread them under that rise up against us.

Psalm 46:1

God is our Refuge and Strength, a very present help in trouble.

Psalm 47:2-3

For the Lord Most High is terrible; He is a great King over all the earth.

He shall subdue the people under us, and the nations under our feet.

Psalm 61:3

For Thou hast been a shelter for me, and a strong tower from the enemy.

Psalm 91:5-8

Thou shalt not be afraid for the terror by night; nor for the arrow that flieth by day;

Nor for the pestilence that walketh in darkness; nor for the destruction that wasteth at noonday.

A thousand shall fall at thy side, and ten thousand at thy right hand; but it shall not come nigh thee.

Only with thine eyes shalt thou behold and see the reward of the wicked.

Psalm 97:10

Ye that love the Lord, hate evil: **He preserveth the souls of His saints; He delivereth them out of the hand of the wicked.**

Psalm 107:2

Let the redeemed of the Lord say so, **whom He hath redeemed from the hand of the enemy;**

Psalm 107:20

He sent His word, and healed them, and **delivered them from their destructions.**

Psalm 118:10

All nations compasseth me about: **but in the name of the Lord will I destroy them.**

Psalm 138:7

Though I walk in the midst of trouble, Thou wilt revive me: **Thou shalt stretch forth Thine hand against the wrath of mine enemies, and Thy right hand shall save me.**

Psalm 144:1

Blessed be the Lord my Strength, **Which teacheth my hands to war, and my fingers to fight:**

Proverbs 3:25-26

Be not afraid of sudden fear, neither of the desolation of the wicked, when it cometh.

For the Lord shall be thy confidence, and shall keep thy foot from being taken.

Isaiah 9:4

For Thou hast broken the yoke of his burden, and the staff of his shoulder, the rod of his oppressor, as in the day of Midian.

Isaiah 10:27

And it shall come to pass in that day, that his burden shall be taken away from off thy shoulder, and his yoke from off thy neck, and **the yoke shall be destroyed because of the anointing.**

Isaiah 43:2

When thou passest through the waters, I will be with thee; and through the rivers, they shall not overflow thee: when thou walkest through the fire, thou shalt not be burned; neither shall the flame kindle upon thee.

Isaiah 54:17

No weapon that is formed against thee shall prosper; and every tongue that shall rise against thee in judgment thou shalt condemn. This is the heritage of the servants of the Lord, and their righteousness is of Me, saith the Lord.

Isaiah 59:19

So shall they fear the name of the Lord from the west, and His glory from the rising of the sun. **When the enemy shall come in like a flood, the Spirit of the Lord shall lift up a standard against him.**

Jeremiah 1:19

And they shall fight against thee; but they shall not prevail against thee; for I am with thee, saith the Lord, to deliver thee.

Jeremiah 12:5

If thou hast run with the footmen, and they have wearied thee, then how canst thou contend with horses? and if in the land of peace, wherein thou trustedst, they wearied thee, then how wilt thou do in the swelling of Jordan?

Jeremiah 15:21

And I will deliver thee out of the hand of the wicked, and I will redeem thee out of the hand of the terrible.

Daniel 11:32

. . . but the people that do know their God shall be strong, and do exploits.

Joel 2:32

And it shall come to pass, that whosoever shall call on the name of the Lord shall be delivered: for in mount Zion and in Jerusalem shall be deliverance, as the Lord hath said, and in the remnant whom the Lord shall call.

Micah 7:8

Rejoice not against me, O mine enemy: **when I fall, I shall arise**; when I sit in darkness, the Lord shall be a light unto me.

Nahum 1:7

The Lord is good, a strong hold in the day of trouble; and He knoweth them that trust in Him.

Zephaniah 3:17

The Lord thy God in the midst of thee is mighty; He will save, He will rejoice over thee with joy; He will rest in His love, He will joy over thee with singing.

Zechariah 2:5

For I, saith the Lord, will be unto her a wall of fire round about, and will be the glory in the midst of her.

Zechariah 4:6-7

. . . This is the word of the Lord unto Zerubbabel, saying, **Not by might, nor by power, but by My Spirit**, saith the Lord of hosts.

Who art thou, O great mountain? before Zerubbabel thou shalt become a plain: and he shall bring forth the headstone thereof with shoutings, crying, Grace, grace unto it.

Matthew 11:12

And from the days of John the Baptist until now the kingdom of heaven suffereth violence, **and the violent take it by force.**

Luke 10:19

Behold, I give unto you power to tread on serpents and scorpions, and over all the power of the enemy: and nothing shall by any means hurt you.

Behold! I have given you authority and power to trample upon serpents and scorpions, and [physical and mental strength and ability] over all the power that the enemy [possesses]; and nothing shall in any way harm you. [AMP]

Luke 11:24-26

When the unclean spirit is gone out of a man, he walketh through dry places, seeking rest; and finding none, he saith, **I will return unto my house whence I came out.**

And when he cometh, he findeth it swept and garnished.

Then goeth he, and taketh to him seven other spirits more wicked than himself; and they enter in, and dwell there: **and the last state of that man is worse than the first.**

John 16:33

These things I have spoken unto you, that in Me ye might have peace. **In the world ye shall have tribulation: but be of good cheer; I have overcome the world.**

II Corinthians 2:11

Lest Satan should get an advantage of us: **for we are not ignorant of his devices.**

II Corinthians 10:3-5

For though we walk in the flesh, we do not war after the flesh:

(For the weapons of our warfare are not carnal, but mighty through God to the pulling down of strong holds;)

Casting down imaginations, and every high thing that exalteth itself against the knowledge of God, and bringing into captivity every thought to the obedience of Christ;

II Thessalonians 3:3

But the Lord is faithful, Who shall stablish you, and keep you from evil.

II Timothy 2:3-4

Thou therefore **endure hardness**, as a good soldier of Jesus Christ.

No man that warreth entangleth himself with the affairs of this life; that he may please him who hath chosen him to be a soldier.

James 4:7

Submit yourselves therefore to God. **Resist** the devil, **and he will flee from you.**

I Peter 5:8-9

Be sober, be vigilant; **because your adversary the devil, as a roaring lion, walketh about, seeking whom he may devour:**

Whom resist stedfast in the faith, . . .

Be well balanced (temperate, sober of mind), be vigilant and cautious at all times; ***for that enemy of yours, the devil, roams around like a lion roaring [in fierce hunger], seeking someone to seize upon and devour.***

Withstand him; be firm in faith [against his onset - rooted, established, strong, immovable, and determined], knowing that the same (identical) sufferings are appointed to your brotherhood (the whole body of Christians) throughout the world. [AMP]

I John 4:1-3

Beloved, believe not every spirit, but try the spirits whether they are of God: because many false prophets are gone out into the world.

Hereby know ye the Spirit of God: Every spirit that confesseth that Jesus Christ is come in the flesh is of God:

And every spirit that confesseth not that Jesus Christ is come in the flesh is not of God: and this is that spirit of antichrist, whereof ye have heard that it should come; and even now already is it in the world.

Revelation 6:2

And I saw, and behold a white horse: and He that sat on him had a bow; and a crown was given unto Him: **and He went forth conquering, and to conquer.**

Revelation 12:11

And they overcame him by the blood of the Lamb, and by the word of their testimony; and they loved not their lives unto the death.

Revelation 17:14

These shall make war with the Lamb, and the Lamb shall overcome them: for He is Lord of lords, and King of kings: and they that are with Him are **called**, and **chosen**, and **faithful**.

B. Jesus' Victory Over Satan

Matthew 8:16

. . . He cast out the spirits **with His word, . . .**

Matthew 12:28-29

But if I cast out devils by the Spirit of God, then the kingdom of God is come unto you.

Or else how can one enter into a strong man's house, and spoil his goods, **except he first bind the strong man**? and then he will spoil his house.

Matthew 28:18

. . . **All power** is given unto Me in heaven and in earth.

Luke 10:17-19

And the seventy returned again with joy, saying, Lord, **even the devils are subject unto us through Thy name.**

And He said unto them, I beheld Satan as lightning fall from heaven.

Behold, I give unto you power to tread on serpents and scorpions, and over all the power of the enemy: and nothing shall by any means hurt you.

Luke 11:20-22

But if I with the finger of God cast out devils, no doubt the kingdom of God is come upon you.

When a strong man armed keepeth his palace, his goods are in peace:

But when a stronger than he shall come upon him, and overcome him, he taketh from him all his armour wherein he trusted, and divideth his spoils.

I Corinthians 15:24

Then cometh the end, when He shall have delivered up the kingdom to God, even the Father; **when He shall have put down all rule and all authority and power.**

Philippians 2:9-11

Wherefore God also hath highly exalted Him, and **given Him a name which is above every name:**

That at the name of Jesus every knee should bow, of things in heaven, and things in earth, and things under the earth;

And that every tongue should confess that Jesus Christ is Lord, to the glory of God the Father.

Colossians 2:10

And ye are complete in Him, **which is the Head of all principality and power:**

Colossians 2:15

And having spoiled principalities and powers, He made a shew of them openly,

triumphing over them in it.

<u>I John 3:8</u>

. . . For this purpose the Son of God was manifested, **that He might destroy the works of the devil.**

. . . *The reason the Son of God was made manifest (visible) was* ***to undo (destroy, loosen, and dissolve) the works the devil [has done].*** *[AMP]*

<u>I John 4:4</u>

Ye are of God, little children, and have overcome them: **because greater is He that is in you, than he that is in the world.**

C. Our Position - Victoriously Seated With Christ!

<u>Ephesians 1:19-23</u>

And what is the exceeding greatness of His power to us-ward who believe, according to the working of His mighty power,

Which He wrought in Christ, when He raised Him from the dead, and set Him at His own right hand in the heavenly places,

Far above all principality, and power, and might, and dominion, and every name that is named, not only in this world, but also in that which is to come:

And **hath put all things under His feet,** and gave Him to be the head over all things to the church,

Which is His body, the fulness of Him that filleth all in all.

<u>Ephesians 2:1-7</u>

And you hath He quickened, who were dead in trespasses and sins;

Wherein in time past ye walked according to the course of this world, according to the prince of the power of the air, the spirit that now worketh in the children of disobedience:

Among whom also we all had our conversation in times past in the lusts of our flesh, fulfilling the desires of the flesh and of the mind; and were by nature the children of wrath, even as others.

But God, Who is rich in mercy, for His great love wherewith He loved us,

Even when we were dead in sins, hath quickened us together with Christ, (by grace ye are saved;)

And hath raised us up together, and made us sit together in heavenly places in Christ Jesus:

That in the ages to come He might shew the exceeding riches of His grace in His kindness toward us through Christ Jesus.

<u>Colossians 1:13</u>

Who hath delivered us from the power of darkness, and hath translated us into the kingdom of His dear Son:

D. Our Authority in Christ

Job 22:28

You shall also decide and decree a thing, and it shall be established for you; *and the light [of God's favor] shall shine upon your ways. [AMP]*

Matthew 10:7-8

And as ye go, preach, saying, The kingdom of heaven is at hand.

Heal the sick, cleanse the lepers, raise the dead, **cast out devils:** freely ye have received, freely give.

Matthew 16:18-19

And I say also unto thee, That thou art Peter, and upon this rock I will build My church; **and the gates of hell shall not prevail against it.**

And I will give unto thee the keys of the kingdom of heaven: and whatsoever thou shalt bind on earth shall be bound in heaven: and whatsoever thou shalt loose on earth shall be loosed in heaven.

Matthew 21:19-21

And when He saw a fig tree in the way, He came to it, and found nothing thereon, but leaves only, and **said unto it**, Let no fruit grow on thee henceforward for ever. And presently the fig tree withered away.

And when the disciples saw it, they marvelled, saying, How soon is the fig tree withered away!

Jesus answered and said unto them, **Verily I say unto you, If ye have faith, and doubt not, ye shall not only do this which is done to the fig tree, but also if ye shall say unto this mountain, Be thou removed, and be thou cast into the sea; it shall be done.**

Mark 16:17-18

And these signs shall follow them that believe; **In My name shall they cast out devils;** they shall speak with new tongues;

They shall take up serpents; and if they drink any deadly thing, it shall not hurt them; they shall lay hands on the sick, and they shall recover.

Luke 9:1

Then He called His twelve disciples together, **and gave them power and authority over all devils**, and to cure diseases.

Luke 10:17-19

And the seventy returned again with joy, saying, Lord, **even the devils are subject unto us through Thy name.**

And He said unto them, I beheld Satan as lightning fall from heaven.

Behold, I give unto you power to tread on serpents and scorpions, and over all the power of the enemy: and nothing shall by any means hurt you.

Luke 10:19

Behold! I have given you authority and power to trample upon serpents and scorpions, and [physical and mental strength and ability] over all the power that the enemy [possesses]; and nothing shall in any way harm you. [AMP]

Romans 5:17

For if by one man's offence death reigned by one; much more they which receive abundance of grace and of the gift of righteousness **shall reign in life** by one, Jesus Christ.)

For if because of one man's trespass (lapse, offense) death reigned through that one, much more surely will those who receive [God's] overflowing grace (unmerited favor) and the free gift of righteousness [putting them into right standing with Himself] ***reign as kings in life*** *through the one Man Jesus Christ (the Messiah, the Anointed One). [AMP]*

E. We Are Conquerors & Overcomers

Romans 8:37

Nay, in all these things **we are more than conquerors** through Him that loved us.

Yet amid all these things ***we are more than conquerors and gain a surpassing victory*** *through Him Who loved us. [AMP]*

I Corinthians 15:57

But thanks be to God, which **giveth us the victory** through our Lord Jesus Christ.

But thanks be to God, Who ***gives us the victory [making us conquerors]*** *through our Lord Jesus Christ. [AMP]*

II Corinthians 2:14

Now thanks be unto God, which **always causeth us to triumph** in Christ, and maketh manifest the savour of His knowledge by us in every place.

But thanks be to God, Who in Christ always leads us in triumph [as trophies of Christ's victory] *and through us spreads and makes evident the fragrance of the knowledge of God everywhere, [AMP]*

I John 4:4

Ye are of God, little children, and **have overcome them**: because greater is He that is in you, than he that is in the world.

I John 5:4-5

For whatsoever is born of God overcometh the world: and this is the victory that overcometh the world, even our faith.

Who is he that **overcometh** the world, but he that believeth that Jesus is the Son of God?

F. Putting on the Armour of God

Isaiah 59:17

For He put on **righteousness as a breastplate**, and **an helmet of salvation upon His head;** and He put on **the garments of vengeance for clothing**, and **was clad with zeal as a cloak.**

Romans 13:12

The night is far spent, the day is at hand: let us therefore cast off the works of darkness, **and let us put on the armour of light.**

II Corinthians 6:7

By the word of truth, by the power of God, **by the armour of righteousness on the right hand and on the left,**

Ephesians 6:10-18

Finally, my brethren, be strong in the Lord, and in the power of His might.

Put on the **whole armour of God,** that ye may be able to stand against the wiles of the devil.

For we wrestle not against flesh and blood, but against principalities, against powers, against the rulers of the darkness of this world, against spiritual wickedness in high places.

Wherefore take unto you the **whole armour of God**, that ye may be able to withstand in the evil day, and having done all, to stand.

Stand therefore, having **your loins girt about with truth**, and having on **the breastplate of righteousness**;

And your feet shod with **the preparation of the Gospel of peace**;

Above all, taking **the shield of faith**, wherewith ye shall be able to quench all the fiery darts of the wicked.

And take **the helmet of salvation**, and **the sword of the Spirit**, which is the word of God:

Praying always with all prayer and supplication in the Spirit, and watching thereunto with all perseverance and supplication for all saints;

In conclusion, be strong in the Lord [be empowered through your union with Him]; draw your strength from Him [that strength which His boundless might provides].

Put on God's whole armor [the armor of a heavy-armed soldier which God supplies], that you may be able successfully to stand up against [all] the strategies and the deceits of the devil.

For we are not wrestling with flesh and blood [contending only with physical opponents], but against the despotisms, against the powers, against [the master spirits who are] the world rulers of this present darkness, against the spirit forces of wickedness in the heavenly (supernatural) sphere.

Therefore put on God's complete armor, that you may be able to resist and stand your ground on the evil day [of danger], and, having done all [the crisis demands], to stand [firmly in your place].

Stand therefore [hold your ground], having tightened ***the belt of truth*** *around your loins and having put on* ***the breastplate of integrity and of moral rectitude and right standing with God.***

And having ***shod your feet in preparation [to face the enemy with the firm-footed stability, the promptness, and the readiness produced by the good news] of the Gospel of peace.***

Lift up over all ***the [covering] shield of saving faith,*** *upon which you can quench all the flaming missiles of the wicked [one].*

And take ***the helmet of salvation*** *and* ***the sword that the Spirit wields, which is the Word of God.***

Pray at all times (on every occasion, in every season) in the Spirit, with all [manner of] prayer and entreaty. To that end keep alert and watch with strong purpose and perseverance, interceding in behalf of all the saints (God's consecrated people). [AMP]

<u>I Thessalonians 5:8</u>

But let us, who are of the day, be sober, **putting on the breastplate of faith and love**; and **for an helmet, the hope of salvation.**

G. The Weapons of our Warfare

<u>I Samuel 17:45</u>

Then said David to the Philistine, Thou comest to me with a sword, and with a spear, and with a shield: but I come to thee in the name of the Lord of hosts, the God of the armies of Israel, Whom thou hast defied.

<u>II Corinthians 10:3-5</u>

For though we walk in the flesh, we do not war after the flesh:

(For the weapons of our warfare are not carnal, but mighty through God to the pulling down of strong holds;)

Casting down imaginations, and every high thing that exalteth itself against the knowledge of God, and bringing into captivity every thought to the obedience of Christ;

<u>Ephesians 6:17</u>

And take the helmet of salvation, and **the sword of the Spirit, which is the word of God**:

<u>Hebrews 4:12</u>

For the word of God is quick, and powerful, and sharper than any twoedged sword, piercing even to the dividing asunder of soul and spirit, and of the joints and marrow, and is a discerner of the thoughts and intents of the heart.

For the Word that God speaks is alive and full of power [making it active, operative, energizing, and effective]; it is sharper than any two-edged sword, penetrating to the dividing line of the breath of life (soul) and [the immortal] spirit, and of joints and marrow [of the deepest parts of our nature], exposing and sifting and analyzing and judging the very thoughts and purposes of the heart. [AMP]

Revelation 1:16

And He had in His right hand seven stars: **and out of His mouth went a sharp twoedged sword:** and His countenance was as the sun shineth in his strength.

Revelation 2:12

And to the angel of the church in Pergamos write; **These things saith He which hath the sharp sword with two edges;**

Revelation 2:16

Repent; or else I will come unto thee quickly, **and will fight against them with the sword of My mouth.**

Revelation 12:11

And they overcame him **by the blood of the Lamb**, and **by the word of their testimony**; and they loved not their lives unto the death.

H. Angels Operating on our Behalf

Exodus 33:2 *(the children of Israel)*

And I will send an Angel before thee; and I will drive out the Canaanite, the Amorite, and the Hittite, and the Perizzite, the Hivite, and the Jebusite:

I Kings 19:4-8 *(Elijah)*

But he himself went a day's journey into the wilderness, and came and sat down under a juniper tree: and he requested for himself that he might die; and said, It is enough; now, O Lord, take away my life; for I am not better than my fathers.

And as he lay and slept under a juniper tree, behold, **then an angel touched him, and said unto him, Arise and eat.**

And he looked, and, behold, there was a cake baken on the coals, and a cruse of water at his head. And he did eat and drink, and laid him down again.

And the angel of the Lord came again the second time, and touched him, and said, Arise and eat; because the journey is too great for thee.

And he arose, and did eat and drink, and went in the strength of that meat forty days and forty nights unto Horeb the mount of God.

<u>II Kings 6:15-17</u> *(Elisha)*

And when the servant of the man of God was risen early, and gone forth, behold, an host compassed the city both with horses and chariots. And his servant said unto him, Alas, my master! how shall we do?

And he answered, Fear not: for they that be with us are more than they that be with them.

And Elisha prayed, and said, Lord, I pray Thee, open his eyes, that he may see. **And the Lord opened the eyes of the young man; and he saw: and, behold, the mountain was full of horses and chariots of fire round about Elisha.**

<u>II Chronicles 32:7-8</u> *(Hezekiah)*

Be strong and courageous, be not afraid nor dismayed for the king of Assyria, nor for all the multitude that is with him: **for there be more with us than with him:**

With him is an arm of flesh; **but with us is the Lord our God to help us, and to fight our battles . . .**

<u>Psalm 34:7</u>

The angel of the Lord encampeth round about them that fear Him, and delivereth them.

<u>Psalm 35:1-6</u> *(David)*

Plead my cause, O Lord, with them that strive with me: **fight against them that fight against me.**

Take hold of shield and buckler, and stand up for mine help.

Draw out also the spear, and stop the way against them that persecute me: say unto my soul, I am thy salvation.

Let them be confounded and put to shame that seek after my soul: let them be turned back and brought to confusion that devise my hurt.

Let them be as chaff before the wind: and **let the Angel of the Lord chase them.**

Let their way be dark and slippery: and **let the Angel of the Lord persecute them.**

<u>Psalm 55:18</u> *(David)*

He hath delivered my soul in peace from the battle that was against me: **for there were many with me.**

<u>Psalm 91:10-12</u>

There shall no evil befall thee, neither shall any plague come nigh thy dwelling.

For He shall give His angels charge over thee, to keep thee in all thy ways.

They shall bear thee up in their hands, lest thou dash thy foot against a stone.

<u>Psalm 103:20</u>

Bless the Lord, ye His angels, that excel in strength, that do His commandments, hearkening unto the voice of His word.

__Daniel 6:22__ *(Daniel)*

My God hath sent His angel, and hath shut the lions' mouths, that they have not hurt me: forasmuch as before Him innocency was found in me; and also before thee, O king, have I done no hurt.

__Daniel 10:11-13,20__ *(Daniel)*

And he said unto me, O Daniel, a man greatly beloved, understand the words that I speak unto thee, and stand upright: for unto thee am I now sent. And when he had spoken this word unto me, I stood trembling.

Then said he unto me, Fear not, Daniel: **for from the first day that thou didst set thine heart to understand, and to chasten thyself before thy God, thy words were heard, and I am come for thy words.**

But the prince of the kingdom of Persia withstood me one and twenty days: but, lo, Michael, one of the chief princes, came to help me; and I remained there with the kings of Persia.

Then said he, Knowest thou wherefore I come unto thee? and now will I return to fight with the prince of Persia: and when I am gone forth, lo, the prince of Grecia shall come.

__Matthew 18:10__

Take heed that ye despise not one of these little ones; for I say unto you, **That in heaven their angels do always behold the face of My Father which is in heaven.**

__Matthew 26:53__ *(Jesus)*

Thinkest thou that I cannot now pray to My Father, and He shall presently give Me more than twelve legions of angels?

__Luke 22:43__ *(Jesus at the garden of Gethsemane)*

And there appeared an angel unto Him from heaven, strengthening Him.

__Acts 5:19-20__ *(the apostles)*

But the angel of the Lord by night opened the prison doors, and brought them forth, and said,

Go, stand and speak in the temple to the people all the words of this life.

__Acts 12:5-11__ *(releasing Peter from prison)*

Peter therefore was kept in prison: but prayer was made without ceasing of the church unto God for him.

And when Herod would have brought him forth, the same night Peter was sleeping between two soldiers, bound with two chains: and the keepers before the door kept the prison.

And, behold, the angel of the Lord came upon him, and a light shined in the prison: and he smote Peter on the side, and raised him up, saying, Arise up quickly. And his chains fell off from his hands.

And the angel said unto him, Gird thyself, and bind on thy sandals. And so he did. And he saith unto him, Cast thy garment about thee, and follow me.

And he went out, and followed him; and wist not that it was true which was done by the angel; but thought he saw a vision.

When they were past the first and the second ward, they came unto the iron gate that leadeth unto the city; which opened to them of his own accord: and they went out, and passed on through one street; and forthwith the angel departed from him.

And when Peter was come to himself, he said, **Now I know of a surety, that the Lord hath sent his angel, and hath delivered me out of the hand of Herod,** and from all the expectation of the people of the Jews.

Hebrews 1:13-14

But to which of the angels said He at any time, Sit on My right hand, until I make thine enemies thy footstool?

Are they not all ministering spirits, sent forth to minister for them who shall be heirs of salvation?

Revelations 12:7-8

And there was war in heaven: **Michael and his angels fought against the dragon; and the dragon fought and his angels,**

And prevailed not; neither was their place found any more in heaven.

I. Examples of Spiritual Warfare from Scripture

I. Moses' & Joshua's Victory over Amalek

Exodus 17:8-13,15

Then came Amalek, and fought with Israel in Rephidim.

And Moses said unto Joshua, Choose us out men, and go out, fight with Amalek: to morrow I will stand on the top of the hill with the rod of God in mine hand.

So Joshua did as Moses had said to him, and fought with Amalek: and Moses, Aaron, and Hur went up to the top of the hill.

And it came to pass, when Moses held up his hand, that Israel prevailed: and when he let down his hand, Amalek prevailed.

But Moses' hands were heavy; and they took a stone, and put it under him, and he sat thereon; and **Aaron and Hur stayed up his hands**, the one on the one side, and the other on the other side; and his hands were steady until the going down of the sun.

And Joshua discomfited Amalek and his people with the edge of the sword.

And Moses built an altar, and called the name of it **Jehovah Nissi** *(The Lord Our Banner).*

II. Gideon & the Midianites

Judges 7:2-7

And the Lord said unto Gideon, **The people that are with thee are too many for Me to**

give the Midianites into their hands, lest Israel vaunt themselves against Me, saying, Mine own hand hath saved me.

Now therefore go to, proclaim in the ears of the people, saying, Whosoever is fearful and afraid, let him return and depart early from mount Gilead. And there returned of the people twenty and two thousand; and there remained ten thousand.

And the Lord said unto Gideon, **The people are yet too many; bring them down unto the water, and I will try them for thee there**: and it shall be, that of whom I say unto thee, This shall go with thee, the same shall go with thee; and of whomsoever I say unto thee, This shall not go with thee, the same shall not go.

So he brought down the people unto the water: and the Lord said unto Gideon, Every one that lappeth of the water with his tongue, as a dog lappeth, him shalt thou set by himself; likewise every one that boweth down upon his knees to drink.

And the number of them that lapped, putting their hand to their mouth, were three hundred men: but all the rest of the people bowed down upon their knees to drink water.

And the Lord said unto Gideon, **By the three hundred men that lapped will I save you, and deliver the Midianites into thine hand**: and let all the other people go every man unto his place.

III. David & Goliath

I Samuel 17:36, 45-47

Thy servant slew both the lion and the bear: and **this uncircumcised Philistine shall be as one of them, seeing he hath defied the armies of the living God.**

Then said David to the Philistine, Thou comest to me with a sword, and with a spear, and with a shield: **but I come to thee in the name of the Lord of hosts, the God of the armies of Israel, Whom thou hast defied.**

This day will the Lord deliver thee into mine hand; and I will smite thee, and take thine head from thee; and I will give the carcases of the host of the Philistines this day unto the fowls of the air, and to the wild beasts of the earth; **that all the earth may know that there is a God in Israel.**

And all this assembly shall know that the Lord saveth not with sword and spear: **for the battle is the Lord's, and He will give you into our hands.**

IV. Jehoshaphat's Victory

II Chronicles 20:15, 17, 20-22

And he said, Hearken ye, all Judah, and ye inhabitants of Jerusalem, and thou king Jehoshaphat, Thus saith the Lord unto you, **Be not afraid nor dismayed by reason of this great multitude; for the battle is not your's, but God's.**

Ye shall not need to fight in this battle: **set yourselves, stand ye still, and see the salvation of the Lord with you**, O Judah and Jerusalem: **fear not, nor be dismayed; to morrow go out against them: for the Lord will be with you.**

And they rose early in the morning, and went forth into the wilderness of Tekoa: and as they went forth, Jehoshaphat stood and said, Hear me, O Judah, and ye inhabitants of Jerusalem; **Believe in the Lord your God, so shall ye be established; believe His prophets, so shall ye prosper.**

And when he had consulted with the people, **he appointed singers unto the Lord, and that should praise the beauty of holiness, as they went out before the army, and to say, Praise the Lord; for His mercy endureth for ever.**

And when they began to sing and to praise, the Lord set ambushments against the children of Ammon, Moab, and mount Seir, which were come against Judah; **and they were smitten.**

Chapter 4

The Blood of Jesus

A. References To The Old Testament Blood Covenant

<u>**Exodus 12:7**</u>

And they shall take of the blood, and strike it on the two side posts and on the upper door post of the houses, wherein they shall eat it.

<u>**Exodus 12:23**</u>

For the Lord will pass through to smite the Egyptians; **and when He seeth the blood upon the lintel, and on the two side posts, the Lord will pass over the door, and will not suffer the destroyer to come in unto your houses to smite you.**

<u>**Exodus 24:6-8**</u>

And Moses took half of the blood, and put it in basins; and half of the blood he sprinkled on the altar.

And he took the book of the covenant, and read in the audience of the people: and they said, All that the Lord hath said will we do, and be obedient.

And Moses took the blood, and sprinkled it on the people, and said, **Behold the blood of the covenant, which the Lord hath made with you concerning all these words.**

<u>**Exodus 29:12-16**</u>

And thou shalt take of the blood of the bullock, and put it upon the horns of the altar with thy finger, and pour all the blood beside the bottom of the altar.

And thou shalt take all the fat that covereth the inwards, and the caul that is above the liver, and the two kidneys, and the fat that is upon them, and burn them upon the altar.

But the flesh of the bullock, and his skin, and his dung, shalt thou burn with fire without the camp: it is a sin offering.

Thou shalt also take one ram; and Aaron and his sons shall put their hands upon the

head of the ram.

And thou shalt slay the ram, and thou shalt take his blood, and sprinkle it round about upon the altar.

Exodus 29:20-21

Then shalt thou kill the ram, and take of his **blood**, and put it upon the tip of the right ear of Aaron, and upon the tip of the right ear of his sons, and upon the thumb of their right hand, and upon the great toe of their right foot, and sprinkle **the blood** upon the altar round about.

And thou shalt take of **the blood** that is upon the altar, and of the anointing oil, and sprinkle it upon Aaron, and upon his garments, and upon his sons, and upon the garments of his sons with him: and he shall be hallowed, and his garments, and his sons, and his sons' garments with him.

Leviticus 4:6-7

And the priest shall dip his finger in the blood, and **sprinkle of the blood seven times** before the Lord, before the vail of the sanctuary.

And the priest shall put some of **the blood** upon the horns of the altar of sweet incense before the Lord, which is in the tabernacle of the congregation; and shall pour all **the blood** of the bullock at the bottom of the altar of the burnt offering, which is at the door of the tabernacle of the congregation.

Leviticus 5:9

And he shall sprinkle of **the blood of the sin offering** upon the side of the altar; and the rest of the blood shall be wrung out at the bottom of the altar: **it is a sin offering.**

Leviticus 7:2

In the place where they kill the burnt offering shall they kill the trespass offering: **and the blood** thereof shall he sprinkle round about upon the altar.

Leviticus 8:23

And he slew it; and Moses took of **the blood** of it, and put it upon the tip of Aaron's right ear, and upon the thumb of his right hand, and upon the great toe of his right foot.

Leviticus 9:12,18,24

And he slew the burnt offering; and Aaron's sons presented unto him **the blood**, which he sprinkled round about upon the altar.

He slew also the bullock and the ram for a sacrifice of peace offerings, which was for the people: and Aaron's sons presented unto him **the blood**, which he sprinkled upon the altar round about,

And there came a fire out from before the Lord, and consumed upon the altar the burnt offering and the fat: which when all the people saw, they shouted, and fell on their faces.

Leviticus 14:25

And he shall kill the lamb of the trespass offering, and the priest shall take some of **the blood of the trespass offering,** and put it upon the tip of the right ear of him that is to be cleansed, and upon the thumb of his right hand, and upon the great toe of his right foot:

Leviticus 17:11-12

For the life of the flesh is in the blood: and I have given it to you upon the altar to make an atonement for your souls: **for it is the blood that maketh an atonement for the soul.**

Therefore I said unto the children of Israel, No soul of you shall eat blood, neither shall any stranger that sojourneth among you eat blood.

Numbers 19:4

And Eleazar the priest shall take of her blood with his finger, and **sprinkle of her blood** directly before the tabernacle of the congregation **seven times:**

Hebrews 9:18-22

Whereupon neither the first testament was dedicated without blood.

For when Moses had spoken every precept to all the people according to the law, he took the **blood** of calves and of goats, with water, and scarlet wool, and hyssop, **and sprinkled both the book, and all the people,**

Saying, **This is the blood of the testament which God hath enjoined unto you.**

Moreover he sprinkled with blood both the tabernacle, and all the vessels of the ministry.

And almost all things are by the law purged with blood; and without shedding of blood is no remission.

Hebrews 11:28 *(Moses)*

Through faith he kept the passover, **and the sprinkling of blood**, lest He that destroyed the firstborn should touch them.

B. Jesus - The Sacrificial Lamb of God

Genesis 22:8

And Abraham said, **My son, God will provide Himself a lamb for a burnt offering: . . .**

Matthew 26:28

For this is My blood of the new testament, which is shed for many for the remission of sins.

Acts 20:28

Take heed therefore unto yourselves, and to all the flock, over the which the Holy Ghost hath made you overseers, to feed the church of God**, which He hath purchased with His own blood.**

Romans 3:25

Whom God hath set forth to be a propitiation through faith in His blood, to declare His righteousness for the remission of sins that are past, through the forbearance of God;

Romans 5:9-10

Much more then, **being now justified by His blood**, we shall be saved from wrath through Him.

For if, when we were enemies, we were reconciled to God by the death of His Son, much more, being reconciled, we shall be saved by His life.

Ephesians 1:7

In Whom we have redemption through His blood, the forgiveness of sins, according to the riches of His grace;

Colossians 1:13-14

Who hath delivered us from the power of darkness, and hath translated us into the kingdom of His dear Son:

In Whom we have redemption through His blood, even the forgiveness of sins:

Colossians 1:20

And, **having made peace through the blood of His cross**, by Him to reconcile all things unto Himself; . . .

Hebrews 7:26-27

For such an high priest became us, Who is holy, harmless, undefiled, separate from sinners, and made higher than the heavens;

Who needeth not daily, as those high priests, to offer up sacrifice, first for His own sins, and then for the people's: **for this He did once, when He offered up Himself.**

Hebrews 9:11-15

But Christ being come an High Priest of good things to come, by a greater and more perfect tabernacle, not made with hands, that is to say, not of this building;

Neither by the blood of goats and calves, **but by His own blood He entered in once into the holy place, having obtained eternal redemption for us.**

For if the blood of bulls and of goats, and the ashes of an heifer sprinkling the unclean, sanctifieth to the purifying of the flesh:

How much more shall the blood of Christ, Who through the eternal Spirit offered Himself without spot to God, purge your conscience from dead works to serve the living God?

And for this cause **He is the Mediator of the new testament,** that by means of death, for the redemption of the transgressions that were under the first testament, they which are called might receive the promise of eternal inheritance.

Hebrews 10:10

By the which will we are sanctified through the offering of the body of Jesus Christ once for all.

Hebrews 10:14-20

For by one offering He hath perfected for ever them that are sanctified.

Whereof the Holy Ghost also is a witness to us: for after that He had said before,

This is the covenant that I will make with them after those days, saith the Lord, I will put My laws into their hearts, and in their minds will I write them;

And their sins and iniquities will I remember no more.

Now where remission of these is, there is no more offering for sin.

Having therefore, brethren, **boldness to enter into the holiest by the blood of Jesus,**

By a new and living way, which He hath consecrated for us, through the veil, that is to say, His flesh;

Hebrews 12:24

And to Jesus the Mediator of the new covenant, and to **the blood of sprinkling**, that speaketh better things than that of Abel.

Hebrews 13:20-21

Now the God of peace, that brought again from the dead our Lord Jesus, that great Shepherd of the sheep, **through the blood of the everlasting covenant**,

Make you perfect in every good work to do His will, working in you that which is well-pleasing in His sight, through Jesus Christ; to Whom be glory for ever and ever. Amen.

I Peter 1:2

Elect according to the foreknowledge of God the Father, through sanctification of the Spirit, **unto obedience and sprinkling of the blood of Jesus Christ:** . . .

I Peter 1:18-19

Forasmuch as ye know that ye were not redeemed with corruptible things, as silver and gold, from your vain conversation received by tradition from your fathers;

But with the precious blood of Christ, as of a lamb without blemish and without spot:

I John 1:7

But if we walk in the light, as He is in the light, we have fellowship one with another, **and the blood of Jesus Christ His Son cleanseth us from all sin.**

I John 5:8-9

And there are three that bear witness in earth, the Spirit, and the water, **and the blood**: and these three agree in one.

If we receive the witness of men, the witness of God is greater: . . .

Revelations 1:5

And from Jesus Christ, Who is the faithful Witness, and the First Begotten of the dead, and the Prince of the kings of the earth. **Unto Him that loved us, and washed us from our sins in His own blood,**

Revelations 5:9

And they sung a new song, saying, Thou art worthy to take the book, and to open the seals thereof: **for Thou wast slain, and hast redeemed us to God by Thy blood out of every kindred, and tongue, and people, and nation;**

Revelations 7:14

. . . These are they which came out of great tribulation**, and have washed their robes, and made them white in the blood of the Lamb.**

Revelations 12:11

And they overcame him **by the blood of the Lamb**, and by the word of their testimony; and they loved not their lives unto the death.

Chapter 5

The Authority of God's Word

<u>**Numbers 23:19**</u>

God is not a man, that He should lie; neither the son of man, that He should repent: hath He said, and shall He not do it? or hath He spoken, and shall He not make it good?

<u>**Deuteronomy 8:3**</u>

And He humbled thee, and suffered thee to hunger, and fed thee with manna, which thou knewest not, neither did thy fathers know; that He might make thee know that **man doth not live by bread only, but by every word that proceedeth out of the mouth of the Lord doth man live.**

<u>**Deuteronomy 11:18-21**</u>

Therefore shall ye lay up these My words in your heart and in your soul, and bind them for a sign upon your hand, that they may be as frontlets between your eyes.

And ye shall teach them your children, speaking of them when thou sittest in thine house, and when thou walkest by the way, when thou liest down, and when thou risest up.

And thou shalt write them upon the door posts of thine house, and upon thy gates:

That your days may be multiplied, and the days of your children, in the land which the Lord sware unto your fathers to give them, **as the days of heaven upon the earth.**

<u>**Joshua 1:8**</u>

This **book of the law** shall not depart out of thy mouth; but thou shalt meditate therein day and night, that thou mayest observe to do according to all that is written therein: for then thou shalt make thy way prosperous, and then thou shalt have good success.

<u>**II Samuel 22:31**</u>

As for God, His way is perfect; **the word of the Lord is tried:** He is a buckler to all them that trust in Him.

I Kings 8:56

Blessed be the Lord, that hath given rest unto His people Israel, according to all that He promised: **there hath not failed one word of all His good promise,** which He promised by the hand of Moses His servant.

Job 23:12

Neither have I gone back from the commandment of His lips; **I have esteemed the words of His mouth more than my necessary food.**

Psalm 12:6

The words of the Lord are pure words: as silver tried in a furnace of earth, purified seven times.

Psalm 17:4

. . . by the word of Thy lips I have kept me from the paths of the destroyer.

Psalm 19:7-11

The law of the Lord is perfect, converting the soul: **the testimony of the Lord is sure,** making wise the simple.

The statutes of the Lord are right, rejoicing the heart: **the commandment of the Lord is pure,** enlightening the eyes.

The fear of the Lord is clean, enduring for ever: **the judgments of the Lord are true and righteous altogether.**

More to be desired are they than gold, yea, than much fine gold: sweeter also than honey and the honeycomb.

Moreover by them is Thy servant warned: and in keeping of them there is great reward.

Psalm 33:6, 9

By the word of the Lord were the heavens made; and all the host of them by the breath of His mouth.

For He spake, and it was done; He commanded, and it stood fast.

Psalm 89:34

My covenant will I not break, nor alter the thing that is gone out of My lips.

Psalm 103:20

Bless the Lord, ye His angels, that excel in strength, **that do His commandments, hearkening unto the voice of His word.**

Psalm 107:20

He sent His word, and healed them, and delivered them from their destructions.

Psalm 119:9

Wherewithal shall a young man cleanse his way? by taking heed thereto according to Thy word.

Psalm 119:11

Thy word have I hid in mine heart, that I might not sin against Thee.

Psalm 119:18

Open Thou mine eyes, that I may behold wondrous things out of Thy law.

Psalm 119:50

This is my comfort in my affliction: for Thy word hath quickened me.

Psalm 119:89

For ever, O Lord, Thy word is settled in heaven.

Psalm 119:103

How sweet are Thy words unto my taste! yea, sweeter than honey to my mouth!

Psalm 119:105

Thy word is a lamp unto my feet, and a light unto my path.

Psalm 119:130

The entrance of Thy words giveth light; it giveth understanding unto the simple.

Psalm 119:133

Order my steps in Thy word: and let not any iniquity have dominion over me.

Psalm 119:140

Thy word is very pure: therefore Thy servant loveth it.

Psalm 119:152

Concerning Thy testimonies, I have known of old that Thou hast founded them for ever.

Psalm 119:165

Great peace have they which love Thy law: and nothing shall offend them.

Psalm 138:2

I will worship toward Thy holy temple, and praise Thy name for Thy lovingkindness and for Thy truth: **for Thou hast magnified Thy word above all Thy name.**

Proverbs 3:1-2

My son, forget not My law; but let thine heart keep My commandments:
For length of days, and long life, and peace, shall they add to thee.

Proverbs 4:20-22

My son, attend to My words; incline thine ear unto My sayings.
Let them not depart from thine eyes; keep them in the midst of thine heart.
For they are life unto those that find them, and health to all their flesh.

Proverbs 6:20-23

My son, keep thy father's commandment, and forsake not the law of thy mother:

Bind them continually upon thine heart, and tie them about thy neck.

When thou goest, it shall lead thee; when thou sleepest, it shall keep thee; and when thou awakest, it shall talk with thee.

For the commandment is a lamp; and the law is light; and reproofs of instruction are the way of life:

Proverbs 13:13

Whoso despiseth the word shall be destroyed: but he that feareth the commandment shall be rewarded.

Proverbs 30:5-6

Every word of God is pure: He is a shield unto them that put their trust in Him.

Add thou not unto His words, lest He reprove thee, and thou be found a liar.

Isaiah 40:8

The grass withereth, the flower fadeth: **but the word of our God shall stand for ever.**

Isaiah 55:10-11

For as the rain cometh down, and the snow from heaven, and returneth not thither, but watereth the earth, and maketh it bring forth and bud, that it may give seed to the sower, and bread to the eater:

So shall My word be that goeth forth out of My mouth: it shall not return unto Me void, but it shall accomplish that which I please, and it shall prosper in the thing whereto I sent it.

Jeremiah 1:12

Then said the Lord to me, ***You have seen well, for I am alert and active, watching over My word to perform it.*** *[AMP]*

Jeremiah 15:16

Thy words were found, and I did eat them; and Thy word was unto me the joy and rejoicing of mine heart: for I am called by Thy name, O Lord God of hosts.

Jeremiah 20:9

. . . But His word was in mine heart as a burning fire shut up in my bones, . . .

Jeremiah 23:29

Is not My word like fire [that consumes all that cannot endure the test]? says the Lord, ***and like a hammer that breaks in pieces the rock [of most stubborn resistance]?*** *[AMP]*

Joel 2:11

. . . for He is strong that executeth His word: . . .

Matthew 4:4

But He answered and said, It is written, Man shall not live by bread alone, but by every word that proceedeth out of the mouth of God.

Matthew 5:18

For verily I say unto you, **Till heaven and earth pass, one jot or one tittle shall in no wise pass from the law, till all be fulfilled.**

Matthew 8:8

The centurion answered and said, Lord, I am not worthy that Thou shouldest come under my roof: **but speak the word only, and my servant shall be healed.**

Matthew 8:16

. . . He cast out the spirits **with His word,** . . .

Mark 13:31

Heaven and earth shall pass away: but My words shall not pass away.

Luke 4:32

And they were astonished at His doctrine: **for His word was with power.**

Luke 16:17

And it is easier for heaven and earth to pass, than one tittle of the law to fail.

John 1:1,3-4

In the beginning was the Word, and the Word was with God, and the Word was God.
All things were made by Him; and without Him was not any thing made that was made.
In Him was life; and the life was the light of men.

John 1:14

And the Word was made flesh, and dwelt among us, (and we beheld His glory, the glory as of the only begotten of the Father,) full of grace and truth.

John 5:39

Search the scriptures; for in them ye think ye have eternal life: and they are they which testify of Me.

John 6:63

It is the Spirit that quickeneth; the flesh profiteth nothing: **the words that I speak unto you, they are spirit, and they are life.**

John 8:31-32

. . . If ye continue in My word, then are ye My disciples indeed;
And ye shall know the truth, and the truth shall make you free.

John 12:48-50

He that rejecteth Me, and receiveth not My words, hath one that judgeth him: **the word that I have spoken, the same shall judge him in the last day.**

For I have not spoken of Myself; but the Father which sent Me, He gave Me a commandment, what I should say, and what I should speak.

And I know that His commandment is life everlasting: whatsoever I speak therefore, even as the Father said unto Me, so I speak.

John 15:3

Now ye are clean through the word which I have spoken unto you.

John 17:17

Sanctify them through Thy truth: **Thy word is truth.**

Acts 20:32

And now, brethren, I commend you to God, and to **the word of His grace, which is able to build you up,** and to give you an inheritance among all them which are sanctified.

Romans 1:16

For I am not ashamed of the gospel of Christ: **for it is the power of God unto salvation to every one that believeth**; to the Jew first, and also to the Greek.

Romans 10:8

But what saith it? The word is nigh thee, even in thy mouth, and in thy heart: that is, the word of faith, which we preach;

Romans 10:17

So then faith cometh by hearing, and hearing by the word of God.

Romans 15:4

For whatsoever things were written aforetime were written for our learning, that we through patience and comfort of the scriptures might have hope.

II Corinthians 1:20

For all the promises of God in Him are yea, and in Him Amen, unto the glory of God by us.

Ephesians 5:26

That He might sanctify and cleanse it with the washing of water by the word,

Ephesians 6:17

And take the helmet of salvation, and **the sword of the Spirit, which is the word of God:**

Philippians 2:16

Holding forth the word of life; that I may rejoice in the day of Christ, that I have not run in vain, neither laboured in vain.

Colossians 3:16

Let the word of Christ dwell in you richly in all wisdom; teaching and admonishing one another in psalms and hymns and spiritual songs, singing with grace in your hearts to the Lord.

II Timothy 3:16-17

All scripture is given by inspiration of God, and is profitable for doctrine, for reproof, for correction, for instruction in righteousness:

That the man of God may be perfect, throughly furnished unto all good works.

Hebrews 1:3

. . . upholding all things by the word of His power, . . .

Hebrews 4:12

For the word of God is quick, and powerful, and sharper than any twoedged sword, piercing even to the dividing asunder of soul and spirit, and of the joints and marrow, and is a discerner of the thoughts and intents of the heart.

For the Word that God speaks is alive and full of power [making it active, operative, energizing, and effective]; it is sharper than any two-edged sword, penetrating to the dividing line of the breath of life (soul) and [the immortal] spirit, and of joints and marrow [of the deepest parts of our nature], exposing and shifting and analyzing and judging the very thoughts and purposes of the heart. [AMP]

Hebrews 11:3

Through faith we understand that the worlds were framed by the word of God, so that things which are seen were not made of things which do appear.

James 1:18

Of His own will begat He us with the word of truth, that we should be a kind of first fruits of His creatures.

James 1:21

Wherefore lay apart all filthiness and superfluity of naughtiness, and **receive with meekness the engrafted word, which is able to save your souls.**

James 1:25

But whoso looketh into the perfect law of liberty, and continueth therein, he being not a forgetful hearer, but a doer of the work, this man shall be blessed in his deed.

I Peter 1:22-25

Seeing ye have purified your souls in obeying the truth through the Spirit unto unfeigned love of the brethren, see that ye love one another with a pure heart fervently:

Being born again, not of corruptible seed, but of incorruptible, by the word of God, which liveth and abideth for ever.

For all flesh is as grass, and all the glory of man as the flower of grass. The grass withereth, and the flower thereof falleth away:

But the word of the Lord endureth for ever. And this is the word which by the gospel is preached unto you.

I Peter 2:2

As newborn babes, desire the sincere milk of the word, that ye may grow thereby:

II Peter 1:4

Whereby are given unto us exceeding great and precious promises: that by these ye might be partakers of the divine nature, having escaped the corruption that is in the world through lust.

II Peter 1:19-21

We have also a more sure word of prophecy; whereunto ye do well that ye take heed, as unto a light that shineth in a dark place, until the day dawn, and the Day Star arise in your hearts:

Knowing this first, **that no prophecy of the scripture is of any private interpretation.**

For the prophecy came not in old time by the will of man: but holy men of God spake as they were moved by the Holy Ghost.

I John 2:14

. . . I have written unto you, young men, because ye are strong, and **the word of God abideth in you,** and ye have overcome the wicked one.

Revelation 1:16

And He had in His right hand seven stars: **and out of His mouth went a sharp two-edged sword:** and His countenance was as the sun shineth in his strength.

Revelation 2:12

And to the angel of the church in Pergamos write; **These things saith He which hath the sharp sword with two edges;**

Revelation 2:16

Repent; or else I will come unto thee quickly, **and will fight against them with the sword of My mouth.**

Revelation 19:13

. . . His name is called The Word of God.

Chapter 6

The Names of God

Psalm 20:1

The Lord hear thee in the day of trouble; **the name of the God of Jacob defend thee**;

Psalm 20:7

Some trust in chariots, and some in horses: **but we will remember the name of the Lord our God.**

Proverbs 18:10

The name of the Lord is a strong tower: the righteous runneth into it, and is safe.

A. God the Father

Genesis 17:1-2

And when Abram was ninety years old and nine, the Lord appeared to Abram, and said unto him, **I am the Almighty God**; walk before Me, and be thou perfect.

And I will make My covenant between Me and thee, and will multiply thee exceedingly.

Genesis 18:25

That be far from Thee to do after this manner, to slay the righteous with the wicked: and that the righteous should be as the wicked, that be far from Thee: Shall not **the Judge of all the earth** do right?

Genesis 22:13-14

And Abraham lifted up his eyes, and looked, and behold behind him a ram caught in a thicket by his horns: and Abraham went and took the ram, and offered him up for a burnt offering in the stead of his son.

And Abraham called the name of that place **Jehovah-Jireh** *(The Lord Will Provide)*: as it is said to this day, In the mount of the Lord it shall be seen.

Exodus 3:14

And God said unto Moses, **I AM THAT I AM**: and He said, Thus shalt thou say unto the children of Israel, **I AM** hath sent me unto you.

*And God said to Moses, **I AM WHO I AM and WHAT I AM, and I WILL BE WHAT I WILL BE;** and He said, You shall say this to the Israelites, **I AM** has sent me to you! [AMP]*

Exodus 6:3

And I appeared unto Abraham, unto Isaac, and unto Jacob, by the name of God Almighty, but by My name **JEHOVAH** was I not known to them.

Exodus 6:3

*I appeared to Abraham, to Isaac, and to Jacob as **God Almighty [El-Shaddai]**, but by My name the Lord [**Yahweh** - the redemptive name of God] I did not make Myself known to them [in acts and great miracles]. [AMP]*

Exodus 15:2

The Lord is **my Strength** and Song, and He is become my Salvation: He is my God, and I will prepare Him an habitation; my father's God, and I will exalt Him.

Exodus 17:15-16

And Moses built an altar, and called the name of it **Jehovah-Nissi** *(The Lord My Banner)*:

For he said, Because the Lord hath sworn that the Lord will have war with Amalek from generation to generation.

Deuteronomy 10:17

For the Lord your God is **God of gods,** and **Lord of lords,** a great God, a mighty, and a terrible, which regardeth not persons, nor taketh reward:

Deuteronomy 32:8

When the **Most High** divided to the nations their inheritance, when He separated the sons of Adam, he set the bounds of the people according to the number of the children of Israel:

Deuteronomy 33:27

The **Eternal God** is thy refuge, and underneath are the everlasting arms: and He shall thrust out the enemy from before thee; and shall say, Destroy them.

Joshua 3:10

And Joshua said, Hereby ye shall know that the **Living God** is among you, and that He will without fail drive out from before you the Canaanites, and the Hittites, and the Hivites, and the Perizzites, and the Girgashites, and the Amorites, and the Jebusites.

Judges 6:22-24

And when Gideon perceived that he was an angel of the Lord, Gideon said, Alas, O Lord God! for because I have seen an angel of the Lord face to face.

And the Lord said unto him, Peace be unto thee; fear not: thou shalt not die.

Then Gideon built an altar there unto the Lord, and called it **Jehovah-Shalom** *(The Lord Send Peace)*: unto this day it is yet in Ophrah of the Abiezrites.

I Samuel 1:11 *(Hannah)*

And she vowed a vow, and said, **O Lord of hosts**, if Thou wilt indeed look on the affliction of Thine handmaid, and remember me, and not forget Thine handmaid, but wilt give unto Thine handmaid a man child, then I will give him unto the Lord all the days of his life, and there shall no razor come upon his head.

II Samuel 22:2-3 *(David)*

He said: The Lord is my Rock [of escape from Saul] and my Fortress [in the wilderness] and my Deliverer;

My God, my Rock, in Him will I take refuge; my Shield and the Horn of my salvation; my Stronghold and my Refuge, my Savior - You save me from violence. [AMP]

I Chronicles 29:10

Wherefore David blessed the Lord before all the congregation: and David said, Blessed be Thou, Lord God of Israel **our Father**, for ever and ever.

Psalm 71:22

I will also praise Thee with the psaltery, even Thy truth, O my God: unto Thee will I sing with the harp, **O Thou Holy One of Israel.**

Isaiah 26:4

Trust ye in the Lord for ever: for in the **Lord Jehovah** is everlasting strength:

So trust in the Lord (commit yourself to Him, lean on Him, hope confidently in Him) forever; for the Lord God is an everlasting Rock ***[the Rock of Ages]****. [AMP]*

Isaiah 33:22

For the Lord is our **Judge**, the Lord is our **Lawgiver**, the Lord is our **King**; He will save us.

Isaiah 41:14

Fear not, thou worm Jacob, and ye men of Israel; I will help thee, saith the Lord, and thy **Redeemer**, the **Holy One of Israel**.

Jeremiah 33:16

In those days shall Judah be saved, and Jerusalem shall dwell safely: and this is the name wherewith she shall be called, **Jehovah-Tsidkenu** *(The Lord Our Righteousness).*

Ezekiel 48:35

It was round about eighteen thousand measures: and the name of the city from that day shall be, **Jehovah-Shammah** *(The Lord is There).*

Matthew 6:9

After this manner therefore pray ye: **Our Father** which art in heaven, Hallowed be Thy name.

Matthew 6:26

Behold the fowls of the air: for they sow not, neither do they reap, nor gather into barns; yet your **heavenly Father** feedeth them. Are ye not much better than they?

James 1:17

Every good gift and every perfect gift is from above, and cometh down from the **Father of lights**, with Whom is no variableness, neither shadow of turning.

James 5:4

Behold, the hire of the labourers who have reaped down your fields, which is of you kept back by fraud, crieth: and the cries of them which have reaped are entered into the ears of the **Lord of Sabaoth.**

B. God the Son

Genesis 3:15

And I will put enmity between you and the woman, and between your offspring and her Offspring; He will bruise and tread your head underfoot, and you will lie in wait and bruise His heel. [AMP]

Genesis 49:10

The sceptre shall not depart from Judah, nor a lawgiver from between his feet, until **Shiloh** come; and unto Him shall the gathering of the people be.

*The scepter or leadership shall not depart from Judah, nor the ruler's staff from between his feet, until **Shiloh [the Messiah, the Peaceful One]** comes to Whom it belongs, and to Him shall be the obedience of the people. [AMP]*

Job 19:25

For I know that my **Redeemer** liveth, and that He shall stand at the latter day upon the earth:

Song of Solomon 2:1

I AM the **Rose of Sharon**, and the **Lily of the Valleys**.

Isaiah 4:2

In that day shall the **Branch of the Lord** be beautiful and glorious, and the fruit of the earth shall be excellent and comely for them that are escaped of Israel.

Isaiah 7:14

Therefore the Lord Himself shall give you a sign; Behold, a virgin shall conceive, and bear a son, and shall call His name **Immanuel** *(God With Us).*

Isaiah 9:6

For unto us a Child is born, unto us a Son is given: and the government shall be upon His shoulder: and His name shall be called **Wonderful, Counsellor, The Mighty God, The Everlasting Father, The Prince of Peace.**

Isaiah 40:3

The voice of him that crieth in the wilderness, Prepare ye the way of the **Lord**, make straight in the desert a highway for our **God**.

Isaiah 42:1

Behold My servant, Whom I uphold; Mine **Elect**, in Whom My soul delighteth; I have put My Spirit upon Him: He shall bring forth judgment to the Gentiles.

Isaiah 51:9

Awake, awake, put on strength, O **arm of the Lord**; awake, as in the ancient days, in the generations of old. Art Thou not It that hath cut Rahab, and wounded the dragon?

Isaiah 53:1

Who hath believed our report? and to whom is the **arm of the Lord** revealed?

Isaiah 53:3

He is despised and rejected of men; a **Man of sorrows**, and acquainted with grief: and we hid as it were our faces from Him; He was despised, and we esteemed Him not.

Isaiah 55:4

Behold, I have given Him for a **Witness** to the people, a **Leader** and **Commander** to the people.

Isaiah 60:16

Thou shalt also suck the milk of the Gentiles, and shalt suck the breast of kings: and thou shalt know that I the Lord am thy **Saviour** and thy **Redeemer**, the **Mighty One of Jacob.**

Jeremiah 23:5-6

Behold, the days come, saith the Lord, that I will raise unto David a righteous **Branch**, and a King shall reign and prosper, and shall execute judgment and justice in the earth.

In His days Judah shall be saved, and Israel shall dwell safely: and this is His name whereby He shall be called, **The Lord Our Righteousness.**

Daniel 9:25

Know therefore and understand, that from the going forth of the commandment to restore and to build Jerusalem unto the **Messiah the Prince** shall be seven weeks, and threescore and two weeks: the street shall be built again, and the wall, even in troublous times.

Micah 5:2

But thou, Bethlehem Ephratah, though thou be little among the thousands of Judah, yet out of thee shall He come forth unto Me that is to be **Ruler in Israel**; Whose goings forth have been from of old, from everlasting.

Zechariah 6:12-13

And speak unto him, saying, Thus speaketh the Lord of hosts, saying, Behold the Man Whose name is **The Branch**; and He shall grow up out of His place, and He shall build the temple of the Lord:

Even He shall build the temple of the Lord; and He shall bear the glory, and shall sit and rule upon His throne; and He shall be a Priest upon His throne: and the counsel of peace shall be between them both.

Zechariah 9:9

Rejoice greatly, O daughter of Zion; shout, O daughter of Jerusalem: behold, thy **King** cometh unto thee: He is just, and having salvation; lowly, and riding upon an ass, and upon a colt the foal of an ass.

Malachi 3:1

Behold, I will send My messenger, and He shall prepare the way before Me: and the Lord, Whom ye seek, shall suddenly come to His temple, even the **Messenger of the covenant**, Whom ye delight in: behold, He shall come, saith the Lord of Hosts.

Malachi 4:2

But unto you that fear My name shall the **Sun of Righteousness** arise with healing in His wings; and ye shall go forth, and grow up as calves of the stall.

Matthew 1:1

The book of the generation of Jesus Christ, the **son of David**, the **son of Abraham**.

The book of the ancestry (genealogy) of Jesus Christ (the Messiah, the Anointed), the son (descendant) of David, the son (descendant) of Abraham. [AMP]

Matthew 1:21

And she shall bring forth a son, and thou shalt call His name **JESUS**: for He shall save His people from their sins.

Matthew 1:23

Behold, a virgin shall be with child, and shall bring forth a son, and they shall call his name **Emmanuel,** which being interpreted is, **God with us.**

Matthew 2:2

Saying, Where is He that is born **King of the Jews**? for we have seen His star in the east, and are come to worship Him.

Matthew 2:6

And thou Bethlehem, in the land of Juda, art not the least among the princes of Juda: for out of thee shall come a **Governor**, that shall rule My people Israel.

Matthew 2:15

And was there until the death of Herod: that it might be fulfilled which was spoken of the Lord by the prophet, saying, Out of Egypt have I call **My Son**.

Matthew 2:23

And He came and dwelt in a city called Nazareth: that it might be fulfilled which was spoken by the prophets, He shall be called a **Nazarene**.

Matthew 8:20

And Jesus saith unto him, The foxes have holes, and the birds of the air have nests; but the **Son of Man** hath not where to lay His head.

Matthew 12:18

Behold **My Servant**, Whom I have chosen; **My Beloved**, in Whom My soul is well pleased: I will put My Spirit upon Him, and He shall shew judgment to the Gentiles.

Matthew 21:11

And the multitude said, This is **Jesus the Prophet of Nazareth** of Galilee.

Matthew 21:42

Jesus asked them, Have you never read in the Scriptures: The very Stone which the builders rejected and threw away has become the ***Cornerstone****; this is the Lord's doing, and it is marvelous in our eyes? [AMP]*

Mark 1:24

Saying, Let us alone; what have we to do with Thee, Thou **Jesus of Nazareth**? art Thou come to destroy us? I know Thee Who Thou art, the **Holy One of God.**

Mark 14:61

But He held His peace, and answered nothing. Again the high priest asked Him, and said unto Him, Art Thou the Christ, the **Son of the Blessed**?

Luke 1:31-32

And, behold, thou shalt conceive in thy womb, and bring forth a son, and shalt call His name **Jesus**.

He shall be great, and shall be called the **Son of the Highest**: and the Lord God shall give unto Him the throne of His father David:

Luke 1:69

And hath raised up an **Horn of salvation** for us in the house of His servant David;

Luke 1:78

Through the tender mercy of our God; whereby the **Dayspring** from on high hath visited us,

Luke 2:11

For unto you is born this day in the city of David a **Saviour**, which is Christ the Lord.

Luke 2:25

And, behold, there was a man in Jerusalem, whose name was Simeon; and the same man was just and devout, waiting for the **Consolation of Israel**: and the Holy Ghost was upon him.

Luke 9:20

He said unto them, But Whom say ye that I am? Peter answering said, **The Christ of God.**

Luke 24:19

And He said unto them, What things? And they said unto Him, Concerning **Jesus of Nazareth**, which was a **Prophet** mighty in deed and word before God and all the people:

John 1:1

In the beginning was the **Word**, and the **Word** was with God, and the **Word** was God.

John 1:9

That was the **true Light**, which lighteth every man that cometh into the world.

John 1:14

And the Word was made flesh, and dwelt among us, (and we beheld His glory, the glory as of the **only begotten of the Father**,) full of grace and truth.

John 1:18

No man hath seen God at any time; the **only begotten Son**, which is in the bosom of the Father, He hath declared Him.

John 1:29

The next day John seeth Jesus coming unto him, and saith, Behold the **Lamb of God**, which taketh away the sin of the world.

John 1:34

And I saw, and bare record that this is the **Son of God.**

John 1:41

He first findeth his own brother Simon, and saith unto him, We have found the **Messias**, which is, being interpreted, the **Christ**.

<u>**John 6:35**</u>

And Jesus said unto them, I am the **Bread of Life:** he that cometh to Me shall never hunger; and he that believeth on Me shall never thirst.

<u>**John 8:12**</u>

Then spake Jesus again unto them, saying, I am the **Light of the world**: He that followeth Me shall not walk in darkness, but shall have the light of life.

<u>**John 8:58**</u>

Jesus said unto them, Verily, verily, I say unto you, Before Abraham was, **I Am.**

<u>**John 10:7**</u>

Then said Jesus unto them again, Verily, verily, I say unto you, I am the **Door of the sheep.**

<u>**John 10:11**</u>

I am the **Good Shepherd**: the Good Shepherd giveth His life for the sheep.

<u>**John 11:25**</u>

Jesus said unto her, I am the **Resurrection, and the Life**: he that believeth in Me, though he were dead, yet shall he live:

<u>**John 14:6**</u>

Jesus saith unto him, I am **the Way, the Truth, and the Life**: no man cometh unto the Father, but by Me.

<u>**John 15:1**</u>

I am the **True Vine**, and My Father is the husbandman.

<u>**John 20:28**</u>

And Thomas answered and said unto Him, **My Lord and my God**.

<u>**Acts 3:14-15**</u>

But ye denied the **Holy One** and the **Just**, and desired a murderer to be granted unto you;

And killed the **Prince of life**, Whom God hath raised from the dead; whereof we are witnesses.

But you denied and rejected and disowned ***the Pure and Holy, the Just and Blameless One****, and demanded [the pardon of] a murderer to be granted to you.*

But you killed ***the very Source (the Author) of life****, Whom God raised from the dead. To this we are witnesses. [AMP]*

<u>**Acts 3:22**</u>

For Moses truly said unto the fathers, **A Prophet** shall the Lord your God raise up unto you of your brethren, like unto me; Him shall ye hear in all things whatsoever He shall say unto you.

Acts 4:27

For of a truth against **Thy holy Child Jesus,** Whom Thou hast anointed, both Herod, and Pontius Pilate, with the Gentiles, and the people of Israel, were gathered together,

Acts 7:52

Which of the prophets have not your fathers persecuted? and they have slain them which shewed before of the coming of the **Just One**; of Whom ye have been now the betrayers and murderers:

Acts 10:36

The word which God sent unto the children of Israel, preaching peace by Jesus Christ: **(He is Lord of all:)**

Romans 11:26

And so all Israel shall be saved: as it is written, There shall come out of Sion **the Deliverer,** and shall turn away ungodliness from Jacob:

I Corinthians 2:8

Which none of the princes of this world knew: for had they known it, they would not have crucified the **Lord of glory**.

I Corinthians 5:7

Purge out therefore the old leaven, that ye may be a new lump, as ye are unleavened. For even **Christ our Passover** is sacrificed for us:

I Corinthians 10:4

And did all drink the same spiritual drink: for they drank of that spiritual **Rock** that followed them: and that **Rock** was Christ.

I Corinthians 15:45

And so it is written, The first man Adam was made a living soul; the **last Adam** was made a quickening Spirit.

II Corinthians 4:4

In whom the god of this world hath blinded the minds of them which believe not, lest the light of the glorious gospel of Christ, Who is the **Image of God**, should shine unto them.

Ephesians 1:22

And hath put all things under His feet, and gave Him to be **the Head over all things** to the church,

Ephesians 2:20

And are built upon the foundation of the apostles and prophets, Jesus Christ Himself being **the chief Corner stone;**

I Timothy 1:17

Now unto the **King Eternal, Immortal, Invisible,** the **Only Wise God**, be honour and glory for ever and ever. Amen.

I Timothy 2:5

For there is one God, and one **Mediator** between God and men, the man Christ Jesus;

I Timothy 6:15

Which in His times He shall shew, Who is the **blessed and only Potentate**, the **King of kings,** and **Lord of lords;**

II Timothy 4:8

Henceforth there is laid up for me a crown of righteousness, which the Lord, the **righteous Judge,** shall give me at that day: and not to me only, but unto all them also that love His appearing.

Hebrews 1:2

Hath in these last days spoken unto us by His Son, Whom He hath appointed **Heir of all things,** by Whom also He made the worlds;

Hebrews 2:10

For it became Him, for Whom are all things, and by Whom are all things, in bringing many sons unto glory, to make the **Captain of their salvation** perfect through sufferings.

Hebrews 3:1

Wherefore, Holy Brethren, partakers of the heavenly calling, consider the **Apostle and High Priest of our profession, Christ Jesus**;

Hebrews 4:14

Seeing then that we have a **great High Priest**, that is passed into the heavens, **Jesus the Son of God,** let us hold fast our profession.

Hebrews 5:9

And being made perfect, He became the **Author of eternal salvation** unto all them that obey Him;

Hebrews 6:20

Whither the **Forerunner** is for us entered, even Jesus, made an High Priest for ever after the order of Melchisedec.

Hebrews 12:2

Looking unto Jesus the **Author and Finisher of our faith**; Who for the joy that was set before Him endured the cross, despising the shame, and is set down at the right hand of the throne of God.

I Peter 2:25

For ye were as sheep going astray; but are now returned unto the **Shepherd and Bishop of your souls.**

I Peter 4:19

Wherefore let them that suffer according to the will of God commit the keeping of their souls to Him in well doing, as unto a faithful **Creator**.

I Peter 5:4

And when the **Chief Shepherd** shall appear, ye shall receive a crown of glory that fadeth not away.

II Peter 2:20

For if after they have escaped the pollutions of the world through the knowledge of the **Lord** and **Saviour** Jesus Christ, they are again entangled therein, and overcome, the latter end is worse with them than the beginning.

I John 1:1

That Which was from the beginning, Which we have heard, Which we have seen with our eyes, Which we have looked upon, and our hands have handled, of the **Word of Life**;

I John 2:1

My little children, these things write I unto you, that ye sin not. And if any man sin, we have an **Advocate** with the Father, Jesus Christ the righteous:

My little children, I write you these things so that you may not violate God's law and sin. But if anyone should sin, we have an ***Advocate (One Who will intercede for us)*** *with the Father - [it is] Jesus Christ [the all] righteous [upright, just, Who conforms to the Father's will in every purpose, thought, and action]. [AMP]*

Revelations 1:5

And from Jesus Christ, Who is the **faithful Witness**, and the **First begotten of the dead,** and the **Prince of the kings of the earth**. Unto Him that loved us, and washed us from our sins in His own blood,

Revelations 1:8

I am **Alpha and Omega**, the **Beginning and the Ending**, saith the Lord, which is, and which was, and which is to come, the **Almighty**.

Revelations 1:17

And when I saw Him, I fell at His feet as dead. And He laid His right hand upon me, saying unto me, Fear not; I am **the First and the Last**:

Revelations 3:14

And unto the angel of the church of the Laodiceans write; These things saith the **Amen,**

the faithful and true Witness, the Beginning of the creation of God;

<u>**Revelations 5:5**</u>

And one of the elders saith unto me, Weep not: behold, the **Lion of the tribe of Juda**, the **Root of David**, hath prevailed to open the book, and to loose the seven seals thereof.

<u>**Revelations 13:8**</u>

And all that dwell upon the earth shall worship Him, whose names are not written in the Book of Life of the **Lamb slain from the foundation of the world.**

<u>**Revelations 15:3**</u>

And they sing the song of Moses the servant of God, and the song of the Lamb, saying, Great and marvellous are Thy works, **Lord God Almighty**; just and true are Thy ways, Thou **King of saints.**

<u>**Revelations 19:11**</u>

*After that I saw heaven opened and behold, a white horse [appeared]! The One Who was riding it is called **Faithful (Trustworthy, Loyal, Incorruptible, Steady) and True,** and He passes judgment and wages war in righteousness (holiness, justice, and uprightness). [AMP]*

<u>**Revelations 19:13**</u>

And He was clothed with a vesture dipped in blood: and His name is called **The Word of God**.

<u>**Revelations 19:16**</u>

And He hath on His vesture and on His thigh a name written, **King of kings, and Lord of lords.**

<u>**Revelations 21:6**</u>

And He said unto me, It is done. I am **Alpha and Omega, the Beginning and the End.** I will give unto him that is athirst of the fountain of the water of Life freely.

<u>**Revelations 22:13**</u>

I am **Alpha and Omega**, the **Beginning and the End**, the **First and the Last**.

<u>**Revelations 22:16**</u>

I Jesus have sent Mine angel to testify unto you these things in the churches. I am the **Root and the Offspring of David**, and the **bright and Morning Star.**

C. The Holy Spirit

<u>**Genesis 1:2**</u>

And the earth was without form, and void; and darkness was upon the face of the deep.

And **the Spirit of God** moved upon the face of the waters.

Psalm 51:11-12

Cast me not away from Thy presence; and take not **Thy Holy Spirit** from me.

Restore unto me the joy of Thy salvation; and uphold me with **Thy Free Spirit.**

Isaiah 11:2

And **the Spirit of the Lord** shall rest upon Him, **the Spirit of wisdom and understanding, the Spirit of counsel and might, the Spirit of knowledge and of the fear of the Lord;**

Isaiah 61:1

The Spirit of the Lord God is upon Me; because the Lord hath anointed Me to preach good tidings unto the meek; He hath sent Me to bind up the brokenhearted, to proclaim liberty to the captives, and the opening of the prison to them that are bound;

Zechariah 12:10

And I will pour upon the house of David, and upon the inhabitants of Jerusalem, **the Spirit of grace and of supplications**: and they shall look upon Me Whom they have pierced, and they shall mourn for Him, as one mourneth for his only son, and shall be in bitterness for Him, as one that is in bitterness for his firstborn.

Matthew 10:19-20

But when they deliver you up, take no thought how or what ye shall speak: for it shall be given you in that same hour what ye shall speak.

For it is not ye that speak, but **the Spirit of your Father** Which speaketh in you.

Luke 1:35

And the angel answered and said unto her, **The Holy Ghost** shall come upon thee, and **the power of the Highest** shall overshadow thee: therefore also that holy Thing which shall be born of thee shall be called the Son of God.

John 14:16-17

And I will ask the Father, and He will give you another ***Comforter (Counselor, Helper, Intercessor, Advocate, Strengthener, and Standby)****, that He may remain with you forever —*

The Spirit of Truth*, Whom the world cannot receive (welcome, take to its heart), because it does not see Him or know and recognize Him. But you know and recognize Him, for He lives with you [constantly] and will be in you. [AMP]*

Romans 1:4

And declared to be the Son of God with power, according to **the Spirit of holiness**, by the resurrection from the dead:

Romans 8:2

For the law of **the Spirit of life** in Christ Jesus hath made me free from the law of sin and death.

Romans 8:15

For ye have not received the spirit of bondage again to fear; but ye have received **the Spirit of adoption**, whereby we cry, Abba, Father.

Galatians 4:6

And because ye are sons, God hath sent forth **the Spirit of His Son** into your hearts, crying, Abba, Father.

Ephesians 1:13

In Whom ye also trusted, after that ye heard the **Word of Truth**, the Gospel of your salvation: in Whom also after that ye believed, ye were sealed with that **Holy Spirit of promise,**

Ephesians 4:30

And grieve not **the Holy Spirit of God**, whereby ye are sealed unto the day of redemption.

Hebrews 9:14

How much more shall the blood of Christ, Who through **the eternal Spirit** offered Himself without spot to God, purge your conscience from dead works to serve the living God?

I Peter 1:11

Searching what, or what manner of time **the Spirit of Christ** Which was in them did signify, when It testified beforehand the sufferings of Christ, and the glory that should follow.

I Peter 4:14

If ye be reproached for the name of Christ, happy are ye; for **the Spirit of glory and of God** resteth upon you: on their part He is evil spoken of, but on your part He is glorified.

Chapter 7

Restoration for Fallen Soldiers

A. What Happens When We Repent of Our Sins?

Psalm 51:7

Purge me with hyssop, and I shall be clean: **wash me, and I shall be whiter than snow.**

Psalm 85:2

Thou hast forgiven the iniquity of Thy people, **Thou hast covered all their sin.** Selah.

Psalm 103:3

Who forgiveth all thine iniquities; Who healeth all thy diseases;

Psalm 103:12

As far as the east is from the west, so far hath He removed our transgressions from us.

Proverbs 28:13

He that covereth his sins shall not prosper: **but whoso confesseth and forsaketh them shall have mercy.**

Isaiah 1:18

Come now, and let us reason together, saith the Lord: **though your sins be as scarlet, they shall be as white as snow; though they be red like crimson, they shall be as wool.**

Isaiah 38:17

Behold, for peace I had great bitterness: but Thou hast in love to my soul delivered it from the pit of corruption: **for Thou hast cast all my sins behind Thy back.**

<u>**Isaiah 43:25**</u>

I, even I, am He that blotteth out thy transgressions for Mine own sake, and will not remember thy sins.

<u>**Isaiah 44:22**</u>

I have blotted out, as a thick cloud, thy transgressions, and, as a cloud, thy sins: return unto Me; for I have redeemed thee.

<u>**Jeremiah 31:34**</u>

And they shall teach no more every man his neighbour, and every man his brother, saying, Know the Lord: for they shall all know me, from the least of them unto the greatest of them, saith the Lord: **for I will forgive their iniquity, and I will remember their sin no more.**

<u>**Jeremiah 33:7-8**</u>

And I will cause the captivity of Judah and the captivity of Israel to return, and will build them, as at the first.

And I will cleanse them from all their iniquity, whereby they have sinned against Me; and I will pardon all their iniquities, whereby they have sinned, and whereby they have transgressed against Me.

<u>**Jeremiah 50:20**</u>

In those days, and in that time, saith the Lord, **the iniquity of Israel shall be sought for, and there shall be none; and the sins of Judah, and they shall not be found:** for I will pardon them whom I reserve.

<u>**Ezekiel 18:21-22**</u>

But if the wicked will turn from all his sins that he hath committed, and keep all My statutes, and do that which is lawful and right, he shall surely live, he shall not die.

All his transgressions that he hath committed, they shall not be mentioned unto him: in his righteousness that he hath done he shall live.

<u>**Ezekiel 33:15-16**</u>

If the wicked restore the pledge, give again that he had robbed, walk in the statutes of life, without committing iniquity; **he shall surely live, he shall not die.**

None of his sins that he hath committed shall be mentioned unto him: he hath done that which is lawful and right; he shall surely live.

<u>**Micah 7:18-19**</u>

Who is a God like unto Thee, **that pardoneth iniquity, and passeth by the transgression of the remnant of His heritage?** He retaineth not His anger for ever, because He delighteth in mercy.

He will turn again, He will have compassion upon us; **He will subdue our iniquities; and Thou wilt cast all their sins into the depths of the sea.**

Zephaniah 3:17

The Lord your God is in the midst of you, a Mighty One, a Savior [Who saves]! He will rejoice over you with joy; He will rest [in silent satisfaction] ***and in His love He will be silent and make no mention [of past sins, or even recall them]****; He will exult over you with singing. [AMP]*

Acts 3:19

Repent ye therefore, and be converted, that your sins may be blotted out, when the times of refreshing shall come from the presence of the Lord;

Romans 4:6-8

Even as David also describeth the blessedness of the man, unto whom God imputeth righteousness without works,

Saying, Blessed are they whose iniquities are forgiven, and whose sins are covered.

Blessed is the man to whom the Lord will not imput sin.

II Corinthians 5:21

For He hath made Him to be sin for us, Who knew no sin; **that we might be made the righteousness of God in Him.**

Ephesians 1:6-7

To the praise of the glory of His grace, **wherein He hath made us accepted in the beloved.**

In whom we have **redemption through His blood, the forgiveness of sins,** according to the riches of His grace;

Colossians 2:13-14

And you, being dead in your sins and the uncircumcision of your flesh, hath He quickened together with Him, having forgiven you all trespasses;

Blotting out the handwriting of ordinances that was against us, which was contrary to us, and took it out of the way, nailing it to His cross;

Hebrews 8:12

For I will be merciful to their unrighteousness, and their sins and their iniquities will I remember no more.

Hebrews 10:16-18

This is the covenant that I will make with them after those days, saith the Lord, I will put My laws in their hearts, and in their minds will I write them;

And their sins and iniquities will I remember no more.

Now where remission of these is, there is no more offering for sin.

I John 1:7, 9

But if we walk in the light, as He is in the light, we have fellowship one with another, **and the blood of Jesus Christ His Son cleanseth us from all sin.**

If we confess our sins, **He is faithful and just to forgive us our sins, and to cleanse us from all unrighteousness.**

<u>**Revelation 1:5**</u>
. . . Unto Him that loved us, **and washed us from our sins in His own blood,**

B. God Promises Restoration to Those Who Return to Him

<u>**Deuteronomy 4:29**</u>
But if from thence thou shalt seek the Lord thy God, thou shalt find Him, if thou seek Him with all thy heart and with all thy soul.

<u>**Deuteronomy 30:6**</u>
And the Lord thy God will circumcise thine heart, and the heart of thy seed, to love the Lord thy God with all thine heart, and with all thy soul, **that thou mayest live.**

<u>**II Chronicles 30:9**</u>
For if ye turn again unto the Lord, your brethren and your children shall find compassion before them that lead them captive, so that they shall come again into this land: **for the Lord your God is gracious and merciful, and will not turn away His face from you, if ye return unto Him.**

<u>**Psalm 23:3**</u>
He restoreth my soul: He leadeth me in the paths of righteousness for His name's sake.

<u>**Psalm 37:23-24**</u>
The steps of a good man are ordered by the Lord: and He delighteth in his way.
Though he fall, he shall not be utterly cast down: for the Lord upholdeth him with His hand.

<u>**Psalm 41:4**</u>
I said, Lord, be merciful unto me: **heal my soul;** for I have sinned against Thee.

<u>**Psalm 51:10**</u>
Create in me a clean heart, O God; and renew a right spirit within me.

<u>**Psalm 51:12**</u>
Restore unto me the joy of Thy salvation; and uphold me with Thy free spirit.

<u>**Psalm 94:14**</u>
For the Lord will not cast off His people, neither will He forsake His inheritance.

Psalm 103:1-5

Bless the Lord, O my soul: and all that is within me, bless His holy name.

Bless the Lord, O my soul, and forget not all His benefits:

Who forgiveth all thine iniquities; Who healeth all thy diseases;

Who redeemeth thy life from destruction; Who crowneth thee with lovingkindness and tender mercies;

Who satisfieth thy mouth with good things; so that thy youth is renewed like the eagle's.

Psalm 103:8-12

The Lord is merciful and gracious, slow to anger, and plenteous in mercy.

He will not always chide: neither will He keep His anger for ever.

He hath not dealt with us after our sins; nor rewarded us according to our iniquities.

For as the heaven is high above the earth, so great is His mercy toward them that fear Him.

As far as the east is from the west, so far hath He removed our transgressions from us.

Psalm 138:8

The Lord will perfect that which concerneth me: Thy mercy, O Lord, endureth for ever: forsake not the works of Thine own hands.

Psalm 145:14

The Lord upholdeth all that fall, and raiseth up all those that be bowed down.

Proverbs 24:16

For a just man falleth seven times, and riseth up again: but the wicked shall fall into mischief.

Isaiah 29:24

They also that erred in spirit shall come to understanding, and they that murmured shall learn doctrine.

Isaiah 43:18-19

Remember ye not the former things, neither consider the things of old.

Behold, I will do a new thing; now it shall spring forth; shall ye not know it? I will even make a way in the wilderness, and rivers in the desert.

Isaiah 49:15-16

Can a woman forget her sucking child, that she should not have compassion on the son of her womb? yea, they may forget, **yet will I not forget thee.**

Behold, I have graven thee upon the palms of My hands; thy walls are continually before Me.

Isaiah 55:7

Let the wicked forsake his way, and the unrighteous man his thoughts: and **let him return unto the Lord, and He will have mercy upon him; and to our God, for He will abun-**

dantly pardon.

__Isaiah 61:3__

. . . to give unto them **beauty for ashes, the oil of joy for mourning, the garment of praise for the spirit of heaviness;** . . .

__Jeremiah 3:14-15__

Turn, O backsliding children, saith the Lord; for I am married unto you: and I will take you one of a city, and two of a family, and I will bring you to Zion:

And I will give you pastors according to Mine heart, which shall feed you with knowledge and understanding.

__Jeremiah 3:22__

Return, ye backsliding children, and I will heal your backslidings . . .

__Jeremiah 29:11-13__

For I know the thoughts that I think toward you, saith the Lord, thoughts of peace, and not of evil, to give you an expected end.

Then shall ye call upon Me, and ye shall go and pray unto Me, and I will hearken unto you.

And ye shall seek Me, and find Me, when ye shall search for Me with all your heart.

__Jeremiah 31:3__

The Lord hath appeared of old unto me, saying, **Yea, I have loved thee with an everlasting love: therefore with lovingkindness have I drawn thee.**

__Jeremiah 32:41__

Yea, I will rejoice over them to do them good, and I will plant them in this land assuredly with My whole heart and with My whole soul.

__Jeremiah 33:10-11__

Thus saith the Lord; Again there shall be heard in this place, . . .

The voice of joy, and the voice of gladness, the voice of the bridegroom, and the voice of the bride, the voice of them that shall say, Praise the Lord of hosts: for the Lord is good; for His mercy endureth for ever: and of them that shall bring the sacrifice of praise into the house of the Lord. For I will cause to return the captivity of the land, as at the first, saith the Lord.

__Lamentations 3:22-23__

It is of the Lord's mercies that we are not consumed, because **His compassions fail not.**

They are new every morning: great is Thy faithfulness.

__Ezekiel 34:16__

I will seek that which was lost, and bring again that which was driven away, and will bind up that which was broken, and will strengthen that which was sick: . . .

<u>**Ezekiel 36:25-27**</u>

Then will I sprinkle clean water upon you, and ye shall be clean: from all your filthiness, and from all your idols, will I cleanse you.

A new heart also will I give you, and a new spirit will I put within you: and I will take away the stony heart out of your flesh, and I will give you an heart of flesh.

And I will put My Spirit within you, and **cause you** to walk in My statutes, and ye shall keep My judgments, and do them.

<u>**Hosea 6:1-3**</u>

Come, and let us return unto the Lord: for He hath torn, and He will heal us; He hath smitten, and He will bind us up.

After two days will He revive us: in the third day He will raise us up, and we shall live in His sight.

Then shall we know, if we follow on to know the Lord: His going forth is prepared as the morning; and **He shall come unto us as the rain, as the latter and former rain unto the earth.**

<u>**Hosea 10:12**</u>

Sow to yourselves in righteousness, reap in mercy; break up your fallow ground: for it is time to seek the Lord, till He come and rain righteousness upon you.

<u>**Hosea 14:4-7**</u>

I will heal their backsliding, I will love them freely: for Mine anger is turned away from him.

I will be as the dew unto Israel: he shall grow as the lily, and cast forth his roots as Lebanon.

His branches shall spread, and his beauty shall be as the olive tree, and his smell as Lebanon.

They that dwell under his shadow shall return; they shall revive as the corn, and grow as the vine: the scent thereof shall be as the wine of Lebanon.

<u>**Joel 2:25**</u>

And I will restore to you the years that the locust hath eaten, the cankerworm, and the caterpiller, and the palmerworm, My great army which I sent among you.

<u>**Micah 7:8**</u>

Rejoice not against me, O mine enemy: **when I fall, I shall arise**; when I sit in darkness, the Lord shall be a light unto me.

<u>**Zechariah 10:6**</u>

And I will strengthen the house of Judah, and I will save the house of Joseph, and I will bring them again to place them; **for I have mercy upon them: and they shall be as though I had not cast them off: for I am the Lord their God, and will hear them.**

<u>**Malachi 3:7**</u>

Even from the days of your fathers ye are gone away from Mine ordinances, and have not kept them. **Return unto Me, and I will return unto you, saith the Lord of hosts . . .**

John 8:32

And ye shall know the truth, and the truth shall make you free.

John 8:36

If the Son therefore shall make you free, ye shall be free indeed.

John 10:10

The thief cometh not, but for to steal, and to kill, and to destroy: **I am come that they might have life, and that they might have it more abundantly.**

Romans 8:1-2

There is therefore now no condemnation to them which are in Christ Jesus, who walk not after the flesh, but after the Spirit.

For the law of the Spirit of life in Christ Jesus hath made me free from the law of sin and death.

Romans 11:29

For the gifts and calling of God are without repentance.

Hebrews 13:5

Let your conversation be without covetousness; and be content with such things as ye have: **for He hath said, I will never leave thee, nor forsake thee.**

Let your character or moral disposition be free from love of money [including greed, avarice, lust, and craving for earthly possessions] and be satisfied with your present [circumstances and with what you have]; ***for He [God] Himself has said, I will not in any way fail you nor give you up nor leave you without support. [I will] not, [I will] not, [I will] not in any degree leave you helpless nor forsake nor let [you] down (relax My hold on you)! [Assuredly not!] [AMP]***

James 5:16

Confess to one another therefore your faults (your slips, your false steps, your offenses, your sins) and pray [also] for one another, ***that you may be healed and restored [to a spiritual tone of mind and heart].*** *The earnest (heartfelt, continued) prayer of a righteous man makes tremendous power available [dynamic in its working]. [AMP]*

I Peter 2:25

For ye were as sheep going astray; **but are now returned unto the Shepherd and Bishop of your souls.**

I John 2:1

My little children, these things write I unto you, that ye sin not. **And if any man sin, we have an advocate with the Father, Jesus Christ the righteous:**

I John 4:4

Ye are of God, little children, and have overcome them: because **greater is He that is in you, than He that is in the world.**

Jude 24

Now unto Him that is able to keep you from falling, and to present you faultless before the presence of His glory with exceeding joy,

Chapter 8

God's Prescription for Physical Well Being

A. God's Healing Power

Exodus 15:26

And said, If thou wilt diligently hearken to the voice of the Lord thy God, and wilt do that which is right in His sight, and wilt give ear to His commandments, and keep all His statutes, **I will put none of these diseases upon thee, which I have brought upon the Egyptians: for I am the Lord that healeth thee**.

Exodus 23:25

And ye shall serve the Lord your God, and He shall bless thy bread, and thy water; **and I will take sickness away from the midst of thee.**

Deuteronomy 7:15

And the Lord will take away from thee all sickness, and will put none of the evil diseases of Egypt, which thou knowest, upon thee; . . .

Job 5:18

For He maketh sore, and bindeth up: He woundeth, and His hands make whole.

Psalm 6:2

. . . O Lord, **heal me**; for my bones are vexed.

Psalm 30:2

O Lord my God, I cried unto Thee, and **Thou hast healed me.**

Psalm 34:19

Many are the afflictions of the righteous: **but the Lord delivereth him out of them all.**

Psalm 41:3

The Lord will strengthen him upon the bed of languishing: Thou wilt make all his bed in his sickness.

Psalm 103:1-5

Bless the Lord, O my soul: and all that is within me, bless His holy name.

Bless the Lord, O my soul, and forget not all His benefits:

Who forgiveth all thine iniquities; **Who healeth all thy diseases;**

Who redeemeth thy life from destruction; who crowneth thee with lovingkindness and tender mercies;

Who satisfieth thy mouth with good things; **so that thy youth is renewed like the eagle's.**

Psalm 107:20

He sent His word, and healed them, and delivered them from their destructions.

Psalm 118:17-18

I shall not die, but live, and declare the works of the Lord.

The Lord hath chastened me sore: but He hath not given me over unto death.

Psalm 146:8

The Lord openeth the eyes of the blind: the Lord raiseth them that are bowed down: . . .

Psalm 147:3

He healeth the broken in heart, and bindeth up their wounds.

Isaiah 32:3

And the eyes of them that see shall not be dim, and the ears of them that hear shall hearken.

Isaiah 42:7

To open the blind eyes, to bring out the prisoners from the prison, and them that sit in darkness out of the prison house.

Isaiah 53:4-5

Surely He hath borne our griefs, and carried our sorrows: yet we did esteem Him stricken, smitten of God, and afflicted.

But He was wounded for our transgressions, He was bruised for our iniquities: the chastisement of our peace was upon Him; **and with His stripes we are healed.**

Surely He has borne our griefs (sicknesses, weaknesses, and distresses) and carried our sorrows and pains [of punishment]. *Yet we [ignorantly] considered Him stricken, smitten, and afflicted by God [as if with leprosy].*

But He was wounded for our transgressions, He was bruised for our guilt and iniquities;

the chastisement [needful to obtain] peace and well-being for us was upon Him, ***and with the stripes [that wounded] Him we are healed and made whole****. [AMP]*

Isaiah 57:19

. . . Peace, peace to him that is far off, and to him that is near, saith the Lord; **and I will heal him.**

Jeremiah 17:14

Heal me, O Lord, and I shall be healed; save me, and I shall be saved: for Thou art my praise.

Ezekiel 16:6

And when I passed by thee, and saw thee polluted in thine own blood, **I said unto thee when thou wast in thy blood, Live; yea, I said unto thee when thou wast in thy blood, Live.**

Hosea 6:1

Come, and let us return unto the Lord: for He hath torn, and He will heal us; He hath smitten, and He will bind us up.

Matthew 10:1 *(the twelve disciples)*

And when He had called unto Him His twelve disciples, He gave them power against unclean spirits, to cast them out, **and to heal all manner of sickness and all manner of disease.**

Matthew 11:5 *(Jesus' ministry)*

The blind receive their sight, and the lame walk, the lepers are cleansed, and the deaf hear, the dead are raised up, and the poor have the gospel preached to them.

Mark 3:15 *(the twelve disciples)*

And to have power to heal sicknesses, and to cast out devils:

Mark 16:17-18 *(all believers)*

And these signs shall follow them that believe; In My name shall they cast out devils; they shall speak with new tongues;

They shall take up serpents; and if they drink any deadly thing, it shall not hurt them; **they shall lay hands on the sick, and they shall recover.**

Luke 6:19

And the whole multitude sought to touch Him: **for there went virtue out of Him, and healed them all.**

John 8:36

If the Son therefore shall make you free, ye shall be free indeed.

Acts 10:38

How God anointed Jesus of Nazareth with the Holy Ghost and with power: Who went about doing good, **and healing all that were oppressed of the devil;** for God was with Him.

Romans 8:2

For the law of the Spirit of life in Christ Jesus hath made me free from the law of sin and death.

Romans 8:11

But if the Spirit of Him that raised up Jesus from the dead dwell in you, **He that raised up Christ from the dead shall also quicken your mortal bodies by His Spirit that dwelleth in you.**

I Corinthians 12:9

To another faith by the same Spirit; **to another the gifts of healing by the same Spirit;**

Galatians 3:13-14

Christ hath redeemed us from the curse of the law, being made a curse for us: for it is written, Cursed is every one that hangeth on a tree:

That the blessing of Abraham might come on the Gentiles through Jesus Christ; that we might receive the promise of the Spirit through faith.

Hebrews 12:12-13

Wherefore lift up the hands which hang down, and the feeble knees;

And make straight paths for your feet, lest that which is lame be turned out of the way; **but let it rather be healed.**

James 5:14-16

Is any sick among you? let him call for the elders of the church; and let them pray over him, anointing him with oil in the name of the Lord:

And the prayer of faith shall save the sick, and the Lord shall raise him up; and if he have committed sins, they shall be forgiven him.

Confess your faults one to another, and pray one for another, **that ye may be healed.** The effectual fervent prayer of a righteous man availeth much.

I Peter 2:24

Who His own self bare our sins in His own body on the tree, that we, being dead to sins, should live unto righteousness: **by Whose stripes ye were healed.**

I John 3:8

. . . For this purpose the Son of God was manifested, **that He might destroy the works of the devil.**

B. Examples of Healing from Scripture

I Kings 13:6 *(Jeroboam's hand)*

And the king answered and said unto the man of God, Intreat now the face of the Lord thy God, and pray for me, that my hand may be restored me again. **And the man of God besought the Lord, and the king's hand was restored him again, and became as it was before.**

II Kings 20:1-5 *(Hezekiah)*

In those days was Hezekiah sick unto death. And the prophet Isaiah the son of Amoz came to him, and said unto him, **Thus saith the Lord, Set thine house in order; for thou shalt die, and not live.**

Then he turned his face to the wall, and prayed unto the Lord, saying,

I beseech Thee, O Lord, remember now how I have walked before Thee in truth and with a perfect heart, and have done that which is good in Thy sight. And Hezekiah wept sore.

And it came to pass, afore Isaiah was gone out into the middle court, that the word of the Lord came to him saying,

Turn again, and tell Hezekiah the captain of My people, Thus saith the Lord, the God of David thy father, I have heard thy prayer, I have seen thy tears: behold, I will heal thee: on the third day thou shalt go up unto the house of the Lord.

Matthew 4:23

And Jesus went about all Galilee, teaching in their synagogues, and preaching the Gospel of the kingdom, and **healing all manner of sickness and all manner of disease** among the people.

Matthew 8:2-3 *(the leper)*

And, behold, there came a leper and worshipped Him, saying, **Lord, if Thou wilt, Thou canst make me clean**.

And Jesus put forth His hand, and touched him, saying, **I will; be thou clean**. And immediately his leprosy was cleansed.

Matthew 8:8 *(the centurion's servant)*

The centurion answered and said, Lord, I am not worthy that Thou shouldest come under my roof: **but speak the word only, and my servant shall be healed.**

Matthew 8:16-17

When the even was come, they brought unto Him many that were possessed with devils: and He cast out the spirits with His word, **and healed all that were sick**:

That it might be fulfilled which was spoken by Esaias the prophet, saying, **Himself took our infirmities, and bare our sicknesses.**

When evening came, they brought to Him many who were under the power of demons, and He drove out the spirits with a word ***and restored to health all who were sick;***

And thus He fulfilled what was spoken by the prophet Isaiah, ***He Himself took [in order to***

carry away] our weaknesses and infirmities and bore away our diseases. *[AMP]*

Matthew 9:35

And Jesus went about all the cities and villages, teaching in their synagogues, and preaching the gospel of the kingdom, and healing **every** sickness and **every** disease among the people.

Matthew 12:9-13 *(the man with the withered hand)*

And when He was departed thence, He went into their synagogue:

And, behold, there was a man which had his hand withered. And they asked Him, saying, Is it lawful to heal on the sabbath days? that they might accuse Him.

And He said unto them, What man shall there be among you, that shall have one sheep, and if it fall into a pit on the sabbath day, will he not lay hold on it, and lift it out?

How much then is a man better than a sheep? Wherefore it is lawful to do well on the sabbath days.

Then saith He to the man, Stretch forth thine hand. And he stretched it forth; and it was restored whole, like as the other.

Matthew 12:22 *(the blind & dumb man)*

Then was brought unto Him one possessed with a devil, blind, and dumb: and He healed him, insomuch that the blind and dumb both spake and saw.

Matthew 14:35-36 *(men healed by touching the hem of Jesus' garment)*

And when the men of that place had knowledge of Him, they sent out into all that country round about, and brought unto Him all that were diseased;

And besought Him that they might only touch the hem of His garment: and as many as touched were made perfectly whole.

Matthew 15:30-31

And great multitudes came unto Him, having with them those that were lame, blind, dumb, maimed, and many others, and cast them down at Jesus' feet; and He healed them:

Insomuch that the multitude wondered, when they saw the dumb to speak, the maimed to be whole, the lame to walk, and the blind to see: and they glorified the God of Israel.

Matthew 17:14-18 *(the lunatic son)*

And when they were come to the multitude, there came to Him a certain man, kneeling down to Him, and saying,

Lord, have mercy on My son: for He is lunatick, and sore vexed: for ofttimes he falleth into the fire, and oft into the water.

And I brought him to Thy disciples, and they could not cure him.

Then Jesus answered and said, O faithless and perverse generation, how long shall I be with you? how long shall I suffer you? bring him hither to Me.

And Jesus rebuked the devil; and he departed out of him: and the child was cured from that very hour.

<u>Matthew 19:1-2</u>

And it came to pass, that when Jesus had finished these sayings, He departed from Galilee, and came into the coasts of Judaea beyond Jordan;

And great multitudes followed Him; and He healed them there.

<u>Matthew 21:14</u> *(the blind & the lame)*

And the blind and the lame came to Him in the temple; **and He healed them.**

<u>Mark 1:32-34</u> *(the city of Capernaum)*

And at even, when the sun did set, they brought unto Him all that were diseased, and them that were possessed with devils.

And all the city was gathered together at the door.

And He healed many that were sick of divers diseases, and cast out many devils; and suffered not the devils to speak, because they knew Him.

<u>Mark 2:3-5,9-12</u> *(the sick of the palsy)*

And they come unto Him, bringing one sick of the palsy, which was borne of four.

And when they could not come nigh unto Him for the press, they uncovered the roof where He was: and when they had broken it up, they let down the bed wherein the sick of the palsy lay.

When Jesus saw their faith, He said unto the sick of the palsy, Son, thy sins be forgiven thee.

Whether is it easier to say to the sick of the palsy, Thy sins be forgiven thee; or to say, Arise, and take up thy bed, and walk?

But that ye may know that the Son of Man hath power on earth to forgive sins, (He saith to the sick of the palsy,)

I say unto thee, Arise, and take up thy bed, and go thy way into thine house.

And immediately he arose, took up the bed, and went forth before them all; insomuch that they were all amazed, and glorified God, saying, We never saw it on this fashion.

<u>Mark 5:25-34</u> *(the woman with the issue of blood)*

And a certain woman, which had an issue of blood twelve years,

And had suffered many things of many physicians, and had spent all that she had, and was nothing bettered, but rather grew worse,

When she had heard of Jesus, came in the press behind, and touched His garment.

For she said, If I may touch but His clothes, I shall be whole.

And straightway the fountain of her blood was dried up; and she felt in her body that she was healed of that plague.

And Jesus, immediately knowing in Himself that virtue had gone out of Him, turned Him about in the press, and said, Who touched My clothes?

And His disciples said unto Him, Thou seest the multitude thronging Thee, and sayest Thou, Who touched Me?

And He looked round about to see her that had done this thing.

But the woman fearing and trembling, knowing what was done in her, came and fell down before Him, and told Him all the truth.

And He said unto her, **Daughter, thy faith hath made thee whole; go in peace, and be whole of thy plague.**

<u>**Mark 7:32-37**</u> *(the deaf man with a speech impediment)*

And they bring unto Him one that was deaf, and had an impediment in his speech; and they beseech Him to put His hand upon him.

And He took him aside from the multitude, and put His fingers into his ears, and He spit, and touched his tongue;

And looking up to heaven, He sighed, and saith unto him, Ephphatha, that is, Be opened.

And straightway his ears were opened, and the string of his tongue was loosed, and he spake plain.

And He charged them that they should tell no man: but the more He charged them, so much the more a great deal they published it;

And were beyond measure astonished, saying, He hath done all things well: He maketh both the deaf to hear, and the dumb to speak.

<u>**Mark 9:25-27**</u> *(the son with the deaf & dumb spirit)*

When Jesus saw that the people came running together, He rebuked the foul spirit, saying unto him, **Thou dumb and deaf spirit, I charge thee, come out of him, and enter no more into him.**

And the spirit cried, and rent him sore, and came out of him: and he was as one dead; insomuch that many said, He is dead.

But Jesus took him by the hand, and lifted him up; and he arose.

<u>**Mark 10:46-52**</u> *(Blind Bartimaeus)*

And they came to Jericho: and as He went out of Jericho with His disciples and a great number of people, blind Bartimaeus, the son of Timaeus, sat by the highway side begging.

And when he heard that it was Jesus of Nazareth, he began to cry out, and say, Jesus, Thou Son of David, have mercy on me.

And many charged him that he should hold his peace: but he cried the more a great deal, Thou Son of David, have mercy on me.

And Jesus stood still, and commanded him to be called. And they call the blind man, saying unto him, Be of good comfort, rise; He calleth thee.

And he, casting away his garment, rose, and came to Jesus.

And Jesus answered and said unto him, What wilt thou that I should do unto thee? The blind man said unto Him, **Lord, that I might receive my sight.**

And Jesus said unto him, Go thy way; thy faith hath made thee whole. And immediately he received his sight, and followed Jesus in the way.

<u>**Luke 4:38-39**</u> *(Simon's wife's mother)*

. . . And Simon's wife's mother was taken with a great fever; and they besought Him for her.

And He stood over her, and rebuked the fever; and it left her: and immediately she arose and ministered unto them.

<u>**Luke 7:11-15**</u> *(the widow's dead son)*

And it came to pass the day after, that He went into a city called Nain; and many of His disciples went with Him, and much people.

Now when He came nigh to the gate of the city, behold, there was a dead man carried out, the only son of his mother, and she was a widow: and much people of the city was with her.

And when the Lord saw her, **He had compassion on her,** and said unto her, Weep not.

And He came and touched the bier: and they that bear him stood still. **And He said, Young man, I say unto thee, Arise.**

And he that was dead sat up, and began to speak. And He delivered him to his mother.

<u>**Luke 7:21**</u>

And in that same hour He cured many of their infirmities and plagues, and of evil spirits; and unto many that were blind He gave sight.

<u>**Luke 8:41-42,49-56**</u> *(Jairus' daughter)*

And, behold, there came a man named Jairus, and he was a ruler of the synagogue: and he fell down at Jesus' feet, and besought Him that He would come into his house:

For he had one only daughter, about twelve years of age, and she lay a dying. But as He went the people thronged Him.

While He yet spake, there cometh one from the ruler of the synagogue's house, saying to him, Thy daughter is dead; trouble not the Master.

But when Jesus heard it, He answered him, saying, **Fear not: believe only, and she shall be made whole.**

And when He came into the house, He suffered no man to go in, save Peter, and James, and John, and the father and the mother of the maiden.

And all wept, and bewailed her: but He said, **Weep not; she is not dead, but sleepeth**.

And they laughed Him to scorn, knowing that she was dead.

And He put them all out, and took her by the hand, and called, saying, **Maid, arise.**

And her spirit came again, and she arose straightway: and He commanded to give her meat.

And her parents were astonished: but He charged them that they should tell no man what was done.

<u>**Luke 13:10-13**</u> *(the woman with the infirmity eighteen years)*

And He was teaching in one of the synagogues on the sabbath.

And, behold, there was a woman which had a spirit of infirmity eighteen years, and was bowed together, and could in no wise lift up herself.

And when Jesus saw her, He called her to Him, and said unto her, **Woman, thou art loosed from thine infirmity**.

And He laid His hands on her: and immediately she was made straight, and glorified God.

<u>**Luke 17:12-14**</u> *(the ten lepers)*

And as He entered into a certain village, there met Him ten men that were lepers, which stood afar off:

And they lifted up their voices, and said, Jesus, Master, have mercy on us.

And when He saw them, **He said unto them, Go shew yourselves unto the priests. And it came to pass, that, as they went, they were cleansed.**

<u>**Luke 22:50-51**</u> *(the high priest's servant)*

And one of them smote the servant of the high priest, and cut off his right ear.

And Jesus answered and said, Suffer ye thus far. **And He touched his ear, and healed him.**

<u>**John 4:46-53**</u> *(the nobleman's son)*

. . . And there was a certain nobleman, whose son was sick at Capernaum.

When he heard that Jesus was come out of Judaea into Galilee, he went unto Him, and besought Him that He would come down, and heal his son: for he was at the point of death.

Then said Jesus unto him, Except ye see signs and wonders, ye will not believe.

The nobleman said unto Him, Sir, come down ere my child die.

Jesus saith unto him, Go thy way; thy son liveth. And the man believed the word that Jesus had spoken unto him, and he went his way.

And as he was now going down, his servants met him, and told him, saying, Thy son liveth.

Then enquired he of them the hour when he began to amend. And they said unto him, Yesterday at the seventh hour the fever left him.

So that father knew that it was at the same hour, in the which Jesus said unto him, Thy son liveth: and himself believed, and his whole house.

<u>**John 5:5-9**</u> *(the man lying at the pool of Bethesda)*

And a certain man was there, which had an infirmity thirty and eight years.

When Jesus saw him lie, and knew that he had been now a long time in that case, He saith unto him, Wilt thou be made whole?

The impotent man answered Him, Sir, I have no man, when the water is troubled, to put me into the pool: but while I am coming, another steppeth down before me.

Jesus saith unto him, Rise, take up thy bed, and walk.

And immediately the man was made whole, and took up his bed, and walked: and on the same day was the sabbath.

<u>**John 9:6-7**</u> *(the blind man near the pool of Siloam)*

When He had thus spoken, **He spat on the ground, and made clay of the spittle, and He anointed the eyes of the blind man with the clay,**

And said unto Him, Go, wash in the pool of Siloam, (which is by interpretation, Sent.) **He went his way therefore, and washed, and came seeing.**

<u>**Acts 3:6-9**</u> *(the lame man at the Beautiful gate)*

Then Peter said, Silver and gold have I none; but such as I have give I thee: In the name of Jesus Christ of Nazareth rise up and walk.

And he took him by the right hand, and lifted him up: and immediately his feet and ankle bones received strength.

And he leaping up stood, and walked, and entered with them into the temple, walking, and leaping, and praising God.

And all the people saw him walking and praising God:

<u>**Acts 5:15-16**</u> *(Peter's shadow)*

Insomuch that they brought forth the sick into the streets, and laid them on beds and couches, that at the least the shadow of Peter passing by might overshadow some of them.

There came also a multitude out of the cities round about unto Jerusalem, bringing sick folks, and them which were vexed with unclean spirits: **and they were healed every one.**

<u>**Acts 9:33-34**</u> *(the healing of Aeneas)*

And there he found a certain man named Aeneas, which had kept his bed eight years, and was sick of the palsy.

And Peter said unto him, Aeneas, Jesus Christ maketh thee whole: arise, and make thy bed. And he arose immediately.

<u>**Acts 9:40-42**</u> *(Peter raising Dorcas from the dead)*

But Peter put them all forth, and kneeled down, and prayed; and turning him to the body said, **Tabitha, arise. And she opened her eyes: and when she saw Peter, she sat up.**

And he gave her his hand, and lifted her up, and when he had called the saints and widows, presented her alive.

And it was known throughout all Joppa; and many believed in the Lord.

<u>**Acts 14:8-10**</u> *(the lame man at Lystra)*

And there sat a certain man at Lystra, impotent in his feet, being a cripple from his mother's womb, who never had walked:

The same heard Paul speak: who stedfastly beholding him, **and perceiving that he had faith to be healed,**

Said with a loud voice, **Stand upright on thy feet. And he leaped and walked.**

<u>**Acts 19:11-12**</u> *(handkerchiefs from Paul)*

And God wrought special miracles by the hands of Paul:

So that from his body were brought unto the sick handkerchiefs or aprons, and the diseases departed from them, and the evil spirits went out of them.

<u>**Acts 28:8**</u> *(the father of Publius)*

And it came to pass, that the father of Publius lay sick of a fever and of a bloody flux: to whom Paul entered in, and prayed, and laid his hands on him, and healed him.

C. Redeemed from the Curse of the Law

<u>**Deuteronomy 28:15**</u>

But it shall come to pass, if thou wilt not hearken unto the voice of the Lord thy God, to observe to do all His commandments and His statutes which I command thee this day; **that all these curses shall come upon thee, and overtake thee:**

<u>**Deuteronomy 28:22**</u>

The Lord shall smite thee with a consumption, and with a fever, and with an inflammation, and with an extreme burning, and with the sword, and with blasting, and with mildew; and they shall pursue thee until thou perish.

<u>**Deuteronomy 28:27-29,35**</u>

The Lord will smite thee with the botch of Egypt, and with the emerods, and with the scab, and with the itch, whereof thou canst not be healed.

The Lord shall smite thee with madness, and blindness, and astonishment of heart:

And thou shalt grope at noonday, as the blind gropeth in darkness, and thou shalt not prosper in thy ways: and thou shalt be only oppressed and spoiled evermore, and no man shall save thee.

The Lord shall smite thee in the knees, and in the legs, with a sore botch that cannot be healed, from the sole of thy foot unto the top of thy head.

<u>**Deuteronomy 28:45**</u>

Moreover all these curses shall come upon thee, and shall pursue thee, and overtake thee, till thou be destroyed; because thou hearkenedst not unto the voice of the Lord thy God, to keep His commandments and His statutes which He commanded thee:

<u>**Deuteronomy 28:58-61**</u>

If thou wilt not observe to do all the words of this law that are written in this book, that thou mayest fear this glorious and fearful name, THE LORD THY GOD;

Then the Lord will make thy plagues wonderful, and the plagues of thy seed, even great plagues, and of long continuance, and sore sicknesses, and of long continuance.

Moreover He will bring upon thee all the diseases of Egypt, which thou wast afraid of; and they shall cleave unto thee.

Also every sickness, and every plague, which is not written in the book of this law, them will the Lord bring upon thee, until thou be destroyed.

<u>**Galatians 3:13-14**</u>

CHRIST HATH REDEEMED US FROM THE CURSE OF THE LAW, being made a curse for us: for it is written, Cursed is every one that hangeth on a tree:

That the blessing of Abraham might come on the Gentiles through Jesus Christ; that we might receive the promise of the Spirit through faith.

D. References to the Laying on of Hands

<u>**Mark 6:5-6**</u>

And He could there do no mighty work, **save that He laid His hands upon a few sick folk, and healed them.**

And He marvelled because of their unbelief. And He went round about the villages, teaching.

<u>Mark 7:32</u>

And they bring unto Him one that was deaf, and had an impediment in his speech; **and they beseech Him to put His hand upon him.**

<u>Mark 16:17-18</u>

And these signs shall follow them that believe; In My name shall they cast out devils; they shall speak with new tongues;

They shall take up serpents; and if they drink any deadly thing, it shall not hurt them; **they shall lay hands on the sick, and they shall recover.**

<u>Luke 4:40</u>

Now when the sun was setting, all they that had any sick with divers diseases brought them unto Him; **and He laid His hands on every one of them, and healed them.**

<u>Luke 13:13</u>

And He laid His hands on her: and immediately she was made straight, and glorified God.

<u>Acts 28:8</u>

And it came to pass, that the father of Publius lay sick of a fever and of a bloody flux: **to whom Paul entered in, and prayed, and laid his hands on him, and healed him.**

E. Maintaining Health

<u>Psalm 42:11</u>

Why art thou cast down, O my soul? and why art thou disquieted within me? hope thou in God: **for I shall yet praise Him, Who is the health of my countenance, and my God.**

<u>Psalm 105:37</u>

He brought them forth also with silver and gold: **and there was not one feeble person among their tribes.**

<u>Proverbs 3:7-8</u>

Be not wise in thine own eyes: fear the Lord, and depart from evil.

It shall be health to thy navel, and marrow to thy bones.

<u>Proverbs 4:20-22</u>

My son, attend to my words; incline thine ear unto my sayings.

Let them not depart from thine eyes; keep them in the midst of thine heart.

For they are life unto those that find them, and health to all their flesh.

<u>Proverbs 12:18</u>

There is that speaketh like the piercings of a sword: **but the tongue of the wise is health.**

Proverbs 14:30

A sound heart is the life of the flesh: but envy the rottenness of the bones.

Proverbs 16:24

Pleasant words are as an honeycomb, sweet to the soul, and **health to the bones.**

Proverbs 17:22

A merry heart doeth good like a medicine: but a broken spirit drieth the bones.

Isaiah 58:7-8 *(as part of fasting)*

Is it not to deal thy bread to the hungry, and that thou bring the poor that are cast out to thy house? when thou seest the naked, that thou cover him; and that thou hide not thyself from thine own flesh?

Then shall thy light break forth as the morning, **and thine health shall spring forth speedily:** and thy righteousness shall go before thee; the glory of the Lord shall be thy rereward.

Isaiah 58:11

And the Lord shall guide thee continually, and satisfy thy soul in drought, and **make fat thy bones: . . .**

Jeremiah 30:17

For I will restore health unto thee, and I will heal thee of thy wounds, saith the Lord ...

Jeremiah 33:6

Behold, **I will bring it health and cure, and I will cure them**, and will reveal unto them the abundance of peace and truth.

John 10:10

The thief cometh not, but for to steal, and to kill, and to destroy: **I am come that they might have life, and that they might have it more abundantly.**

I Corinthians 6:19-20

What? know ye not that **your body is the temple of the Holy Ghost** which is in you, which ye have of God, and **ye are not your own?**

For ye are bought with a price: **therefore glorify God in your body, and in your spirit, which are God's.**

III John 2

Beloved, I wish above all things that thou mayest prosper **and be in health,** even as thy soul prospereth.

F. Receiving Strength from the Lord

Deuteronomy 33:25

Thy shoes shall be iron and brass; and **as thy days, so shall thy strength be.**

II Samuel 22:40

For Thou hast girded me with strength to battle: them that rose up against me hast Thou subdued under me.

Nehemiah 8:10

Then he said unto them, Go your way, eat the fat, and drink the sweet, and send portions unto them for whom nothing is prepared: for this day is holy unto our Lord: neither be ye sorry; **for the joy of the Lord is your strength.**

Job 17:9

The righteous also shall hold on his way, **and he that hath clean hands shall be stronger and stronger.**

Job 23:6

Will He plead against me with His great power? No; **but He would put strength in me.**

Psalm 18:2

The Lord is my Rock, and my Fortress, and my Deliverer; my God, **my Strength**, in Whom I will trust; my Buckler, and the Horn of my salvation, and my High Tower.

Psalm 27:1

The Lord is my Light and my Salvation; whom shall I fear? **the Lord is the Strength of my life;** of whom shall I be afraid?

Psalm 28:7-8

The Lord is my Strength and my Shield; my heart trusted in Him, and I am helped: therefore my heart greatly rejoiceth; and with my song will I praise Him.

The Lord is their Strength, and He is the saving Strength of His anointed.

Psalm 29:11

The Lord will give strength unto His people; the Lord will bless His people with peace.

Psalm 41:3

The Lord will strengthen him upon the bed of languishing: Thou wilt make all his bed in his sickness.

Psalm 46:1

God is our Refuge and Strength, a very present help in trouble.

Psalm 68:28

Thy God hath commanded thy strength: strengthen, O God, that which Thou hast wrought for us.

Psalm 73:26

My flesh and my heart may fail, ***but God is the Rock and firm Strength of my heart*** *and my Portion forever. [AMP]*

Psalm 118:14

The Lord is my Strength and Song, and is become my Salvation.

Psalm 119:28

My soul melteth for heaviness: **strengthen Thou me according unto Thy word.**

Psalm 138:3

In the day when I cried Thou answeredst me, and **strengthenedst me with strength in my soul.**

Proverbs 8:14 *(Wisdom from God)*

Counsel is mine, and sound wisdom: I am understanding; **I have strength.**

Isaiah 30:15

For thus saith the Lord God, the Holy One of Israel; In returning and rest shall ye be saved; **in quietness and in confidence shall be your strength**: . . .

Isaiah 35:3

Strengthen ye the weak hands, and confirm the feeble knees.

Isaiah 40:29

He gives power to the faint and weary, and to him who has no might He increases strength [causing it to multiply and making it to abound]. [AMP]

Isaiah 40:31

But they that wait upon the Lord shall renew their strength; they shall mount up with wings as eagles; they shall run, and not be weary; and they shall walk, and not faint.

But those who wait for the Lord [who expect, look for, and hope in Him] shall change and renew their strength and power; they shall lift their wings and mount up [close to God] as eagles [mount up to the sun]; they shall run and not be weary, they shall walk and not faint or become tired. [AMP]

Isaiah 41:10

Fear thou not; for I am with thee: be not dismayed; for I am thy God: **I will strengthen thee;** yea, I will help thee; yea, I will uphold thee with the right hand of My righteousness.

Daniel 10:19

And said, O man greatly beloved, fear not: peace be unto thee, **be strong, yea, be strong. And when he had spoken unto me, I was strengthened, and said, Let my lord speak; for thou hast strengthened me.**

Daniel 11:32

. . . **but the people that do know their God shall be strong**, and do exploits.

Joel 3:10

Beat your plowshares into swords, and your pruninghooks into spears: **let the weak say, I am strong.**

Habakkuk 3:19

The Lord God is my strength, and He will make my feet like hinds' feet, and He will make me to walk upon mine high places. . .

II Corinthians 12:9-10

And He said unto me, My grace is sufficient for thee: **for My strength is made perfect in weakness.** Most gladly therefore will I rather glory in my infirmities, that the power of Christ may rest upon me.

Therefore I take pleasure in infirmities, in reproaches, in necessities, in persecutions, in distresses for Christ's sake: **for when I am weak, then am I strong.**

Ephesians 3:16

That He would grant you, according to the riches of His glory, **to be strengthened with might by His Spirit in the inner man;**

Ephesians 6:10

Finally, my brethren, **be strong in the Lord, and in the power of His might.**

Philippians 4:13

I can do all things through Christ which strengtheneth me.

Colossians 1:10-12

That ye might walk worthy of the Lord unto all pleasing, being fruitful in every good work, and increasing in the knowledge of God;

Strengthened with all might, according to His glorious power, unto all patience and longsuffering with joyfulness;

Giving thanks unto the Father, which hath made us meet to be partakers of the inheritance of the saints in light:

Hebrews 11:33-34

Who through faith subdued kingdoms, wrought righteousness, obtained promises, stopped the mouths of lions,

Quenched the violence of fire, escaped the edge of the sword, **out of weakness were**

made strong, waxed valiant in fight, turned to flight the armies of the aliens.

Chapter 9

Prospering God's Way

A. General References from Scripture

<u>Deuteronomy 8:18</u>

But thou shalt remember the Lord thy God: for it is He that giveth thee power to get wealth, that He may establish His covenant which He sware unto thy fathers, as it is this day.

<u>Psalm 105:37</u>

He brought them forth also with silver and gold: and there was not one feeble person among their tribes.

<u>Psalm 113:7-8</u>

He raiseth up the poor out of the dust, and lifteth the needy out of the dunghill;
That He may set him with princes, even with the princes of His people.

<u>Proverbs 10:22</u>

The blessing of the Lord, it maketh rich, and He addeth no sorrow with it.

<u>Ecclesiastes 5:19</u>

Every man also to whom **God hath given riches and wealth**, and **hath given him power to eat thereof,** and **to take his portion**, and **to rejoice in his labour;** this is the gift of God.

<u>Isaiah 45:3</u>

And I will give thee the treasures of darkness, and hidden riches of secret places, that thou mayest know that I, the Lord, which call thee by thy name, am the God of Israel.

Isaiah 48:17

Thus saith the Lord, thy Redeemer, the Holy One of Israel; **I am the Lord thy God which teachest thee to profit, which leadeth thee by the way that thou shouldest go.**

Isaiah 61:6

But ye shall be named the Priests of the Lord: men shall call you the Ministers of our God: **ye shall eat the riches of the Gentiles**, and in their glory shall ye boast yourselves.

I Timothy 6:17

Charge them that are rich in this world, that they be not highminded, nor trust in uncertain riches, but in the living God, **Who giveth us richly all things to enjoy;**

James 1:17

Every good gift and every perfect gift is from above, and cometh down from the Father of lights, with Whom is no variableness, neither shadow of turning.

III John 2

Beloved, I wish above all things that thou mayest **prosper** and be in health, **even as thy soul prospereth.**

B. What are God's Resources?

I Chronicles 29:11-12

Thine, O Lord, is the greatness, and the power, and the glory, and the victory, and the majesty: **for all that is in the heaven and in the earth is Thine;** Thine is the kingdom, O Lord, and Thou art exalted as Head above all.

Both riches and honour come of Thee, and Thou reignest over all; and in Thine hand is power and might; and in Thine hand it is to make great, and to give strength unto all.

Psalm 50:10,12

For every beast of the forest is Mine, and the cattle upon a thousand hills.

. . . for the world is Mine, and the fulness thereof.

Psalm 104:24

O Lord, how manifold are Thy works! in wisdom hast Thou made them all: **the earth is full of Thy riches.**

Haggai 2:8

The silver is Mine, and the gold is Mine, saith the Lord of hosts.

Philippians 4:19

But my God shall supply all your need **according to His riches in glory by Christ Jesus**.

C. God's Daily Provision

Psalm 23:1

The Lord is my Shepherd; **I shall not want.**

Psalm 37:18-19

The Lord knoweth the days of the upright: and their inheritance shall be for ever.

They shall not be ashamed in the evil time: **and in the days of famine they shall be satisfied.**

Psalm 37:25-26

I have been young, and now am old; **yet have I not seen the righteous forsaken, nor his seed begging bread.**

He is ever merciful, and lendeth; and his seed is blessed.

Psalm 68:19

Blessed be the Lord, **Who daily loadeth us with benefits,** even the God of our salvation. Selah.

Isaiah 40:11

He shall feed His flock like a shepherd: He shall gather the lambs with His arm, and carry them in His bosom, and shall gently lead those that are with young.

Matthew 6:25-33

Therefore I say unto you, **Take no thought for your life**, what ye shall eat, or what ye shall drink; nor yet for your body, what ye shall put on. **Is not the life more than meat, and the body than raiment?**

Behold the fowls of the air: for they sow not, neither do they reap, nor gather into barns; yet your heavenly Father feedeth them. **Are ye not much better than they?**

Which of you by taking thought can add one cubit unto his stature?

And why take ye thought for raiment? Consider the lilies of the field, how they grow; they toil not, neither do they spin:

And yet I say unto you, That even Solomon in all his glory was not arrayed like one of these.

Wherefore, if God so clothe the grass of the field, which to day is, and to morrow is cast into the oven, shall He not much more clothe you, O ye of little faith?

Therefore take no thought, saying, What shall we eat? or, What shall we drink? or, Wherewithal shall we be clothed?

(For after all these things do the Gentiles seek:) for your heavenly Father knoweth that ye have need of all these things.

But seek ye first the kingdom of God, and His righteousness; and all these things shall be added unto you.

Matthew 7:7-11

Ask, and it shall be given you; seek, and ye shall find; knock, and it shall be opened

unto you:

For every one that asketh receiveth; and he that seeketh findeth; and to him that knocketh it shall be opened.

Or what man is there of you, whom if his son ask bread, will he give him a stone?

Or if he ask a fish, will he give him a serpent?

If ye then, being evil, know how to give good gifts unto your children, how much more shall your Father which is in heaven give good things to them that ask Him?

Romans 8:32

He that spared not His own Son, but delivered Him up for us all, **how shall He not with Him also freely give us all things?**

Philippians 4:19

But my God shall supply all your need according to His riches in glory by Christ Jesus.

D. God's Blessing on Those Who Seek Him

Genesis 39:23 *(Joseph)*

. . . **the Lord was with him**, and that which he did, **the Lord made it to prosper.**

II Chronicles 26:5 *(Uzziah)*

. . . and as long as he sought the Lord, God made him to prosper.

II Chronicles 31:21 *(Hezekiah)*

And in every work that he began in the service of the house of God, and in the law, and in the commandments, to seek his God, **he did it with all his heart, and prospered.**

Psalm 1:2-3

But his delight is in the law of the Lord; and in His law doth he meditate day and night.

And he shall be like a tree planted by the rivers of water, that bringeth forth his fruit in his season; his leaf also shall not wither; and whatsoever he doeth shall prosper.

Psalm 34:9-10

O fear the Lord, ye His saints: **for there is no want to them that fear Him.**

The young lions do lack, and suffer hunger: **but they that seek the Lord shall not want any good thing.**

Proverbs 8:21

That I may cause those that love Me to inherit substance; and I will fill their treasures.

Isaiah 58:14 *(those who fast unto the Lord)*

Then shalt thou delight thyself in the Lord; and **I will cause thee to ride upon the high places of the earth, and feed thee with the heritage of Jacob thy father:** for the mouth of the Lord hath spoken it.

Daniel 6:28 (Daniel)
So this Daniel prospered in the reign of Darius, and in the reign of Cyrus the Persian.

Matthew 6:33
But seek ye first the kingdom of God, and His righteousness; **and all these things shall be added unto you.**

E. God's Blessing on Those Who Obey Him

Leviticus 26:3-5
If ye walk in My statutes, and keep My commandments, and do them;
Then I will give you rain in due season, and the land shall yield her increase, and the trees of the field shall yield their fruit.
And your threshing shall reach unto the vintage, and the vintage shall reach unto the sowing time: **and ye shall eat your bread to the full, and dwell in your land safely.**

Deuteronomy 7:12-14
Wherefore it shall come to pass, **if ye hearken to these judgments, and keep, and do them,** that the Lord thy God shall keep unto thee the covenant and the mercy which He sware unto thy fathers:
And He will love thee, and bless thee, and multiply thee: He will also bless the fruit of thy womb, and the fruit of thy land, thy corn, and thy wine, and thine oil, the increase of thy kine, and the flocks of thy sheep, in the land which He sware unto thy fathers to give thee.
Thou shalt be blessed above all people: there shall not be male or female barren among you, or among your cattle.

Deuteronomy 11:26-28
Behold, I set before you this day a blessing and a curse;
A blessing, if ye obey the commandments of the Lord your God, which I command you this day:
And a curse, if ye will not obey the commandments of the Lord your God, but turn aside out of the way which I command you this day, to go after other gods, which ye have not known.

Deuteronomy 28:1-6
And it shall come to pass, if thou shalt hearken diligently unto the voice of the Lord thy God, to observe and to do all His commandments which I command thee this day, **that the Lord thy God will set thee on high above all nations of the earth:**
And all these blessings shall come on thee, and overtake thee, if thou shalt hearken unto the voice of the Lord thy God.
Blessed shalt thou be in the city, and blessed shalt thou be in the field.
Blessed shall be the fruit of thy body, and the fruit of thy ground, and the fruit of thy

cattle, the increase of thy kine, and the flocks of thy sheep.

Blessed shall be thy basket and thy store.

Blessed shalt thou be when thou comest in, and blessed shalt thou be when thou goest out.

Deuteronomy 28:8

The Lord shall command the blessing upon thee in thy storehouses, and in all that thou settest thine hand unto; and He shall bless thee in the land which the Lord thy God giveth thee.

Deuteronomy 28:11-13

And the Lord shall make thee plenteous in goods, in the fruit of thy body, and in the fruit of thy cattle, and in the fruit of thy ground, in the land which the Lord sware unto thy fathers to give thee.

The Lord shall open unto thee His good treasure, the heaven to give the rain unto thy land in His season, and to bless all the work of thine hand: and thou shalt lend unto many nations, and thou shalt not borrow.

And the Lord shall make thee the head, and not the tail; and thou shalt be above only, and thou shalt not be beneath; if that thou hearken unto the commandments of the Lord thy God, which I command thee this day, to observe and to do them:

Deuteronomy 29:9

Keep therefore the words of this covenant, and do them, **that ye may prosper in all that ye do**.

Joshua 1:8

This book of the law shall not depart out of thy mouth; but thou shalt **meditate** therein day and night, that thou mayest observe **to do** according to all that is written therein: **for then thou shalt make thy way prosperous, and then thou shalt have good success.**

Job 36:11

If they obey and serve Him, they shall spend their days in prosperity, and their years in pleasures.

Job 42:10

And the Lord turned the captivity of Job, when he prayed for his friends: **also the Lord gave Job twice as much as he had before.**

Psalm 1:1-3

Blessed is the man that walketh not in the counsel of the ungodly, nor standeth in the way of sinners, nor sitteth in the seat of the scornful.

But his delight is in the law of the Lord; and in his law doth he meditate day and night.

And he shall be like a tree planted by the rivers of water, that bringeth forth his fruit in his season; his leaf also shall not wither; and whatsoever he doeth shall prosper.

<u>**Psalm 112:1-3**</u>

Praise ye the Lord. Blessed is the man that feareth the Lord, that delighteth greatly in His commandments.

His seed shall be mighty upon earth: the generation of the upright shall be blessed.

Wealth and riches shall be in his house: and his righteousness endureth for ever.

<u>**Proverbs 22:4**</u>

By humility and the fear of the Lord are **riches, and honor, and life.**

F. God's Blessing on The Righteous

<u>**Job 27:16-17**</u>

Though he heap up silver as the dust, and prepare raiment as the clay;

He may prepare it, **but the just shall put it on, and the innocent shall divide the silver.**

<u>**Psalm 84:11**</u>

For the Lord God is a sun and shield: the Lord will give grace and glory: **no good thing will He withhold from them that walk uprightly.**

<u>**Proverbs 13:22**</u>

A good man leaveth an inheritance to his children's children: **and the wealth of the sinner is laid up for the just.**

A good man leaves an inheritance [of moral stability and goodness] to his children's children, and ***the wealth of the sinner [finds its way eventually] into the hands of the righteous, for whom it was laid up.*** *[AMP]*

<u>**Ecclesiastes 2:26**</u>

For God giveth to a man that is good in His sight wisdom, and knowledge, and joy: **but to the sinner He giveth travail, to gather and to heap up, that he may give to him that is good before God . . .**

G. God's Blessing on Tithe Payers

<u>**Proverbs 3:9-10**</u>

Honour the Lord with thy substance, and with the first-fruits of all thine increase:

So shall thy barns be filled with plenty, and thy presses shall burst out with new wine.

<u>**Malachi 3:10-12**</u>

Bring ye all the tithes into the storehouse, that there may be meat in Mine house, and prove Me now herewith, saith the Lord of hosts, if I will not open you the

windows of heaven, and pour you out a blessing, that there shall not be room enough to receive it.

And I will rebuke the devourer for your sakes, and he shall not destroy the fruits of your ground; neither shall your vine cast her fruit before the time in the field, saith the Lord of hosts.

And all nations shall call you blessed: for ye shall be a delightsome land, saith the Lord of hosts.

H. God's Blessing on Liberal Givers

Proverbs 11:24-25

There is that scattereth, and yet increaseth; and there is that withholdeth more than is meet, but it tendeth to poverty.

The liberal soul shall be made fat: and he that watereth shall be watered also himself.

Ecclesiastes 11:1

Cast thy bread upon the waters: for thou shalt find it after many days.

Mark 12:41-44

And Jesus sat over against the treasury, and beheld how the people cast money into the treasury: and many that were rich cast in much.

And there came a certain poor widow, and she threw in two mites, which make a farthing.

And He called unto Him His disciples, and saith unto them, **Verily I say unto you, That this poor widow hath cast more in, than all they which have cast into the treasury:**

For all they did cast in of their abundance; **but she of her want did cast in all that she had, even all her living.**

Luke 6:38

Give, and it shall be given unto you; good measure, pressed down, and shaken together, and running over, shall men give into your bosom. For with the same measure that ye mete withal it shall be measured to you again.

Acts 20:35

. . . remember the words of the Lord Jesus, how He said, **It is more blessed to give than to receive.**

II Corinthians 9:6-12

But this I say, **He which soweth sparingly shall reap also sparingly; and he which soweth bountifully shall reap also bountifully.**

Every man according as he purposeth in his heart, so let him give; not grudgingly, or of necessity: for God loveth a cheerful giver.

And God is able to make all grace abound toward you; that ye, **always having all sufficiency in all things, may abound to every good work:**

(As it is written, He hath dispersed abroad; he hath given to the poor: his righteousness remaineth for ever.

Now He that ministereth seed to the sower both minister bread for your food, and multiply your seed sown, and increase the fruits of your righteousness;)

Being enriched in every thing to all bountifulness, which causeth through us thanksgiving to God.

For the administration of this service not only supplieth the want of saints, but is abundant also by many thanksgivings unto God;

[Remember] this: ***he who sows sparingly and grudgingly will also reap sparingly and grudgingly, and he who sows generously [that blessings may come to someone] will also reap generously and with blessings.***

Let each one [give] as he has made up his own mind and purposed in his heart, not reluctantly or sorrowfully or under compulsion, for God loves (He takes pleasure in, prizes above other things, and is unwilling to abandon or to do without) a cheerful (joyous, "prompt to do it") giver [whose heart is in his giving].

And God is able to make all grace (every favor and earthly blessing) come to you in abundance, so that you may always and under all circumstances and whatever the need be self-sufficient [possessing enough to require no aid or support and furnished in abundance for every good work and charitable donation].

As it is written, He [the benevolent person] scatters abroad; He gives to the poor; His deeds of justice and goodness and kindness and benevolence will go on and endure forever!

And [God] Who provides seed for the sower and bread for eating will also provide and multiply your [resources for] sowing and increase the fruits of your righteousness [which manifests itself in active goodness, kindness and charity].

Thus you will be enriched in all things and in every way, so that you can be generous, and [your generosity as it is] administered by us will bring forth thanksgiving to God.

For the service the ministering of this fund renders does not only fully supply what is lacking to the saints (God's people), but it also overflows in many [cries of] thanksgiving to God. [AMP]

Galatians 6:7,9

Be not deceived; God is not mocked: **for whatsoever a man soweth, that shall he also reap.**

And let us not be weary in well doing: **for in due season we shall reap, if we faint not.**

I. References to the Hundred Fold Return

Matthew 19:29-30

And every one that hath forsaken houses, or brethren, or sisters, or father, or mother, or wife, or children, or lands, for My name's sake, **shall receive an hundredfold,** and shall inherit everlasting life.

But many that are first shall be last; and the last shall be first.

<u>Mark 10:29-31</u>
. . . Verily I say unto you, There is no man that hath left house, or brethren, or sisters, or father, or mother, or wife, or children, or lands, for My sake, and the Gospel's.
But he shall receive an hundredfold now in this time, houses, and brethren, and sisters, and mothers, and children, and lands, with persecutions; and in the world to come eternal life.
But many that are first shall be last; and the last first.

J. God's Blessing on Those Who Give to the Poor

<u>Proverbs 19:17</u>
He that hath pity upon the poor lendeth unto the Lord; **and that which he hath given will He pay him again.**

<u>Proverbs 22:9</u>
He that hath a bountiful eye shall be blessed; for he giveth of his bread to the poor.

<u>Proverbs 28:8</u>
He that by usury and unjust gain increaseth his substance, **he shall gather it for him that will pity the poor.**

<u>Proverbs 28:27</u>
He that giveth unto the poor shall not lack: but he that hideth his eyes shall have many a curse.

<u>Isaiah 58:10-11</u> *(as part of fasting)*
And if thou draw out thy soul to the hungry, and satisfy the afflicted soul; **then shall thy light rise in obscurity, and thy darkness be as the noon day:**
And the Lord shall guide thee continually, and satisfy thy soul in drought, and make fat thy bones: and thou shalt be like a watered garden, and like a spring of water, whose waters fail not.

<u>Matthew 6:3-4</u>
But when thou doest alms, let not thy left hand know what thy right hand doeth:
That thine alms may be in secret: **and thy Father which seeth in secret Himself shall reward thee openly.**

<u>Matthew 19:21</u>
Jesus said unto him, **If thou wilt be perfect, go and sell that thou hast, and give to the poor, and thou shalt have treasure in heaven:** and come and follow Me.

Matthew 25:40

And the King shall answer and say unto them, **Verily I say unto you, Inasmuch as ye have done it unto one of the least of these My brethren, ye have done it unto Me.**

Luke 12:33

Sell that ye have, and give alms; provide yourselves bags which wax not old, a treasure in the heavens that faileth not, where no thief approacheth, neither moth corrupteth.

Luke 18:22

Now when Jesus heard these things, He said unto him, Yet lackest thou one thing: **sell all that thou hast, and distribute unto the poor, and thou shalt have treasure in heaven: and come, follow Me.**

Acts 20:35

I have shewed you all things, **how that so labouring ye ought to support the weak,** and to remember the words of the Lord Jesus, how He said, **It is more blessed to give than to receive.**

Chapter 10

Enduring Through Tribulation

Deuteronomy 4:30-31

When thou art in tribulation, and all these things are come upon thee, even in the latter days, if thou turn to the Lord thy God, and shalt be obedient unto His voice;

(For the Lord thy God is a merciful God;) **He will not forsake thee, neither destroy thee,** nor forget the covenant of thy fathers which He sware unto them.

Psalm 7:1

O Lord my God, in Thee do I put my trust: **save me from all them that persecute me, and deliver me:**

Psalm 31:14-15

But I trusted in Thee, O Lord: I said, Thou art my God.

My times are in Thy hand: **deliver me from the hand of mine enemies, and from them that persecute me.**

Psalm 57:1

. . . **yea, in the shadow of Thy wings will I make my refuge,** until these calamities be overpast.

Psalm 119:86

All Thy commandments are faithful: they persecute me wrongfully; help Thou me.

Psalm 119:153

Consider mine affliction, and deliver me: for I do not forget Thy law.

Psalm 119:157

Many are my persecutors and mine enemies; yet do I not decline from Thy testimonies.

Psalm 143:3

For the enemy hath persecuted my soul; he hath smitten my life down to the ground; he hath made me to dwell in darkness, as those that have been long dead.

Isaiah 43:2

When thou passest through the waters, **I will be with thee;** and through the rivers, **they shall not overflow thee:** when thou walkest through the fire, **thou shalt not be burned; neither shall the flame kindle upon thee.**

Isaiah 48:10

Behold, I have refined thee, but not with silver; **I have chosen thee in the furnace of affliction.**

Jeremiah 15:15

O Lord, Thou knowest: remember me, and visit me, and revenge me of my persecutors; take me not away in Thy longsuffering: know that for Thy sake I have suffered rebuke.

Lamentations 5:5

Our necks are under persecution: we labour, and have no rest.

Matthew 5:11-12

Blessed are ye, when men shall revile you, and persecute you, and shall say all manner of evil against you falsely, for My sake.

Rejoice, and be exceeding glad: for great is your reward in heaven: for so persecuted they the prophets which were before you.

Matthew 10:16-22

Behold, I send you forth as sheep in the midst of wolves: be ye therefore wise as serpents, and harmless as doves.

But beware of men: for they will deliver you up to the councils, and they will scourge you in their synagogues;

And ye shall be brought before governors and kings for My sake, for a testimony against them and the Gentiles.

But when they deliver you up, take no thought how or what ye shall speak: for it shall be given you in that same hour what ye shall speak.

For it is not ye that speak, but the Spirit of your Father which speaketh in you.

And brother shall deliver up the brother to death, and the father the child: and the children shall rise up against their parents, and cause them to be put to death.

And ye shall be hated of all men for My name's sake: **but he that endureth to the end shall be saved.**

Matthew 10:24-28

The disciple is not above his master, nor the servant above his lord.

It is enough for the disciple that he be as his master, and the servant as his lord. **If they have called the Master of the house Beelzebub, how much more shall they call them of**

His household?

Fear them not therefore: for there is nothing covered, that shall not be revealed; and hid, that shall not be known.

What I tell you in darkness, that speak ye in light: and what ye hear in the ear, that preach ye upon the housetops.

And fear not them which kill the body, but are not able to kill the soul: but rather fear Him which is able to destroy both soul and body in hell.

Matthew 24:21-22

For then shall be great tribulation, such as was not since the beginning of the world to this time, no, nor ever shall be.

And except those days should be shortened, there should no flesh be saved: but for the elect's sake those days shall be shortened.

Luke 21:12-19

But before all these, **they shall lay their hands on you, and persecute you, delivering you up to the synagogues, and into prisons, being brought before kings and rulers for My name's sake.**

And it shall turn to you for a testimony.

Settle it therefore in your hearts, not to meditate before what ye shall answer:

For I will give you a mouth and wisdom, which all your adversaries shall not be able to gainsay nor resist.

And ye shall be betrayed both by parents, and brethren, and kinsfolks, and friends; and some of you shall they cause to be put to death.

And ye shall be hated of all men for My name's sake.

But there shall not an hair of your head perish.

In your patience possess ye your souls.

John 15:20

Remember the word that I said unto you, The servant is not greater than his lord. **If they have persecuted Me, they will also persecute you;** if they have kept My saying, they will keep your's also.

John 16:2

They shall put you out of the synagogues: **yea, the time cometh, that whosoever killeth you will think that he doeth God service.**

John 16:33

These things I have spoken unto you, that in Me ye might have peace. **In the world ye shall have tribulation: but be of good cheer; I have overcome the world.**

Acts 14:22

. . . that **we must through much tribulation enter into the kingdom of God.**

Romans 5:3-5

And not only so, **but we glory in tribulations also: knowing that tribulation worketh patience;**

And patience, experience; and experience, hope:

And hope maketh not ashamed; because the love of God is shed abroad in our hearts by the Holy Ghost which is given unto us.

Romans 8:18

For I reckon that the sufferings of this present time are not worthy to be compared with the glory which shall be revealed in us.

Romans 8:35-39

Who shall separate us from the love of Christ? shall tribulation, or distress, or persecution, or famine, or nakedness, or peril, or sword?

As it is written, For Thy sake we are killed all the day long; we are accounted as sheep for the slaughter.

Nay, in all these things we are more than conquerors through Him that loved us.

For I am persuaded, that neither death, nor life, nor angels, nor principalities, nor powers, nor things present, nor things to come,

Nor height, nor depth, nor any other creature, shall be able to separate us from the love of God, which is in Christ Jesus our Lord.

Romans 12:12

Rejoicing in hope; **patient in tribulation**; continuing instant in prayer;

Romans 12:14

Bless them which persecute you: bless, and curse not.

II Corinthians 1:3-4

Blessed be God, even the Father of our Lord Jesus Christ, the Father of mercies, and the God of all comfort;

Who comforteth us in all our tribulation, that we may be able to comfort them which are in any trouble, by the comfort wherewith we ourselves are comforted of God.

II Corinthians 1:7

And our hope of you is stedfast, knowing, that as ye are partakers of the sufferings, so shall ye be also of the consolation.

II Corinthians 4:8-11

We are troubled on every side, yet not distressed; we are perplexed, but not in despair;

Persecuted, but not forsaken; cast down, but not destroyed;

Always bearing about in the body the dying of the Lord Jesus, that the life also of Jesus might be made manifest in our body.

For we which live are alway delivered unto death for Jesus' sake, that the life also of Jesus might be made manifest in our mortal flesh.

II Corinthians 4:16-18

For which cause we faint not; but though our outward man perish, yet the inward man is renewed day by day.

For our light affliction, which is but for a moment, worketh for us a far more exceeding and eternal weight of glory;

While we look not at the things which are seen, but at the things which are not seen: for the things which are seen are temporal; but the things which are not seen are eternal.

II Corinthians 6:4-10

But in all things approving ourselves as the ministers of God, in much patience, in afflictions, in necessities, in distresses,

In stripes, in imprisonments, in tumults, in labours, in watchings, in fastings;

By pureness, by knowledge, by longsuffering, by kindness, by the Holy Ghost, by love unfeigned,

By the word of truth, by the power of God, by the armour of righteousness on the right hand and on the left,

By honour and dishonour, by evil report and good report: as deceivers, and yet true;

As unknown, and yet well known; as dying, and, behold, we live; as chastened, and not killed;

As sorrowful, yet alway rejoicing; as poor, yet making many rich; as having nothing, and yet possessing all things.

II Corinthians 6:4

But we commend ourselves in every way as [true] servants of God: through great endurance, in tribulation and suffering, in hardships and privations, in sore straits and calamities, [AMP]

II Corinthians 7:4

Great is my boldness of speech toward you, great is my glorying of you: I am filled with comfort, **I am exceeding joyful in all our tribulation.**

Ephesians 3:13

Wherefore I desire that ye faint not at my tribulations for you, which is your glory.

I Thessalonians 3:4

For verily, when we were with you, we told you before that we should suffer tribulation; even as it came to pass, and ye know.

II Thessalonians 1:4-6

So that we ourselves glory in you in the churches of God **for your patience and faith in all your persecutions and tribulations that ye endure:**

Which is a manifest token of the righteous judgment of God, **that ye may be counted worthy of the kingdom of God, for which ye also suffer:**

Seeing it is a righteous thing with God to recompense tribulation to them that trouble you;

II Timothy 3:12

Yea, and all that will live godly in Christ Jesus shall suffer persecution.

Hebrews 11:24-27

By faith Moses, when he was come to years, **refused** to be called the son of Pharaoh's daughter;

Choosing rather to suffer affliction with the people of God, than to enjoy the pleasures of sin for a season;

Esteeming the reproach of Christ greater riches than the treasures in Egypt: for he had respect unto the recompence of the reward.

By faith he forsook Egypt, not fearing the wrath of the king: **for he endured, as seeing Him Who is invisible.**

Hebrews 11:35-39

. . . others were tortured, not accepting deliverance; that they might obtain a better resurrection:

And others had trial of cruel mockings and scourgings, yea, moreover of bonds and imprisonment:

They were stoned, they were sawn asunder, were tempted, were slain with the sword: they wandered about in sheepskins and goatskins; being destitute, afflicted, tormented;

(Of whom the world was not worthy:) they wandered in deserts, and in mountains, and in dens and caves of the earth.

And these all, having obtained a good report through faith, received not the promise:

James 5:11

Behold, we count them happy which endure. Ye have heard of the patience of Job, and have seen the end of the Lord; that the Lord is very pitiful, and of tender mercy.

I Peter 4:12-14

Beloved, think it not strange concerning the fiery trial which is to try you, as though some strange thing happened unto you:

But rejoice, inasmuch as ye are partakers of Christ's sufferings; that, when His glory shall be revealed, ye may be glad also with exceeding joy.

If ye be reproached for the name of Christ, happy are ye; for the spirit of glory and of God resteth upon you: . . .

I Peter 4:17-19

For the time is come that judgment must begin at the house of God: and if it first begin at us, what shall the end be of them that obey not the Gospel of God?

And if the righteous scarcely be saved, where shall the ungodly and the sinner appear?

Wherefore let them that suffer according to the will of God commit the keeping of their souls to Him in well doing, as unto a faithful Creator.

I John 4:4

Ye are of God, little children, and have overcome them: **because greater is He that is in**

you, than he that is in the world.

Jude 24

Now unto Him that is able to keep you from falling, and to present you faultless before the presence of His glory with exceeding joy,

Revelation 2:7

. . . **To him that overcometh will I give to eat of the tree of life,** which is in the midst of the paradise of God.

Revelation 2:9-11

I know thy works, and tribulation, and poverty, (but thou art rich) and I know the blasphemy of them which say they are Jews, and are not, but are the synagogue of Satan.

Fear none of those things which thou shalt suffer: behold, the devil shall cast some of you into prison, that ye may be tried; and ye shall have tribulation ten days: be thou faithful unto death, and I will give thee a crown of life.

. . . **He that overcometh shall not be hurt of the second death.**

Revelation 2:17

. . . **To him that overcometh will I give to eat of the hidden manna, and will give him a white stone, and in the stone a new name written, which no man knoweth saving he that receiveth it.**

Revelation 2:26-28

And he that overcometh, and keepeth My works unto the end, to him will I give power over the nations:

And he shall rule them with a rod of iron; as the vessels of a potter shall they be broken to shivers: even as I received of My Father.

And I will give him the Morning Star.

Revelation 3:5

He that overcometh, the same shall be clothed in white raiment; and I will not blot out his name out of the Book of Life, but I will confess his name before My Father, and before His angels.

Revelation 3:12

Him that overcometh will I make a pillar in the temple of My God, and he shall go no more out: and I will write upon him the name of My God, and the name of the city of My God, which is New Jerusalem, which cometh down out of heaven from My God: and **I will write upon him My new name.**

Revelation 3:21

To him that overcometh will I grant to sit with Me in My throne, even as I also overcame, and am set down with My Father in His throne.

Revelations 6:9

. . . I saw under the altar the souls of them that were slain for the Word of God, and for the testimony which they held:

Revelation 7:13-17

And one of the elders answered, saying unto me, What are these which are arrayed in white robes? and whence came they?

And I said unto him, Sir, thou knowest. And he said to me, **These are they which came out of great tribulation, and have washed their robes, and made them white in the blood of the Lamb.**

Therefore are they before the throne of God, and serve Him day and night in His temple: and He that sitteth on the throne shall dwell among them.

They shall hunger no more, neither thirst any more; neither shall the sun light on them, nor any heat.

For the Lamb which is in the midst of the throne shall feed them, and shall lead them unto living fountains of waters: and God shall wipe away all tears from their eyes.

Revelation 12:11

And they overcame him by the blood of the Lamb, and by the word of their testimony; **and they loved not their lives unto the death.**

Revelation 20:4

. . . and I saw the souls of them that were beheaded for the witness of Jesus, and for the Word of God, and which had not worshipped the beast, neither his image, neither had received his mark upon their foreheads, or in their hands; **and they lived and reigned with Christ a thousand years.**

Revelation 21:7

He that overcometh shall inherit all things; and I will be his God, and he shall be My son.

Chapter 11

Righteous Responses to the Lord

A. Thanksgiving

I Chronicles 16:8

Give thanks unto the Lord, call upon His name, make known His deeds among the people.

II Chronicles 31:2

And Hezekiah appointed the courses of the priests and the Levites after their courses, every man according to his service, the priests and Levites for burnt offerings and for peace offerings, to minister, and **to give thanks**, and to praise in the gates of the tents of the Lord.

Nehemiah 12:31

Then I brought up the princes of Judah upon the wall, **and appointed two great companies of them that gave thanks**, whereof one went on the right hand upon the wall toward the dung gate:

Psalm 18:49

Therefore will I give thanks unto Thee, O Lord, among the heathen, and sing praises unto Thy name.

Psalm 35:18

I will give Thee thanks in the great congregation: I will praise Thee among much people.

Psalm 50:14

Offer unto God thanksgiving; and pay thy vows unto the Most High:

Psalm 69:30

I will praise the name of God with a song, **and will magnify Him with thanksgiving.**

Psalm 79:13

So we Thy people and sheep of Thy pasture will give Thee thanks for ever: we will shew forth Thy praise to all generations.

Psalm 92:1

It is a good thing to give thanks unto the Lord, and to sing praises unto Thy name, O Most High:

Psalm 95:2

Let us come before His presence with thanksgiving, and make a joyful noise unto Him with psalms.

Psalm 100:1-4

Make a joyful noise unto the Lord, all ye lands.

Serve the Lord with gladness: come before His presence with singing.

Know ye that the Lord He is God: it is He that hath made us, and not we ourselves; we are His people, and the sheep of His pasture.

Enter into His gates with thanksgiving, and into His courts with praise: **be thankful unto Him, and bless His name.**

Psalm 106:1

Praise ye the Lord. **O give thanks unto the Lord; for He is good:** for His mercy endureth for ever.

Psalm 116:17

I will offer to Thee the sacrifice of thanksgiving, and will call upon the name of the Lord.

Psalm 118:1

O give thanks unto the Lord; for He is good: because His mercy endureth for ever.

Psalm 136:26

O give thanks unto the God of heaven: for His mercy endureth for ever.

Psalm 147:7

Sing unto the Lord with thanksgiving; sing praise upon the harp unto our God:

Luke 17:15-16

And one of them, when he saw that he was healed, turned back, and **with a loud voice glorified God,**

And fell down on his face at His feet, giving Him thanks: and he was a Samaritan.

II Corinthians 1:11

Ye also helping together by prayer for us, that for the gift bestowed upon us by the means of many persons **thanks may be given by many on our behalf.**

Ephesians 5:19-20

Speaking to yourselves in psalms and hymns and spiritual songs, singing and making melody in your heart to the Lord;

Giving thanks always for all things unto God and the Father in the name of our Lord Jesus Christ;

Philippians 4:6

Be careful for nothing; but in every thing by prayer and supplication **with thanksgiving** let your requests be made known unto God.

Colossians 2:7

Rooted and built up in Him, and stablished in the faith, as ye have been taught, **abounding therein with thanksgiving.**

Colossians 3:17

And whatsoever ye do in word or deed, do all in the name of the Lord Jesus, **giving thanks to God and the Father by Him.**

Colossians 4:2

Continue in prayer, and **watch in the same with thanksgiving;**

I Thessalonians 5:18

In every thing give thanks: for this is the will of God in Christ Jesus concerning you.

II Thessalonians 2:13

But we are bound to give thanks alway to God for you, brethren beloved of the Lord, because God hath from the beginning chosen you to salvation through sanctification of the Spirit and belief of the truth:

I Timothy 4:4

For every creature of God is good, and nothing to be refused, **if it be received with thanksgiving:**

Hebrews 13:15

By Him therefore let us offer the sacrifice of praise to God continually, that is, **the fruit of our lips giving thanks to His name.**

B. Praise

II Samuel 22:4

I will call on the Lord, Who is worthy to be praised: so shall I be saved from mine enemies.

II Chronicles 5:13-14

It came even to pass, as the trumpeters and singers were as one, **to make one sound to be heard in praising and thanking the Lord;** and when they lifted up their voice with the trumpets and cymbals and instruments of musick, and **praised the Lord**, saying, For He is good; for His mercy endureth for ever: **that then the house was filled with a cloud,** even the house of the Lord;

So that the priests could not stand to minister by reason of the cloud: for the glory of the Lord had filled the house of God.

II Chronicles 20:21-22

And when he had consulted with the people, **he appointed singers unto the Lord, and that should praise the beauty of holiness,** as they went out before the army, and to say, Praise the Lord; for His mercy endureth for ever.

And when they began to sing and to praise, the Lord set ambushments against the children of Ammon, Moab, and mount Seir, which were come against Judah; and they were smitten.

Psalm 9:1-2

I will praise Thee, O Lord, with my whole heart; I will shew forth all Thy marvellous works.

I will be glad and rejoice in Thee: **I will sing praise to Thy name, O Thou Most High.**

Psalm 22:3

But Thou art holy, **O Thou that inhabitest the praises of Israel.**

Psalm 29:2

Give unto the Lord the glory due unto His name; **worship the Lord in the beauty of holiness.**

Psalm 33:1

Rejoice in the Lord, O ye righteous: **for praise is comely for the upright.**

Psalm 34:1

I will bless the Lord at all times: **His praise shall continually be in my mouth.**

Psalm 40:3

And He hath put a new song in my mouth, even praise unto our God: many shall see it, and fear, and shall trust in the Lord.

Psalm 47:6-7

Sing praises to God, sing praises: sing praises unto our King, sing praises.

For God is the King of all the earth: sing ye praises with understanding.

Psalm 50:23

Whoso offereth praise glorifieth Me: and to him that ordereth his conversation aright will I shew the salvation of God.

Psalm 56:4

In God I will praise His word, in God I have put my trust; I will not fear what flesh can do unto me.

Psalm 57:9

I will praise Thee, O Lord, among the people: I will sing unto Thee among the nations.

Psalm 63:3-5

Because Thy lovingkindness is better than life, **my lips shall praise Thee.**

Thus will I bless Thee while I live: I will lift up my hands in Thy name.

My soul shall be satisfied as with marrow and fatness; and **My mouth shall praise Thee with joyful lips:**

Psalm 66:2

Sing forth the honour of His name; make His praise glorious.

Psalm 71:8

Let my mouth be filled with Thy praise and with Thy honor all the day.

Psalm 79:13

. . . we will shew forth Thy praise to all generations.

Psalm 96:4

For the Lord is great, and greatly to be praised: . . .

Psalm 104:33

I will sing unto the Lord as long as I live: **I will sing praise to my God while I have my being.**

Psalm 107:8

Oh that men would praise the Lord for His goodness, and for His wonderful works to the children of men!

Psalm 113:3

From the rising of the sun unto the going down of the same the Lord's name is to be praised.

<u>**Psalm 119:171**</u>

My lips shall utter praise, when Thou hast taught me Thy statutes.

<u>**Psalm 134:2**</u>

Lift up your hands in the sanctuary, and bless the Lord.

<u>**Psalm 138:1**</u>

I will praise Thee with my whole heart: before the gods will I sing praise unto Thee.

<u>**Psalm 145:2-4**</u>

Every day will I bless Thee; and I will praise Thy name for ever and ever.

Great is the Lord, and greatly to be praised; and His greatness is unsearchable.

One generation shall praise Thy works to another, and shall declare Thy mighty acts.

<u>**Psalm 145:10**</u>

All Thy works shall praise Thee, O Lord; and Thy saints shall bless Thee.

<u>**Psalm 147:1**</u>

Praise ye the Lord: **for it is good to sing praises unto our God**; for it is pleasant; and **praise is comely.**

<u>**Psalm 149:1**</u>

Praise ye the Lord. Sing unto the Lord a new song, and His praise in the congregation of saints.

<u>**Psalm 150:1-2**</u>

Praise ye the Lord. Praise God in His sanctuary: praise Him in the firmament of His power.

Praise Him for His mighty acts: praise Him according to His excellent greatness.

<u>**Psalm 150:6**</u>

Let every thing that hath breath praise the Lord. Praise ye the Lord.

<u>**Isaiah 25:1**</u>

O Lord, Thou art my God; I will exalt Thee, **I will praise Thy name;** for Thou hast done wonderful things; Thy counsels of old are faithfulness and truth.

<u>**Isaiah 43:21**</u>

This people have I formed for Myself; **they shall shew forth My praise.**

<u>**Isaiah 61:3**</u>

. . . to give unto them beauty for ashes, the oil of joy for mourning, **the garment of praise for the spirit of heaviness;** . . .

Matthew 21:16

. . . Yea; have ye never read, **Out of the mouth of babes and sucklings Thou hast perfected praise?**

Luke 18:43

And immediately he received his sight, and followed Him, glorifying God: **and all the people, when they saw it, gave praise unto God.**

Luke 19:37-38

. . . the whole multitude of the disciples began **to rejoice and praise God with a loud voice** for all the mighty works that they had seen;

Saying, **Blessed be the King that cometh in the name of the Lord: peace in heaven, and glory in the highest.**

Luke 24:52-53

And they worshipped Him, and returned to Jerusalem with great joy:

And were continually in the temple, **praising and blessing God**. Amen.

Acts 2:46-47

And they, continuing daily with one accord in the temple, and breaking bread from house to house, did eat their meat with gladness and singleness of heart,

Praising God, and having favour with all the people. And the Lord added to the church daily such as should be saved.

Acts 3:8

And he leaping up stood, and walked, and entered with them into the temple**, walking, and leaping, and praising God.**

Acts 16:25

And at midnight Paul and Silas **prayed, and sang praises unto God**: and the prisoners heard them.

Hebrews 13:15

By Him therefore let us offer **the sacrifice of praise** to God continually, that is, **the fruit of our lips giving thanks to His Name.**

I Peter 2:9

But ye are a chosen generation, a royal priesthood, an holy nation, a peculiar people; **that ye should shew forth the praises of Him who hath called you out of darkness into His marvellous light:**

Revelation 19:5

And a voice came out of the throne, saying, **Praise our God, all ye His servants, and ye that fear Him, both small and great.**

C. Worship

Exodus 34:14

For thou shalt worship no other god: for the Lord, Whose name is Jealous, is a jealous God:

Deuteronomy 26:10

And now, behold, I have brought the firstfruits of the land, which Thou, O Lord, hast given me. **And thou shalt set it before the Lord thy God, and worship before the Lord thy God:**

II Kings 17:36

But the Lord, Who brought you up out of the land of Egypt with great power and a stretched out arm, **Him shall ye fear, and Him shall ye worship, and to Him shall ye do sacrifice.**

I Chronicles 16:29

Give unto the Lord the glory due unto His name: bring an offering, and come before Him: **worship the Lord in the beauty of holiness.**

Psalm 29:2

Give unto the Lord the glory due unto His name; worship the Lord in the beauty of holiness.

Psalm 95:6-7

O come, let us worship and bow down: let us kneel before the Lord our Maker.

For He is our God; and we are the people of His pasture, and the sheep of His hand . . .

Psalm 96:8-9

Give unto the Lord the glory due unto His name: bring an offering, and come into His courts.

O worship the Lord in the beauty of holiness: fear before Him, all the earth.

Psalm 99:5,9

Exalt ye the Lord our God, and **worship at His footstool;** for He is holy.

Exalt the Lord our God, and **worship at His holy hill;** for the Lord our God is holy.

Isaiah 27:13

And it shall come to pass in that day, that the great trumpet shall be blown, and they shall come which were ready to perish in the land of Assyria, and the outcasts in the land of Egypt, **and shall worship the Lord in the holy mount at Jerusalem.**

Matthew 4:10

Then saith Jesus unto him, **Get thee hence, Satan: for it is written, Thou shalt worship the Lord thy God, and Him only shalt thou serve.**

John 4:23-24

But the hour cometh, and now is, when the true worshippers shall worship the Father in spirit and in truth: for the Father seeketh such to worship Him.

God is a Spirit: and they that worship Him must worship Him in spirit and in truth.

Philippians 3:3

For we are the circumcision, **which worship God in the spirit,** and rejoice in Christ Jesus, and have no confidence in the flesh.

Revelation 4:10-11

The four and twenty elders fall down before Him that sat on the throne, and worship Him that liveth for ever and ever, and cast their crowns before the throne, saying,

Thou art worthy, O Lord, to receive glory and honour and power: for Thou hast created all things, and for Thy pleasure they are and were created.

Revelations 5:11-14

And I beheld, and I heard the voice of many angels round about the throne and the beasts and the elders: and the number of them was ten thousand times ten thousand, and thousands of thousands;

Saying with a loud voice, **Worthy is the Lamb that was slain to receive power, and riches, and wisdom, and strength, and honour, and glory, and blessing.**

And every creature which is in heaven, and on the earth, and under the earth, and such as are in the sea, and all that are in them, heard I saying, **Blessing, and honour, and glory, and power, be unto Him that sitteth upon the throne, and unto the Lamb for ever and ever.**

And the four beasts said, Amen. And the four and twenty elders fell down and worshipped Him that liveth for ever and ever.

Revelations 14:6-7

And I saw another angel fly in the midst of heaven, having the everlasting gospel to preach unto them that dwell on the earth, and to every nation, and kindred, and tongue, and people,

Saying with a loud voice, **Fear God, and give glory to Him; for the hour of His judgment is come: and worship Him that made heaven, and earth, and the sea, and the fountains of waters.**

Revelations 22:8-9

. . . And when I had heard and seen, I fell down to worship before the feet of the angel which shewed me these things.

Then saith he unto me, See thou do it not: for I am thy fellowservant, and of thy brethren the prophets, and of them which keep the sayings of this book: **worship God.**

Part II

Character Development For Believers

Chapter 12

Walking in Integrity

<u>**Genesis 20:2-6**</u> *(Abimelech)*

And Abraham said of Sarah his wife, She is my sister: and Abimelech king of Gerar sent, and took Sarah.

But God came to Abimelech in a dream by night, and said to him, Behold, thou art but a dead man, for the woman which thou hast taken; for she is a man's wife.

But Abimelech had not come near her: and he said, Lord, wilt Thou slay also a righteous nation?

Said he not unto me, She is my sister? and she, even she herself said, He is my brother: **in the integrity of my heart and innocency of my hands have I done this.**

And God said unto him in a dream, **Yea, I know that thou didst this in the integrity of thy heart, for I also withheld thee from sinning against Me: therefore suffered I thee not to touch her.**

<u>**Genesis 39:6-12**</u> *(Joseph)*

And he *(Potiphar)* left all that he had in Joseph's hand; and he knew not ought he had, save the bread which he did eat. And Joseph was a goodly person, and well favoured.

And it came to pass after these things, that his master's wife cast her eyes upon Joseph; and she said, Lie with me.

But he refused, and said unto his master's wife, Behold, my master wotteth not what is with me in the house, and he hath committed all that he hath to my hand;

There is none greater in this house than I; neither hath he kept back any thing from me but thee, because thou art his wife: **how then can I do this great wickedness, and sin against God?**

And it came to pass, as she spake to Joseph day by day, that he hearkened not unto her, to lie by her, or to be with her.

And it came to pass about this time, that Joseph went into the house to do his business; and there was none of the men of the house there within.

And she caught him by his garment, saying, Lie with me: and **he left his garment in her hand, and fled, and got him out.**

Leviticus 19:11

You shall not steal, or deal falsely, or lie one to another. [AMP]

Leviticus 19:35-36

You shall do no unrighteousness in judgment, in measures of length or weight or quantity.

You shall have accurate and just balances, just weights, just ephah and hin measures. *I am the Lord your God, Who brought you out of the land of Egypt. [AMP]*

Deuteronomy 25:14-16

You shall not have in your house true and false measures, a large and a small.

But you shall have a perfect and just weight and a perfect and just measure, that your days may be prolonged in the land which the Lord your God gives you.

For all who do such things, all who do unrighteously, are an abomination to the Lord your God. [AMP]

Job 2:3

And the Lord said unto Satan, Hast thou considered My servant Job, that there is none like him in the earth, a perfect and an upright man, one that feareth God, and escheweth evil? and **still he holdeth fast his integrity,** although thou movedst me against him, to destroy him without cause.

Job 17:9

The righteous also shall hold on his way, and he that hath clean hands shall be stronger and stronger.

Job 27:4-6

My lips shall not speak wickedness, nor my tongue utter deceit.

God forbid that I should justify you: **till I die I will not remove mine integrity from me.**

My righteousness I hold fast, and will not let it go: my heart shall not reproach me so long as I live.

Job 31:6

Let me be weighed in an even balance, that God may know mine integrity.

Psalm 7:8

The Lord judges the people; judge me, O Lord, and do me justice according to my righteousness [my rightness, justice, and right standing with You] and according to the integrity that is in me. [AMP]

Psalm 15:1-5

Lord, who shall abide in Thy tabernacle? who shall dwell in Thy holy hill?

He that walketh uprightly, and worketh righteousness, and speaketh the truth in his heart.

He that backbiteth not with his tongue, nor doeth evil to his neighbour, nor taketh up a reproach against his neighbour.

In whose eyes a vile person is contemned; but he honoureth them that fear the Lord. He that sweareth to his own hurt, and changeth not.

He that putteth not out his money to usury, nor taketh reward against the innocent. He that doeth these things shall never be moved.

Psalm 24:3-5

Who shall ascend into the hill of the Lord? or who shall stand in His holy place?

He that hath clean hands, and a pure heart; who hath not lifted up his soul unto vanity, nor sworn deceitfully.

He shall receive the blessing from the Lord, and righteousness from the God of his salvation.

Psalms 25:21

Let integrity and uprightness preserve me; for I wait on Thee.

Psalms 26:1

Judge me, O Lord; for I have walked in mine integrity: I have trusted also in the Lord; therefore I shall not slide.

Psalm 26:11

But as for me, I will walk in mine integrity: redeem me, and be merciful unto me.

Psalms 41:12

And as for me, Thou upholdest me in mine integrity, and settest me before Thy face for ever.

Proverbs 1:3

Receive instruction in wise dealing and the discipline of wise thoughtfulness, righteousness, justice, and integrity, [AMP]

Proverbs 4:18

But the path of the just is as the shining light, that shineth more and more unto the perfect day.

Proverbs 4:25-27

Let thine eyes look right on, and let thine eyelids look straight before thee.

Ponder the path of thy feet, and let all thy ways be established.

Turn not to the right hand nor to the left: remove thy foot from evil.

Proverbs 11:3

The integrity of the upright shall guide them: . . .

Proverbs 12:22

Lying lips are abomination to the Lord: but they that deal truly are His delight.

Proverbs 19:1

Better is the poor that walketh in his integrity, than he that is perverse in his lips, and is a fool.

Proverbs 20:7

The just man walketh in his integrity: his children are blessed after him.

Proverbs 21:3

To do justice and judgment is more acceptable to the Lord than sacrifice.

Isaiah 33:15-16

He that walketh righteously, and speaketh uprightly; he that despiseth the gain of oppressions, that shaketh his hands from holding of bribes, that stoppeth his ears from hearing of blood, and shutteth his eyes from seeing evil;

He shall dwell on high: his place of defence shall be the munitions of rocks: bread shall be given him; his waters shall be sure.

Jeremiah 7:5-7

For if ye throughly amend your ways and your doings; if ye throughly execute judgment between a man and his neighbour;

If ye oppress not the stranger, the fatherless, and the widow, and shed not innocent blood in this place, neither walk after other gods to your hurt:

Then will I cause you to dwell in this place, in the land that I gave to your fathers, for ever and ever.

Micah 6:8

He hath shewed thee, O man, what is good; and what doth the Lord require of thee, but to do justly, and to love mercy, and to walk humbly with thy God?

Malachi 1:14

But cursed be the deceiver, which hath in his flock a male, and voweth, and sacrificeth unto the Lord a corrupt thing: for I am a great King, saith the Lord of hosts, and My name is dreadful among the heathen.

Luke 3:13-14

And He said unto them, **Exact no more than that which is appointed you.**

And the soldiers likewise demanded of Him, saying, And what shall we do? And He said unto them, **Do violence to no man, neither accuse any falsely; and be content with your wages.**

Luke 16:10

He that is faithful in that which is least is faithful also in much: and he that is unjust in the least is unjust also in much.

<u>**Luke 19:8-10**</u>

And Zacchaeus stood, and said unto the Lord; **Behold, Lord, the half of my goods I give to the poor; and if I have taken any thing from any man by false accusation, I restore him fourfold.**

And Jesus said unto him, This day is salvation come to this house, forsomuch as he also is a son of Abraham.

For the Son of man is come to seek and to save that which was lost.

<u>**Acts 5:1-5**</u> *(Ananias & Sapphira)*

But a certain man named Ananias, with Sapphira his wife, sold a possession,

And kept back part of the price, his wife also being privy to it, and brought a certain part, and laid it at the apostles' feet.

But Peter said, **Ananias, why hath Satan filled thine heart to lie to the Holy Ghost, and to keep back part of the price of the land?**

Whiles it remained, was it not thine own? and after it was sold, was it not in thine own power? why hast thou conceived this thing in thine heart? thou hast not lied unto men, but unto God.

And Ananias hearing these words fell down, and gave up the ghost: and great fear came on all them that heard these things.

<u>**Acts 24:16**</u>

And herein do I exercise myself, to have always a conscience void of offence toward God, and toward men.

<u>**Romans 12:17**</u>

. . . Provide things honest in the sight of all men.

<u>**Romans 13:13**</u>

Let us walk honestly, as in the day, . . .

<u>**II Corinthians 8:20-21**</u>

[For] we are on our guard, intending that no one should find anything for which to blame us in regard to our administration of this large contribution.

For we take thought beforehand and aim to be honest and absolutely above suspicion, not only in the sight of the Lord but also in the sight of men. [AMP]

<u>**Ephesians 4:28**</u>

Let him that stole steal no more: but rather let him labour, working with his hands the thing which is good, that he may have to give to him that needeth.

<u>**Ephesians 5:8-11**</u>

For ye were sometimes darkness, but now are ye light in the Lord: walk as children of light:

(For the fruit of the Spirit is in all goodness and righteousness and truth;)

Proving what is acceptable unto the Lord.

And have no fellowship with the unfruitful works of darkness, but rather reprove them.

Ephesians 6:14

Stand therefore [hold your ground], having tightened the belt of truth around your loins and having put on the breastplate of integrity and of moral rectitude and right standing with God, [AMP]

Colossians 3:9-10

Lie not one to another, seeing that ye have put off the old man with his deeds;
And have put on the new man, which is renewed in knowledge after the image of him that created him:

I Thessalonians 4:11-12

And that ye study to be quiet, and to do your own business, and to work with your own hands, as we commanded you;
That ye may walk honestly toward them that are without, and that ye may have lack of nothing.

Titus 1:6

[These elders should be] men who are of unquestionable integrity and are irreproachable... [AMP]

Hebrews 13:18

Keep praying for us, for we are convinced that ***we have a good (clear) conscience, that we want to walk uprightly*** *and live a noble life,* ***acting honorably and in complete honesty in all things.*** *[AMP]*

Chapter 13

Walking in Humility

II Chronicles 7:14

If My people, which are called by My name, **shall humble themselves**, and pray, and seek My face, and turn from their wicked ways; then will I hear from heaven, and will forgive their sin, and will heal their land.

Job 5:11

To set up on high those that be low; that those which mourn may be exalted to safety.

Job 22:29

When men are cast down, then thou shalt say, **There is lifting up; and He shall save the humble person.**

Psalm 9:12

. . . He forgetteth not the cry of the humble.

Psalm 10:17

Lord, **Thou hast heard the desire of the humble:** Thou wilt prepare their heart, Thou wilt cause Thine ear to hear:

Psalms 22:26

The meek shall eat and be satisfied: they shall praise the Lord that seek Him: your heart shall live for ever.

Psalms 25:9

The meek will He guide in judgment: and the meek will He teach His way.

<u>**Psalms 37:11**</u>

But the meek shall inherit the earth; and shall delight themselves in the abundance of peace.

<u>**Psalm 69:32**</u>

The humble shall see this, and be glad: and your heart shall live that seek God.

<u>**Psalm 131:1-2**</u>

Lord, my heart is not haughty, nor mine eyes lofty: neither do I exercise myself in great matters, or in things too high for me.

Surely I have behaved and quieted myself, as a child that is weaned of his mother: my soul is even as a weaned child.

<u>**Psalms 138:6**</u>

Though the Lord be high, yet hath He respect unto the lowly: but the proud He knoweth afar off.

<u>**Psalms 147:6**</u>

The Lord lifteth up the meek: He casteth the wicked down to the ground.

<u>**Psalms 149:4**</u>

For the Lord taketh pleasure in His people: **He will beautify the meek with salvation**.

<u>**Proverbs 3:34**</u>

Surely He scorneth the scorners: **but He giveth grace unto the lowly.**

<u>**Proverbs 11:2**</u>

When pride cometh, then cometh shame: **but with the lowly is wisdom.**

<u>**Proverbs 13:10**</u>

Only by pride cometh contention: but **with the well advised is wisdom.**

<u>**Proverbs 15:33**</u>

The fear of the Lord is the instruction of wisdom; and **before honour is humility.**

<u>**Proverbs 16:19**</u>

Better it is to be of an humble spirit with the lowly, than to divide the spoil with the proud.

<u>**Proverbs 22:4**</u>

By humility and the fear of the Lord are riches, and honour, and life.

<u>**Proverbs 25:6-7**</u>

Put not forth thyself in the presence of the king, and stand not in the place of great men:

For better it is that it be said unto thee, Come up hither; than that thou shouldest be put lower in the presence of the prince whom thine eyes have seen.

Proverbs 27:2

Let another man praise thee, and not thine own mouth; a stranger, and not thine own lips.

Proverbs 29:23

A man's pride shall bring him low: **but honour shall uphold the humble in spirit.**

Isaiah 29:19

The meek also shall increase their joy in the Lord, and the poor among men shall rejoice in the Holy One of Israel.

Isaiah 57:15

For thus saith the high and lofty One that inhabiteth eternity, Whose name is Holy; **I dwell in the high and holy place, with him also that is of a contrite and humble spirit, to revive the spirit of the humble, and to revive the heart of the contrite ones.**

Isaiah 66:2

For all those things hath Mine hand made, and all those things have been, saith the Lord: **but to this man will I look, even to him that is poor and of a contrite spirit, and trembleth at My word.**

Jeremiah 9:23-24

Thus saith the Lord, Let not the wise man glory in his wisdom, neither let the mighty man glory in his might, let not the rich man glory in his riches:

But let him that glorieth glory in this, that he understandeth and knoweth Me, that I am the Lord which exercise lovingkindness, judgment, and righteousness, in the earth: for in these things I delight, saith the Lord.

Micah 6:8

He hath shewed thee, O man, what is good; and **what doth the Lord require of thee, but to do justly, and to love mercy, and to walk humbly with thy God?**

Matthew 5:3

Blessed are the poor in spirit: for their's is the kingdom of heaven.

Matthew 11:29-30

Take My yoke upon you, and learn of Me; for I am meek and lowly in heart: and ye shall find rest unto your souls.

For My yoke is easy, and My burden is light.

Matthew 18:4

Whoever will humble himself therefore and become like this little child [trusting, lowly, loving, forgiving] is greatest in the kingdom of heaven. [AMP]

Matthew 20:26-28

. . . but whosoever will be great among you, let him be your minister;

And whosoever will be chief among you, let him be your servant:

Even as the Son of man came not to be ministered unto, but to minister, and to give His life a ransom for many.

Matthew 23:11-12

But he that is greatest among you shall be your servant.

And whosoever shall exalt himself shall be abased; and he that shall humble himself shall be exalted.

Luke 1:52

He hath put down the mighty from their seats, and **exalted them of low degree.**

Luke 14:10

But when thou art bidden, go and sit down in the lowest room; that when he that bade thee cometh, he may say unto thee, Friend, go up higher: then shalt thou have worship in the presence of them that sit at meat with thee.

Luke 17:10

So likewise ye, when ye shall have done all those things which are commanded you, say, **We are unprofitable servants:** we have done that which was our duty to do.

Luke 18:14

. . . for every one that exalteth himself shall be abased; and **he that humbleth himself shall be exalted.**

Luke 22:24-27

And there was also a strife among them, which of them should be accounted the greatest.

And He said unto them, The kings of the Gentiles exercise lordship over them; and they that exercise authority upon them are called benefactors.

But ye shall not be so: **but he that is greatest among you, let him be as the younger; and he that is chief, as He that doth serve.**

For whether is greater, he that sitteth at meat, or he that serveth? is not he that sitteth at meat? but **I am among you as He that serveth**.

John 8:50 (Jesus)

And I seek not Mine own glory: . . .

John 13:14-16

If I then, your Lord and Master, have washed your feet; ye also ought to wash one another's feet.

For I have given you an example, that ye should do as I have done to you.

Verily, verily, I say unto you, The servant is not greater than his lord; neither he that is sent greater than he that sent him.

__Acts 20:19__ *(Apostle Paul)*

Serving the Lord will all humility of mind, . . .

__Romans 12:3__

For I say, through the grace given unto me, to every man that is among you, **not to think of himself more highly than he ought to think; but to think soberly,** according as God hath dealt to every man the measure of faith.

__Romans 12:10__

Be kindly affectioned one to another with brotherly love; **in honour preferring one another;**

__Romans 12:16__

Be of the same mind one toward another. **Mind not high things, but condescend to men of low estate. Be not wise in your own conceits.**

__I Corinthians 1:26-29__

For ye see your calling, brethren, how that not many wise men after the flesh, not many mighty, nor many noble, are called:

But God hath chosen the foolish things of the world to confound the wise; and God hath chosen the weak things of the world to confound the things which are mighty;

And base things of the world, and things which are despised, hath God chosen, yea, and things which are not, to bring to nought things that are:

That no flesh should glory in His presence.

__Galatians 2:20__

I am crucified with Christ: nevertheless I live; yet not I, but Christ liveth in me: and the life which I now live in the flesh I live by the faith of the Son of God, Who loved me, and gave Himself for me.

__Ephesians 4:1-3__

I therefore, the prisoner of the Lord, beseech you that ye walk worthy of the vocation wherewith ye are called,

With all lowliness and meekness, with longsuffering, forbearing one another in love;

Endeavouring to keep the unity of the Spirit in the bond of peace.

__Philippians 2:3-9__

Let nothing be done through strife or vainglory; **but in lowliness of mind let each esteem other better than themselves.**

Look not every man on his own things, but every man also on the things of others.

Let this mind be in you, which was also in Christ Jesus:

Who, being in the form of God, thought it not robbery to be equal with God:

But made Himself of no reputation, and took upon Him the form of a servant, and was made in the likeness of men:

And being found in fashion as a man, **He humbled Himself, and became obedient unto**

death, even the death of the cross.

Wherefore God also hath highly exalted Him, and given Him a name which is above every name:

Do nothing from factional motives [through contentiousness, strife, selfishness, or for unworthy ends] or prompted by conceit and empty arrogance. ***Instead, in the true spirit of humility (lowliness of mind) let each regard the others as better than and superior to himself [thinking more highly of one another than you do of yourselves].***

Let each of you esteem and look upon and be concerned for not [merely] his own interests, but also each for the interests of others.

Let this same attitude and purpose and [humble] mind be in you which was in Christ Jesus: [Let Him be your example in humility:]

Who, although being essentially one with God and in the form of God [possessing the fullness of the attributes which make God God], did not think this equality with God was a thing to be eagerly grasped or retained,

But stripped Himself [of all privileges and rightful dignity], ***so as to assume the guise of a servant (slave),*** *in that He became like men and was born a human being.*

And after He had appeared in human form, ***He abased and humbled Himself [still further]*** *and carried* ***His obedience*** *to the extreme of death, even the death of the cross!*

Therefore [because He stooped so low] God has highly exalted Him *and has freely bestowed on Him the name that is above every name,*

<u>Colossians 3:12</u>

Put on therefore, as the elect of God, holy and beloved, bowels of mercies, kindness, **humbleness of mind**, meekness, longsuffering;

<u>Titus 3:2</u>

To speak evil of no man, to be no brawlers, but gentle, **shewing all meekness unto all men.**

<u>James 1:9-10</u>

Let the brother of low degree rejoice in that he is exalted:

But the rich, in that he is made low: because as the flower of the grass he shall pass away.

<u>James 1:21</u>

Wherefore lay apart all filthiness and superfluity of naughtiness, and **receive with meekness the engrafted word, which is able to save your souls.**

<u>James 3:13</u>

Who is a wise man and endued with knowledge among you? let him shew out of a good conversation his works with **meekness of wisdom.**

<u>James 4:6</u>

But He giveth more grace. Wherefore He saith, **God resisteth the proud, but giveth grace unto the humble.**

But He gives us more and more grace (power of the Holy Spirit, to meet this evil tendency and all others fully). That is why He says, God sets Himself against the proud and haughty, but gives grace [continually] to the lowly ***(those who are humble enough to receive it).*** *[AMP]*

James 4:10

Humble yourselves in the sight of the Lord, and He shall lift you up.

I Peter 5:5-6

Likewise, ye younger, submit yourselves unto the elder. Yea, all of you be subject one to another, and **be clothed with humility**: for God resisteth the proud, and **giveth grace to the humble.**

Humble yourselves therefore under the mighty hand of God, that He may exalt you in due time:

Likewise, you who are younger and of lesser rank, be subject to the elders (the ministers and spiritual guides of the church) - [giving them due respect and yielding to their counsel]. ***Clothe (apron) yourselves, all of you, with humility [as the garb of a servant, so that its covering cannot possibly be stripped from you, with freedom from pride and arrogance] toward one another.*** *For God sets Himself against the proud (the insolent, the overbearing, the disdainful, the presumptuous, the boastful) - [and He opposes, frustrates, and defeats them],* ***but gives grace (favor, blessing) to the humble.***

Therefore humble yourselves [demote, lower yourselves in your own estimation] under the mighty hand of God, that in due time He may exalt you. [AMP]

Chapter 14

Developing a Fear of the Lord

Deuteronomy 4:10

. . . Gather Me the people together, and I will make them hear My words, **that they may learn to fear Me all the days that they shall live upon the earth**, and that they may teach their children.

Deuteronomy 5:29

O that there were such an heart in them, **that they would fear Me,** and keep all My commandments always, **that it might be well with them, and with their children for ever!**

Deuteronomy 6:1-2

Now these are the commandments, the statutes, and the judgments, which the Lord your God commanded to teach you, that ye might do them in the land whither ye go to possess it:

That thou mightest fear the Lord thy God, to keep all His statutes and His commandments, which I command thee, thou, and thy son, and thy son's son, all the days of thy life; and that thy days may be prolonged.

Deuteronomy 6:13-15

Thou shalt fear the Lord thy God, and serve Him, and shalt swear by His name.

Ye shall not go after other gods, of the gods of the people which are round about you;

(For the Lord thy God is a jealous God among you) lest the anger of the Lord thy God be kindled against thee, and destroy thee from off the face of the earth.

Deuteronomy 17:19-20

And it shall be with him, and he shall read therein all the days of his life: **that he may learn to fear the Lord his God,** to keep all the words of this law and these statutes, to do them:

That his heart be not lifted up above his brethren, and that he turn not aside from the commandment, to the right hand, or to the left: **to the end that he may prolong his days in his kingdom, he, and his children, in the midst of Israel.**

<u>I Samuel 12:24</u>

Only fear the Lord, and serve Him in truth with all your heart: for consider how great things He hath done for you.

<u>Job 28:28</u>

*But to man He said, **Behold, the reverential and worshipful fear of the Lord - that is Wisdom;** and to depart from evil is understanding. [AMP]*

<u>Psalm 19:9</u>

The fear of the Lord is clean, enduring for ever: . . .

<u>Psalm 25:12-14</u>

*Who is the man who reverently fears and worships the Lord? **Him shall He teach in the way that he should choose.***

He himself shall dwell at ease, and his offspring shall inherit the land.

The secret [of the sweet, satisfying companionship] of the Lord have they who fear (revere and worship) Him, and He will show them His covenant and reveal to them its [deep, inner] meaning. [AMP]

<u>Psalm 31:19-20</u>

Oh how great is Thy goodness, which Thou hast laid up for them that fear Thee; which Thou hast wrought for them that trust in Thee before the sons of men!

Thou shalt hide them in the secret of Thy presence from the pride of man: Thou shalt keep them secretly in a pavilion from the strife of tongues.

<u>Psalm 33:8</u>

Let all the earth fear the Lord: let all the inhabitants of the world stand in awe of Him.

<u>Psalm 33:18-19</u>

Behold, **the eye of the Lord is upon them that fear Him,** upon them that hope in His mercy;

To deliver their soul from death, and to keep them alive in famine.

<u>Psalm 34:9-11</u>

O fear the Lord, ye His saints: **for there is no want to them that fear Him.**

The young lions do lack, and suffer hunger: **but they that seek the Lord shall not want any good thing.**

Come, ye children, hearken unto me: I will teach you the fear of the Lord.

<u>Psalm 86:11</u>

Teach me Thy way, O Lord; I will walk in Thy truth: **unite my heart to fear Thy name.**

Psalm 111:10

The fear of the Lord is the beginning of wisdom: a good understanding have all they that do His commandments: His praise endureth for ever.

Psalm 145:19

He will fulfil the desire of them that fear Him: He also will hear their cry, and will save them.

Psalm 147:11

The Lord taketh pleasure in them that fear Him, in those that hope in His mercy.

Proverbs 2:1-5

My son, if thou wilt receive My words, and hide My commandments with thee;
So that thou incline thine ear unto wisdom, and apply thine heart to understanding;
Yea, if thou criest after knowledge, and liftest up thy voice for understanding;
If thou seekest her as silver, and searchest for her as for hid treasures;
Then shalt thou understand the fear of the Lord, and find the knowledge of God.

Proverbs 3:7

Be not wise in thine own eyes: **fear the Lord, and depart from evil.**

Proverbs 8:13

The fear of the Lord is to hate evil: pride, and arrogancy, and the evil way, and the froward mouth, do I hate.

Proverbs 10:27

The fear of the Lord prolongeth days: but the years of the wicked shall be shortened.

Proverbs 14:26-27

In the fear of the Lord is strong confidence: and His children shall have a place of refuge.

The fear of the Lord is a fountain of life, to depart from the snares of death.

Proverbs 15:33

The fear of the Lord is the instruction of wisdom; and before honour is humility.

Proverbs 19:23

The reverent, worshipful fear of the Lord leads to life, and he who has it rests satisfied; he cannot be visited with [actual] evil. *[AMP]*

Proverbs 23:17

Let not thine heart envy sinners: **but be thou in the fear of the Lord all the day long.**

Proverbs 24:21-22

My son, fear thou the Lord and the king: and meddle not with them that are given to change:

For their calamity shall rise suddenly; and who knoweth the ruin of them both?

Proverbs 28:14

Blessed (happy, fortunate, and to be envied) is the man who reverently and worshipfully fears [the Lord] at all times [regardless of circumstances], *but he who hardens his heart will fall into calamity. [AMP]*

Ecclesiastes 5:7

For in the multitude of dreams and many words there are also divers vanities: **but fear thou God.**

Ecclesiastes 12:13-14

Let us hear the conclusion of the whole matter: **Fear God, and keep His commandments:** for this is the whole duty of man.

For God shall bring every work into judgment, with every secret thing, whether it be good, or whether it be evil.

Isaiah 59:19

So shall they fear the name of the Lord from the west, and His glory from the rising of the sun. When the enemy shall come in like a flood, the Spirit of the Lord shall lift up a standard against him.

Jeremiah 32:39-40

And I will give them one heart, and one way, **that they may fear Me for ever,** for the good of them, and of their children after them:

And I will make an everlasting covenant with them, that I will not turn away from them, to do them good; **but I will put My fear in their hearts, that they shall not depart from Me**.

Malachi 3:16-18

Then they that feared the Lord spake often one to another: and the Lord hearkened, and heard it, and **a book of remembrance was written before Him for them that feared the Lord, and that thought upon His name.**

And they shall be Mine, saith the Lord of hosts, in that day when I make up My jewels; and I will spare them, as a man spareth his own son that serveth him.

Then shall ye return, and discern between the righteous and the wicked, between him that serveth God and him that serveth Him not.

Malachi 4:2

But unto you that fear My name shall the Sun of Righteousness arise with healing in His wings; and ye shall go forth, and grow up as calves of the stall.

Matthew 10:28

And fear not them which kill the body, but are not able to kill the soul: **but rather fear Him which is able to destroy both soul and body in hell.**

Luke 12:4-5

And I say unto you My friends, Be not afraid of them that kill the body, and after that have no more that they can do.

But I will forewarn you Whom ye shall fear: **Fear Him, which after He hath killed hath power to cast into hell; yea, I say unto you, Fear Him.**

Luke 23:39-40

And one of the malefactors which were hanged railed on Him, saying, If Thou be Christ, save Thyself and us.

But the other answering rebuked him, saying, **Dost not thou fear God, seeing thou art in the same condemnation?**

Acts 9:31

Then had the churches rest throughout all Judaea and Galilee and Samaria, and were edified; **and walking in the fear of the Lord,** and in the comfort of the Holy Ghost, were multiplied.

Romans 11:19-22

Thou wilt say then, The branches were broken off, that I might be graffed in.

Well; because of unbelief they were broken off, and thou standest by faith. **Be not high-minded, but fear:**

For if God spared not the natural branches, take heed lest He also spare not thee.

Behold therefore the goodness and severity of God: on them which fell, severity; but toward thee, goodness, if thou continue in His goodness: otherwise thou also shalt be cut off.

Hebrews 5:7

Who in the days of His flesh, when He had offered up prayers and supplications with strong crying and tears unto Him that was able to save Him from death, **and was heard in that He feared;**

In the days of His flesh [Jesus] offered up definite, special petitions [for that which He not only wanted but needed] and supplications with strong crying and tears to Him Who was [always] able to save Him [out] from death, and ***He was heard because of His reverence toward God [His godly fear, His piety, in that He shrank from the horrors of separation from the bright presence of the Father].*** *[AMP]*

I Peter 2:17

Honour all men. Love the brotherhood. **Fear God.** Honour the king.

Chapter 15

Desiring to Please God

<u>**Psalm 147:11**</u>

The Lord taketh pleasure in them that fear Him, in those that hope in His mercy.

<u>**Psalm 149:4**</u>

For the Lord taketh pleasure in His people: He will beautify the meek with salvation.

<u>**Proverbs 16:7**</u>

When a man's ways please the Lord, He maketh even his enemies to be at peace with him.

<u>**Jeremiah 9:23-24**</u>

Thus saith the Lord, Let not the wise man glory in his wisdom, neither let the mighty man glory in his might, let not the rich man glory in his riches:

But let him that glorieth glory in this, that he understandeth and knoweth Me, that I am the Lord which exercise lovingkindness, judgment, and righteousness, in the earth: for in these things I delight, saith the Lord.

<u>**John 5:30**</u>

I am able to do nothing from Myself [independently, of My own accord - but only as I am taught by God and as I get His orders]. Even as I hear, I judge [I decide as I am bidden to decide. As the voice comes to Me, so I give a decision], and My judgment is right (just, righteous), ***because I do not seek or consult My own will [I have no desire to do what is pleasing to Myself, My own aim, My own purpose] but only the will and pleasure of the Father Who sent Me.*** *[AMP]*

<u>**John 8:29**</u>

And He that sent Me is with Me: the Father hath not left Me alone; **for I do always those things that please Him.**

Romans 8:8-9

So then they that are in the flesh **cannot** please God.

But ye are not in the flesh, but in the Spirit, if so be that the Spirit of God dwell in you...

I Corinthians 7:32-33

But I would have you without carefulness. **He that is unmarried careth for the things that belong to the Lord, how he may please the Lord:**

But he that is married careth for the things that are of the world, how he may please his wife.

Galatians 1:10

For do I now persuade men, or God? or do I seek to please men? **for if I yet pleased men, I should not be the servant of Christ.**

Philippians 2:13

For it is God which worketh in you **both to will and to do of His good pleasure.**

Philippians 4:18

But I have all, and abound: I am full, having received of Epaphroditus the things which were sent from you, **an odour of a sweet smell, a sacrifice acceptable, well-pleasing to God.**

Colossians 1:10

That ye might walk worthy of the Lord unto all pleasing, being fruitful in every good work, and increasing in the knowledge of God;

Colossians 3:20

Children, obey your parents in all things: **for this is well pleasing unto the Lord.**

I Thessalonians 2:4

But as we were allowed of God to be put in trust with the Gospel, even so we speak; **not as pleasing men, but God, which trieth our hearts.**

I Thessalonians 4:1

Furthermore then we beseech you, brethren, and exhort you by the Lord Jesus, **that as ye have received of us how ye ought to walk and to please God,** so ye would abound more and more.

Hebrews 11:5-6

By faith Enoch was translated that he should not see death; and was not found, because God had translated him**: for before his translation he had this testimony, that he pleased God.**

But without faith it is impossible to please Him: for he that cometh to God must believe that He is, and that He is a rewarder of them that diligently seek Him.

Hebrews 13:16

But to do good and to communicate forget not: **for with such sacrifices God is well pleased.**

Hebrews 13:20-21

Now the God of peace, that brought again from the dead our Lord Jesus, that great Shepherd of the sheep, through the blood of the everlasting covenant,

Make you perfect in every good work to do His will, **working in you that which is well-pleasing in His sight, through Jesus Christ**; to Whom be glory for ever and ever. Amen.

I John 3:22

And whatsoever we ask, we receive of Him, because we keep His commandments, and **do those things that are pleasing in His sight.**

Chapter 16

Being a Servant

Exodus 23:25-26

And ye shall serve the Lord your God, and He shall bless thy bread, and thy water; and I will take sickness away from the midst of thee.

There shall nothing cast their young, nor be barren, in thy land: the number of thy days I will fulfill.

Deuteronomy 10:12

And now, Israel, what doth the Lord thy God require of thee, but to fear the Lord thy God, to walk in all His ways, and to love Him, **and to serve the Lord thy God with all thy heart and with all thy soul,**

Deuteronomy 11:13-15

And it shall come to pass, if ye shall hearken diligently unto My commandments which I command you this day, **to love the Lord your God, and to serve Him with all your heart and with all your soul,**

That I will give you the rain of your land in his due season, the first rain and the latter rain, that thou mayest gather in thy corn, and thy wine, and thine oil.

And I will send grass in thy fields for thy cattle, that thou mayest eat and be full.

Deuteronomy 13:4

Ye shall walk after the Lord your God, and fear Him, and keep His commandments, and obey His voice, and **ye shall serve Him, and cleave unto Him.**

Deuteronomy 28:47 *(regarding the curse of the law)*

Because thou servedst not the Lord thy God with joyfulness, and with gladness of heart, for the abundance of all things;

Joshua 22:5

But take diligent heed to do the commandment and the law, which Moses the servant of the Lord charged you, to love the Lord your God, and to walk in all His ways, and to keep His commandments, and to cleave unto Him, **and to serve Him with all your heart and with all your soul.**

Joshua 24:14-15

Now therefore fear the Lord, and **serve Him in sincerity and in truth:** and put away the gods which your fathers served on the other side of the flood, and in Egypt; and serve ye the Lord.

And if it seem evil unto you to serve the Lord, **choose you this day whom ye will serve;** whether the gods which your fathers served that were on the other side of the flood, or the gods of the Amorites, in whose land ye dwell: **but as for me and my house, we will serve the Lord.**

I Samuel 12:20-22

And Samuel said unto the people, Fear not: ye have done all this wickedness: yet turn not aside from following the Lord, but **serve the Lord with all your heart**;

And turn ye not aside: for then should ye go after vain things, which cannot profit nor deliver; for they are vain.

For the Lord will not forsake His people for His great name's sake: because it hath pleased the Lord to make you His people.

I Chronicles 28:9

And thou, Solomon my son, know thou the God of thy father, and **serve Him with a perfect heart** and with a willing mind: for the Lord searcheth all hearts, and understandeth all the imaginations of the thoughts: if thou seek Him, He will be found of thee; but if thou forsake Him, He will cast thee off for ever.

Psalm 2:11

Serve the Lord with reverent awe and worshipful fear*; rejoice and be in high spirits with trembling [lest you displease Him]. [AMP]*

Psalm 100:2

Serve the Lord with gladness: come before His presence with singing.

Proverbs 27:18

Whoso keepeth the fig tree shall eat the fruit thereof: **so he that waiteth on his master shall be honoured.**

Joel 2:28-29

And it shall come to pass afterward, that I will pour out My Spirit upon all flesh; and your sons and your daughters shall prophesy, your old men shall dream dreams, your young men shall see visions:

And also upon the servants and upon the handmaids in those days will I pour out

My Spirit.

Matthew 4:10

Then saith Jesus unto him, Get thee hence, Satan: for it is written, Thou shalt worship the Lord thy God, **and Him only shalt thou serve**.

Matthew 6:24

No one can serve two masters*; for either he will hate the one and love the other, or he will stand by and be devoted to the one and despise and be against the other. You cannot serve God and mammon (deceitful riches, money, possessions, or whatever is trusted in). [AMP]*

Matthew 10:41-42

He that receiveth a prophet in the name of a prophet shall receive a prophet's reward; and he that receiveth a righteous man in the name of a righteous man shall receive a righteous man's reward.

And whosoever shall give to drink unto one of these little ones a cup of cold water only in the name of a disciple, verily I say unto you, he shall in no wise lose his reward.

Matthew 20:25-28

And Jesus called them to Him and said, You know that the rulers of the Gentiles lord it over them, and their great men hold them in subjection [tyrannizing over them].

Not so shall it be among you; ***but whoever wishes to be great among you must be your servant,***

And whoever desires to be first among you must be your slave -

Just as the Son of Man came not to be waited on but to serve, and to give His life as a ransom for many [the price paid to set them free]. [AMP]

Matthew 23:11

But he that is greatest among you shall be your servant.

Matthew 25:23

His lord said unto him, **Well done, good and faithful servant; thou hast been faithful over a few things, I will make thee ruler over many things: enter thou into the joy of thy Lord.**

Mark 10:43-45

But so shall it not be among you: **but whosoever will be great among you, shall be your minister:**

And whosoever of you will be the chiefest, shall be servant of all.

For even the Son of man came not to be ministered unto, but to minister, and to give His life a ransom for many.

Luke 10:36-37

Which now of these three, thinkest thou, was neighbour unto him that fell among the thieves?

And he said, He that shewed mercy on him. Then said Jesus unto him, Go, and do thou likewise.

Luke 16:12-13

And if ye have not been faithful in that which is another man's, who shall give you that which is your own?

No servant can serve two masters: for either he will hate the one, and love the other; or else he will hold to the one, and despise the other. Ye cannot serve God and mammon.

Luke 17:7-10

But which of you, having a servant plowing or feeding cattle, will say unto him by and by, when he is come from the field, Go and sit down to meat?

And will not rather say unto him, Make ready wherewith I may sup, and gird thyself, and serve me, till I have eaten and drunken; and afterward thou shalt eat and drink?

Doth he thank that servant because he did the things that were commanded him? I trow not.

So likewise ye, when ye shall have done all those things which are commanded you, say, We are unprofitable servants: we have done that which was our duty to do.

Luke 22:27

For whether is greater, he that sitteth at meat, or he that serveth? is not he that sitteth at meat? **but I am among you as He that serveth.**

John 12:26

If anyone serves Me, he must continue to follow Me [to cleave steadfastly to Me, conform wholly to My example in living and, if need be, in dying] and wherever I am, there will My servant be also. ***If anyone serves Me, the Father will honor him.*** *[AMP]*

John 13:14

If I then, your Lord and Master, have washed your feet; **ye also ought to wash one another's feet.**

John 21:16

He saith to him again the second time, Simon, son of Jonas, lovest thou Me? He saith unto Him, Yea, Lord; Thou knowest that I love Thee. He saith unto him, **Feed My sheep.**

Acts 2:17-18

And it shall come to pass in the last days, saith God, I will pour out of My Spirit upon all flesh: and your sons and your daughters shall prophesy, and your young men shall see visions, and your old men shall dream dreams:

And on My servants and on My handmaidens I will pour out in those days of My Spirit; and they shall prophesy:

Acts 20:19

Serving the Lord with all humility of mind, and with many tears, and temptations, . . .

Acts 27:23

For there stood by me this night the angel of God, Whose I am, **and Whom I serve,**

Romans 1:9

For God is my witness, **Whom I serve with my spirit in the Gospel of His Son,** . . .

Romans 6:22

But now being made free from sin, and become servants to God, ye have your fruit unto holiness, and the end everlasting life.

Romans 7:6

But now we are delivered from the law, that being dead wherein we were held; **that we should serve in newness of spirit, and not in the oldness of the letter.**

Romans 12:1

I beseech you therefore, brethren, by the mercies of God, that ye present your bodies a living sacrifice, holy, acceptable unto God, which is your reasonable service.

Romans 12:10-11,13

Be kindly affectioned one to another with brotherly love; in honour preferring one another;

Not slothful in business; fervent in spirit; **serving the Lord;**

Distributing to the necessity of saints; given to hospitality.

Romans 15:8

For I tell you that ***Christ (the Messiah) became a servant and a minister to the circumcised (the Jews)*** *in order to show God's truthfulness and honesty by confirming (verifying) the promises [given] to our fathers, [AMP]*

I Corinthians 3:5

What then is Apollos? What is Paul? ***Ministering servants*** *[not heads of parties] through whom you believed, even as the Lord appointed to each his task: [AMP]*

I Corinthians 4:1

So then, let us [apostles] be looked upon as ministering servants of Christ *and stewards (trustees) of the mysteries (the secret purposes) of God. [AMP]*

I Corinthians 7:20-23

Let every man abide in the same calling wherein he was called.

Art thou called being a servant? care not for it: but if thou mayest be made free, use it rather.

For he that is called in the Lord, being a servant, is the Lord's freeman: **likewise also he that is called, being free, is Christ's servant.**

Ye are bought with a price; be not ye the servants of men.

I Corinthians 7:35

And this I speak for your own profit; not that I may cast a snare upon you, but for that which is comely, **and that ye may attend upon the Lord without distraction.**

I Corinthians 9:19

For although I am free in every way from anyone's control, I have made myself a bond servant to everyone, so that I might gain the more [for Christ]. [AMP]

I Corinthians 16:15

I beseech you, brethren, (ye know the house of Stephanas, that it is the firstfruits of Achaia, and that **they have addicted themselves to the ministry of the saints,)**

II Corinthians 6:4

But we commend ourselves in every way as [true] servants of God: *through great endurance, in tribulation and suffering, in hardships and privations, in sore straits and calamities, [AMP]*

Galatians 1:10

For do I now persuade men, or God? or do I seek to please men? **for if I yet pleased men, I should not be the servant of Christ.**

Galatians 5:13

For, brethren, ye have been called unto liberty; only use not liberty for an occasion to the flesh, **but by love serve one another.**

Galatians 6:2

Bear ye one another's burdens, and so fulfil the law of Christ.

Galatians 6:10

As we have therefore opportunity, let us do good unto all men, especially unto them who are of the household of faith.

Ephesians 2:10

For we are His workmanship, created in Christ Jesus unto good works, which God hath before ordained that we should walk in them.

Ephesians 6:5-8

Servants, be obedient to them that are your masters according to the flesh, with fear and trembling, in singleness of your heart, as unto Christ;

Not with eyeservice, as menpleasers; **but as the servants of Christ, doing the will of God from the heart;**

With good will doing service, as to the Lord, and not to men:

Knowing that whatsoever good thing any man doeth, the same shall he receive of the Lord, whether he be bond or free.

Philippians 2:4

Look not every man on his own things, but every man also on the things of others.

Philippians 2:7 *(Jesus)*

But made Himself of no reputation, and took upon Him the form of a servant, and was made in the likeness of men:

Colossians 3:24

Knowing that of the Lord ye shall receive the reward of the inheritance: f**or ye serve the Lord Christ.**

I Thessalonians 1:9

. . . how ye turned to God from idols to serve the living and true God;

Hebrews 9:14

How much more shall the blood of Christ, Who through the eternal Spirit offered Himself without spot to God, **purge your conscience from dead works to serve the living God?**

Hebrews 12:28

Wherefore we receiving a kingdom which cannot be moved, let us have grace, whereby we may serve God acceptably with reverence and godly fear:

I Peter 2:16

As free, and not using your liberty for a cloke of maliciousness, **but as the servants of God.**

I Peter 4:11

Whoever speaks, [let him do it as one who utters] oracles of God; ***whoever renders service, [let him do it] as with the strength which God furnishes abundantly,*** *so that in all things God may be glorified through Jesus Christ (the Messiah). . . . [AMP]*

Revelation 7:15

Therefore are they before the throne of God, **and serve Him day and night in His temple:** and He that sitteth on the throne shall dwell among them.

Chapter 17

Forgiving Others

<u>**Psalm 37:8**</u>

Cease from anger, and **forsake wrath**: fret not thyself in any wise to do evil.

<u>**Proverbs 20:22**</u>

Say not thou, I will recompense evil; **but wait on the Lord, and He shall save thee.**

<u>**Proverbs 25:21-22**</u>

If thine enemy be hungry, give him bread to eat; and if he be thirsty, give him water to drink:

For thou shalt heap coals of fire upon his head, and the Lord shall reward thee.

<u>**Matthew 5:7**</u>

Blessed are the merciful: for they shall obtain mercy.

<u>**Matthew 5:44**</u>

But I say unto you, **Love your enemies, bless them that curse you, do good to them that hate you, and pray for them which despitefully use you, and persecute you;**

<u>**Matthew 6:14-15**</u>

For if ye forgive men their trespasses, your heavenly Father will also forgive you:

But if ye forgive not men their trespasses, neither will your Father forgive your trespasses.

For if you forgive people their trespasses [their reckless and willful sins, leaving them, letting them go, and giving up resentment], your heavenly Father will also forgive you.

But if you do not forgive others their trespasses [their reckless and willful sins, leaving them, letting them go, and giving up resentment], neither will your Father forgive you your trespasses. [AMP]

<u>**Matthew 18:21-22**</u>

Then came Peter to Him, and said, **Lord, how oft shall my brother sin against me, and I forgive him?** till seven times?

Jesus saith unto him, I say not unto thee, Until seven times: **but, Until seventy times seven.**

<u>**Matthew 18:35**</u>

So likewise shall My heavenly Father do also unto you, if ye from your hearts forgive not every one his brother their trespasses.

<u>**Mark 11:25-26**</u>

And when ye stand praying, forgive, if ye have ought against any: that your Father also which is in heaven may forgive you your trespasses.

But if ye do not forgive, neither will your Father which is in heaven forgive your trespasses.

And whenever you stand praying, if you have anything against anyone, forgive him and let it drop (leave it, let it go), *in order that your Father Who is in heaven may also forgive you your [own] failings and shortcomings and let them drop.*

But if you do not forgive, neither will your Father in heaven forgive your failings and shortcomings. [AMP]

<u>**Luke 6:35-37**</u>

But love ye your enemies, and do good, and lend, hoping for nothing again; and your reward shall be great, and ye shall be the children of the Highest: for He is kind unto the unthankful and to the evil.

Be ye therefore merciful, as your Father also is merciful.

Judge not, and ye shall not be judged: condemn not, and ye shall not be condemned: **forgive, and ye shall be forgiven:**

<u>**Luke 17:3-4**</u>

Take heed to yourselves: **If thy brother trespass against thee, rebuke him; and if he repent, forgive him.**

And if he trespass against thee seven times in a day, and seven times in a day turn again to thee, saying, I repent; thou shalt forgive him.

Pay attention and always be on your guard [looking out for one another]. If your brother sins (misses the mark), solemnly tell him so and reprove him, and if he repents (feels sorry for having sinned), forgive him.

And even if he sins against you seven times in a day, and turns to you seven times and says, I repent [I am sorry], you must forgive him (give up resentment and consider the offense as recalled and annulled). [AMP]

<u>**John 20:23**</u>

Whose soever sins ye remit, they are remitted unto them; and whose soever sins ye retain, they are retained.

<u>Romans 12:14</u>

Bless them which persecute you: bless, and curse not.

Bless those who persecute you [who are cruel in their attitude toward you]; bless and do not curse them. [AMP]

<u>Romans 12:20-21</u>

Therefore if thine enemy hunger, feed him; if he thirst, give him drink: for in so doing thou shalt heap coals of fire on his head.

Be not overcome of evil, but overcome evil with good.

<u>Ephesians 4:26-27</u>

Be ye angry, and sin not: let not the sun go down upon your wrath:

Neither give place to the devil.

<u>Ephesians 4:31-32</u>

Let all bitterness, and wrath, and anger, and clamour, and evil speaking, be put away from you, with all malice:

And be ye kind one to another, tenderhearted, forgiving one another, even as God for Christ's sake hath forgiven you.

Let all bitterness and indignation and wrath (passion, rage, bad temper) and resentment (anger, animosity) and quarreling (brawling, clamor, contention) and slander (evil-speaking, abusive or blasphemous language) be banished from you, with all malice (spite, ill will, or baseness of any kind).

And become useful and helpful and kind to one another, tenderhearted (compassionate, understanding, loving-hearted), forgiving one another [readily and freely], as God in Christ forgave you. [AMP]

<u>Colossians 3:13</u>

Forbearing one another, and forgiving one another, if any man have a quarrel against any: even as Christ forgave you, so also do ye.

Be gentle and forbearing with one another and, if one has a difference (a grievance or complaint) against another, readily pardoning each other; even as the Lord has [freely] forgiven you, so must you also [forgive]. [AMP]

<u>Hebrews 10:30</u>

For we know Him that hath said, **Vengeance belongeth unto Me, I will recompense, saith the Lord.** And again, The Lord shall judge His people.

<u>Hebrews 12:1-4</u>

Wherefore seeing we also are compassed about with so great a cloud of witnesses, **let us**

lay aside every weight, and the sin which doth so easily beset us, and let us run with patience the race that is set before us,

Looking unto Jesus the Author and Finisher of our faith; who for the joy that was set before Him endured the cross, despising the shame, and is set down at the right hand of the throne of God.

For consider Him that endured such contradiction of sinners against Himself, lest ye be wearied and faint in your minds.

Ye have not yet resisted unto blood, striving against sin.

I Peter 2:19-23

For this is thankworthy, if a man for conscience toward God endure grief, suffering wrongfully.

For what glory is it, if, when ye be buffeted for your faults, ye shall take it patiently? but if, when ye do well, and suffer for it, ye take it patiently, this is acceptable with God.

For even hereunto were ye called: **because Christ also suffered for us, leaving us an example, that ye should follow His steps:**

Who did no sin, neither was guile found in His mouth:

Who, when He was reviled, reviled not again; when He suffered, He threatened not; but committed Himself to Him that judgeth righteously:

I Peter 3:9-10

Not rendering evil for evil, or railing for railing: but contrariwise blessing; knowing that ye are thereunto called, that ye should inherit a blessing.

For he that will love life, and see good days, let him refrain his tongue from evil, and his lips that they speak no guile:

Never return evil for evil or insult for insult (scolding, tongue-lashing, berating), but on the contrary blessing [praying for their welfare, happiness, and protection, and truly pitying and loving them]. *For know that to this you have been called, that you may yourselves inherit a blessing [from God - that you may obtain a blessing as heirs, bringing welfare and happiness and protection].*

For let him who wants to enjoy life and see good days [good - whether apparent or not] keep his tongue free from evil and his lips from guile (treachery, deceit). [AMP]

I Peter 4:8

Above all things have intense and unfailing love for one another, ***for love covers a multitude of sins [forgives and disregards the offenses of others].*** *[AMP]*

I Peter 4:14

If ye be reproached for the name of Christ, happy are ye; for the spirit of glory and of God resteth upon you: . . .

Chapter 18

Developing Godly Attributes

A. Purity

Psalm 18:26
With the pure Thou wilt shew Thyself pure; and with the froward Thou wilt shew Thyself froward.

Psalm 24:3-4
Who shall ascend into the hill of the Lord? or who shall stand in His holy place?
He that hath clean hands, and a pure heart; who hath not lifted up his soul unto vanity, nor sworn deceitfully.

Song of Solomon 4:7
Thou art all fair, my love; **there is no spot in thee.**

Matthew 5:8
Blessed are the pure in heart: for they shall see God.

John 17:17
Sanctify them through Thy truth: Thy word is truth.

John 17:19
And for their sakes I sanctify Myself, **that they also might be sanctified through the truth.**

I Corinthians 1:30
But of Him are ye in **Christ Jesus, Who of God is made unto us** wisdom, and righteous-

ness, and **sanctification**, and redemption:

But it is from Him that you have your life in Christ Jesus, Whom God made our Wisdom from God, [revealed to us a knowledge of the divine plan of salvation previously hidden, manifesting itself as] our Righteousness [thus making us upright and putting us in right standing with God], and ***our Consecration [making us pure and holy],*** *and our Redemption [providing our ransom from eternal penalty for sin]. [AMP]*

I Corinthians 6:11

And such were some of you: but ye are washed, but ye are sanctified, but ye are justified in the name of the Lord Jesus, and by the Spirit of our God.

I Thessalonians 5:23

And the very God of peace sanctify you wholly; and I pray God your whole spirit and soul and body be preserved blameless unto the coming of our Lord Jesus Christ.

I Timothy 1:5

Now the end of the commandment is charity out of a pure heart, and of a good conscience, and of faith unfeigned:

I Timothy 5:22

Lay hands suddenly on no man, neither be partaker of other men's sins: **keep thyself pure.**

II Timothy 2:20-22

But in a great house there are not only vessels of gold and of silver, but also of wood and of earth; and some to honour, and some to dishonour.

If a man therefore purge himself from these, **he shall be a vessel unto honour, sanctified, and meet for the master's use, and prepared unto every good work.**

Flee also youthful lusts: but follow **righteousness**, faith, charity, peace, **with them that call on the Lord out of a pure heart.**

Titus 1:15

Unto the pure all things are pure: but unto them that are defiled and unbelieving is nothing pure; but even their mind and conscience is defiled.

To the pure [in heart and conscience] all things are pure, *but to the defiled and corrupt and unbelieving nothing is pure; their very minds and consciences are defiled and polluted. [AMP]*

Titus 2:14

Who gave Himself for us, that He might redeem us from all iniquity, **and purify unto Himself a peculiar people, zealous of good works.**

James 1:27

Pure religion and undefiled before God and the Father is this, **To visit the fatherless and**

widows in their affliction, and to keep himself unspotted from the world.

I Peter 1:22

Seeing ye have **purified your souls in obeying the truth** through the Spirit unto unfeigned love of the brethren, **see that ye love one another with a pure heart fervently:**

II Peter 3:14

Wherefore, beloved, seeing that ye look for such things, be diligent that ye may be found of Him in peace, **without spot, and blameless.**

I John 3:2-3

Beloved, now are we the sons of God, and it doth not yet appear what we shall be: but we know that, when He shall appear, we shall be like Him; for we shall see Him as He is.

And every man that hath this hope in him purifieth himself, even as He is pure.

Beloved, we are [even here and] now God's children; it is not yet disclosed (made clear) what we shall be [hereafter], but we know that when He comes and is manifested, we shall [as God's children] resemble and be like Him, for we shall see Him just as He [really] is.

And everyone who has this hope [resting] on Him cleanses (purifies) himself just as He is pure (chaste, undefiled, guiltless). [AMP]

B. Righteousness

Hosea 10:12

Sow to yourselves in righteousness, reap in mercy; break up your fallow ground: **for it is time to seek the Lord, till He come and rain righteousness upon you.**

Matthew 5:20

For I say unto you, **That except your righteousness shall exceed the righteousness of the scribes and Pharisees,** ye shall in no case enter into the kingdom of heaven.

For I tell you, ***unless your righteousness (your uprightness and your right standing with God) is more than that of the scribes and Pharisees,*** *you will never enter the kingdom of heaven. [AMP]*

Luke 1:74-75

That He would grant unto us, that we being delivered out of the hand of our enemies **might serve Him without fear,**

In holiness and righteousness before Him, all the days of our life.

Romans 8:10

And if Christ be in you, the body is dead because of sin; **but the spirit is life because of righteousness.**

But if Christ lives in you, [then although] your [natural] body is dead by reason of sin and guilt, ***the spirit is alive because of [the] righteousness [that He imputes to you].*** *[AMP]*

I Corinthians 1:30

But of Him are ye in **Christ Jesus, Who of God is made unto us** wisdom, and **righteousness**, and sanctification, and redemption:

But it is from Him that you have your life in Christ Jesus, Whom God made our Wisdom from God, [revealed to us a knowledge of the divine plan of salvation previously hidden, manifesting itself as] ***our Righteousness [thus making us upright and putting us in right standing with God],*** *and our Consecration [making us pure and holy], and our Redemption [providing our ransom from eternal penalty for sin]. [AMP]*

II Corinthians 5:21

For He hath made Him to be sin for us, Who knew no sin; **that we might be made the righteousness of God in Him.**

Ephesians 6:14

Stand therefore, having your loins girt about with truth, **and having on the breastplate of righteousness:**

Stand therefore [hold your ground], having tightened the belt of truth around your loins and having put on ***the breastplate of integrity and of moral rectitude and right standing with God,*** *[AMP]*

Philippians 1:11

Being filled with the fruits of righteousness, which are by Jesus Christ, unto the glory and praise of God.

May you abound in and be filled with the fruits of righteousness (of right standing with God and right doing) which come through Jesus Christ (the Anointed One), *to the honor and praise of God [that His glory may be both manifested and recognized]. [AMP]*

I Timothy 6:11

But thou, O man of God, flee these things; and **follow after righteousness,** godliness, faith, love, patience, meekness.

But as for you, O man of God, flee from all these things; ***aim at and pursue righteousness (right standing with God and true goodness),*** *godliness (which is the loving fear of God and being Christlike), faith, love, steadfastness (patience), and gentleness of heart. [AMP]*

II Timothy 2:20-22

But in a great house there are not only vessels of gold and of silver, but also of wood and of earth; and some to honour, and some to dishonour.

If a man therefore purge himself from these, **he shall be a vessel unto honour, sanctified, and meet for the master's use, and prepared unto every good work.**

Flee also youthful lusts: but follow **righteousness**, faith, charity, peace, with them that call on the Lord out of a pure heart.

Titus 2:12

Teaching us that, denying ungodliness and worldly lusts, **we should live soberly, righteously, and godly, in this present world;**

I John 2:28-29

And now, little children, abide in Him; that, when He shall appear, we may have confidence, and not be ashamed before Him at His coming.

If ye know that He is righteous, **ye know that every one that doeth righteousness is born of Him.**

I John 2:29

If you know (perceive and are sure) that He [Christ] is [absolutely] righteous [conforming to the Father's will in purpose, thought, and action], ***you may also know (be sure) that everyone who does righteously [and is therefore in like manner conformed to the divine will] is born (begotten) of Him [God].*** *[AMP]*

I John 3:7

Little children, let no man deceive you: **he that doeth righteousness is righteous,** even as He is righteous.

Boys (lads), let no one deceive and lead you astray. ***He who practices righteousness [who is upright, conforming to the divine will in purpose, thought, and action, living a consistently conscientious life] is righteous,*** *even as He is righteous. [AMP]*

Revelation 14:5

And in their mouth was found no guile: **for they are without fault before the throne of God.**

C. Godliness

Psalm 4:3

But know that the Lord hath set apart him that is godly for Himself: the Lord will hear when I call unto Him.

I Timothy 2:1-2

I exhort therefore, that, first of all, supplications, prayers, intercessions, and giving of thanks, be made for all men;

For kings, and for all that are in authority; **that we may lead a quiet and peaceable life in all godliness and honesty.**

I Timothy 4:7-8

But refuse profane and old wives' fables, **and exercise thyself rather unto godliness.**

For bodily exercise profiteth little: **but godliness is profitable unto all things,** having promise of the life that now is, and of that which is to come.

But refuse and avoid irreverent legends (profane and impure and godless fictions, mere grandmothers' tales) and silly myths, and express your disapproval of them. Train yourself toward godliness (piety), [keeping yourself spiritually fit].

For physical training is of some value (useful for a little), but godliness (spiritual training) is useful and of value in everything and in every way, for it holds promise for the present life and also for the life which is to come. [AMP]

I Timothy 6:11

But thou, O man of God, flee these things; and **follow after** righteousness, **godliness,** faith, love, patience, meekness.

I Timothy 6:11

But as for you, O man of God, flee from all these things; ***aim at and pursue*** *righteousness (right standing with God and true goodness),* ***godliness (which is the loving fear of God and being Christlike),*** *faith, love, steadfastness (patience), and gentleness of heart. [AMP]*

II Timothy 3:12

Yea, and all that will live godly in Christ Jesus shall suffer persecution.

Titus 1:1

Paul, a servant of God, and an apostle of Jesus Christ, according to the faith of God's elect, **and the acknowledging of the truth which is after godliness;**

Titus 2:12

Teaching us that, denying ungodliness and worldly lusts, **we should live soberly, righteously, and godly, in this present world;**

II Peter 1:3

According as His divine power hath given unto us all things that pertain unto life and godliness, through the knowledge of Him that hath called us to glory and virtue:

II Peter 1:5-8

And beside this, giving all diligence, add to your faith virtue; and to virtue knowledge;

And to knowledge temperance; and to temperance patience; and to patience **godliness;**

And to **godliness** brotherly kindness; and to brotherly kindness charity.

For if these things be in you, and abound, they make you that ye shall neither be barren nor unfruitful in the knowledge of our Lord Jesus Christ.

II Peter 2:9

The Lord knoweth how to deliver the godly out of temptations, . . .

II Peter 3:11

Seeing then that all these things shall be dissolved, **what manner of persons ought ye to be in all holy conversation and godliness,**

Since all these things are thus in the process of being dissolved, ***what kind of person ought [each of] you to be [in the meanwhile] in consecrated and holy behavior and devout and godly qualities,*** *[AMP]*

D. Holiness

Isaiah 35:8

And an highway shall be there, and a way, and it shall be called **The Way of Holiness;** the unclean shall not pass over it; but it shall be for those: the wayfaring men, though fools, shall not err therein.

Isaiah 35:8

And a highway shall be there, and a way; and it shall be called ***the Holy Way****. The unclean shall not pass over it, but it shall be for the redeemed; the wayfaring men, yes, the simple ones and fools, shall not err in it and lose their way. [AMP]*

Luke 1:74-75

That He would grant unto us, that we being delivered out of the hand of our enemies **might serve Him without fear,**

In holiness and righteousness before Him, all the days of our life.

Romans 6:22

But now being made free from sin, and become servants to God, **ye have your fruit unto holiness,** and the end everlasting life.

I Corinthians 1:30

But of Him are ye in **Christ Jesus, Who of God is made unto us** wisdom, and righteousness, and **sanctification**, and redemption:

But it is from Him that you have your life in Christ Jesus, Whom God made our Wisdom from God, [revealed to us a knowledge of the divine plan of salvation previously hidden, manifesting itself as] our Righteousness [thus making us upright and putting us in right standing with God], and ***our Consecration [making us pure and holy],*** *and our Redemption [providing our ransom from eternal penalty for sin]. [AMP]*

Ephesians 4:24

And put on the new nature (the regenerate self) created in God's image, [Godlike] in true righteousness and holiness. [AMP]

Ephesians 5:27

That He might present it to Himself a glorious church, not having spot, or wrinkle, or any such thing; **but that it should be holy and without blemish.**

Colossians 1:21-22

And you, that were sometime alienated and enemies in your mind by wicked works, yet now hath He reconciled

In the body of His flesh through death, **to present you holy and unblameable and unreproveable in His sight:**

I Thessalonians 3:13

So that He may strengthen and confirm and establish your hearts faultlessly pure and unblamable in holiness in the sight of our God and Father, *at the coming of our Lord Jesus Christ (the Messiah) with all His saints (the holy and glorified people of God)! Amen, (so be it)! [AMP]*

Hebrews 12:10

For [our earthly fathers] disciplined us for only a short period of time and chastised us as seemed proper and good to them; ***but He disciplines us for our certain good, that we may become sharers in His own holiness.*** *[AMP]*

Hebrews 12:14

Strive to live in peace with everybody ***and pursue that consecration and holiness without which no one will [ever] see the Lord.*** *[AMP]*

I Peter 1:15-16

But as He which hath called you is holy, so be ye holy in all manner of conversation;

Because it is written, **Be ye holy; for I am holy.**

II Peter 3:11

Seeing then that all these things shall be dissolved, **what manner of persons ought ye to be in all holy conversation** and godliness,

Since all these things are thus in the process of being dissolved, what kind of person ought [each of] you to be [in the meanwhile] ***in consecrated and holy behavior*** *and devout and godly qualities, [AMP]*

Chapter 19

Growing in Love

A. God's Love & Care for Us

<u>Exodus 20:5-6</u>

. . . **for I the Lord thy God am a jealous God,** visiting the iniquity of the fathers upon the children unto the third and fourth generation of them that hate Me;

And shewing mercy unto thousands of them that love Me, and keep My commandments.

<u>Deuteronomy 7:8-9</u>

But **because the Lord loved you**, and because He would keep the oath which He had sworn unto your fathers, hath the Lord brought you out with a mighty hand, and redeemed you out of the house of bondmen, from the hand of Pharaoh king of Egypt.

Know therefore that the Lord thy God, He is God, the faithful God, which keepeth covenant and mercy with them that love Him and keep His commandments to a thousand generations;

<u>Deuteronomy 7:13</u>

And He will love thee, and bless thee, and multiply thee: He will also bless the fruit of thy womb, and the fruit of thy land, thy corn, and thy wine, and thine oil, the increase of thy kine, and the flocks of thy sheep, in the land which He sware unto thy fathers to give thee.

<u>Nehemiah 1:5</u>

And said, I beseech Thee, O Lord God of heaven, the great and terrible God, **that keepeth covenant and mercy for them that love Him and observe His commandments:**

<u>Psalm 42:8</u>

Yet the Lord will command His lovingkindness in the daytime, and in the night His song shall be with me, and my prayer unto the God of my life.

<u>Psalm 145:20</u>

The Lord preserveth all them that love Him: but all the wicked will He destroy.

<u>Psalm 146:8</u>

The Lord openeth the eyes of the blind: the Lord raiseth them that are bowed down: **the Lord loveth the righteous:**

<u>Proverbs 3:11-12</u>

My son, despise not the chastening of the Lord; neither be weary of His correction:

For whom the Lord loveth He correcteth; even as a father the son in whom he delighteth.

<u>Proverbs 8:17</u>

I love them that love Me; and those that seek Me early shall find Me.

<u>Proverbs 15:9</u>

The way of the wicked is an abomination unto the Lord: **but He loveth him that followeth after righteousness.**

<u>Isaiah 38:17</u>

Behold, for peace I had great bitterness: **but Thou hast in love to my soul delivered it from the pit of corruption**: for Thou hast cast all my sins behind Thy back.

<u>Isaiah 49:15-16</u>

Can a woman forget her sucking child, that she should not have compassion on the son of her womb? yea, they may forget, **yet will I not forget thee.**

Behold, I have graven thee upon the palms of My hands; thy walls are continually before Me.

<u>Isaiah 62:5</u>

For as a young man marrieth a virgin, so shall thy sons marry thee: **and as the bridegroom rejoiceth over the bride, so shall thy God rejoice over thee.**

<u>Jeremiah 31:3</u>

The Lord hath appeared of old unto me, saying, **Yea, I have loved thee with an everlasting love: therefore with lovingkindness have I drawn thee.**

<u>Hosea 2:19-20</u>

And I will betroth thee unto Me for ever: yea, I will betroth thee unto Me in righteousness, and in judgment, and in lovingkindness, and in mercies.

I will even betroth thee unto Me in faithfulness: and thou shalt know the Lord.

Hosea 14:4

I will heal their backsliding, **I will love them freely**: for Mine anger is turned away from him.

Zephaniah 3:17

The Lord thy God in the midst of thee is mighty; He will save, He will rejoice over thee with joy; **He will rest in His love,** He will joy over thee with singing.

John 3:16

For God so loved the world, that He gave His only begotten Son, that whosoever believeth in Him should not perish, but have everlasting life.

John 14:21

He that hath My commandments, and keepeth them, **he it is that loveth Me: and he that loveth Me shall be loved of My Father, and I will love him, and will manifest Myself to him.**

John 15:9-10

As the Father hath loved Me, **so have I loved you: continue ye in My love.**

If ye keep My commandments, ye shall abide in My love; even as I have kept My Father's commandments, and abide in His love.

John 16:27

For the Father Himself loveth you, because ye have loved Me, and have believed that I came out from God.

John 17:26

And I have declared unto them Thy name, and will declare it: **that the love wherewith Thou hast loved Me may be in them, and I in them.**

Romans 5:8

But God commendeth His love toward us, in that, while we were yet sinners, Christ died for us.

Romans 8:37-39

Nay, in all these things we are more than conquerors through Him that loved us.

For I am persuaded, that neither death, nor life, nor angels, nor principalities, nor powers, nor things present, nor things to come,

Nor height, nor depth, nor any other creature, **shall be able to separate us from the love of God, which is in Christ Jesus our Lord.**

I Corinthians 2:9

But as it is written, Eye hath not seen, nor ear heard, neither have entered into the heart of man, **the things which God hath prepared for them that love Him.**

II Corinthians 13:11

Finally, brethren, farewell. Be perfect, be of good comfort, be of one mind, live in peace; **and the God of love and peace shall be with you.**

Ephesians 2:4,6

But God, Who is rich in mercy, for His great love wherewith He loved us,

. . . hath raised us up together, and made us sit together in heavenly places in Christ Jesus:

Ephesians 3:19

And to know **the love of Christ, which passeth knowledge,** that ye might be filled with all the fulness of God.

II Thessalonians 2:16-17

Now our Lord Jesus Christ Himself, and God, even our Father, which hath loved us, and hath given us everlasting consolation and good hope through grace,

Comfort your hearts, and stablish you in every good word and work.

I Peter 5:7

Casting all your care upon Him; **for He careth for you.**

I John 4:9-10

In this was manifested the love of God toward us, because that God sent His only begotten Son into the world, that we might live through Him.

Herein is love, not that we loved God, but that He loved us, and sent His Son to be the propitiation for our sins.

I John 4:16

And we have known and believed **the love that God hath to us.** God is love; and he that dwelleth in love dwelleth in God, and God in him.

I John 4:19

We love Him, because He first loved us.

B. Our Love for God

Exodus 20:6

And shewing mercy unto thousands of them that love Me, and keep My commandments.

Deuteronomy 7:9

Know therefore that the Lord thy God, He is God, the faithful God, **which keepeth covenant and mercy with them that love Him and keep His commandments** to a thousand generations;

Deuteronomy 11:13-15

And it shall come to pass, if ye shall hearken diligently unto My commandments which I command you this day, **to love the Lord your God, and to serve Him with all your heart and with all your soul,**

That I will give you the rain of your land in his due season, the first rain and the latter rain, that thou mayest gather in thy corn, and thy wine, and thine oil.

And I will send grass in thy fields for thy cattle, that thou mayest eat and be full.

Deuteronomy 30:6

And the Lord thy God will circumcise thine heart, and the heart of thy seed, **to love the Lord thy God with all thine heart, and with all thy soul,** that thou mayest live.

Judges 5:31

So let all Thine enemies perish, O Lord: **but let them that love Him be as the sun when he goeth forth in his might. . . .**

Nehemiah 1:5

And said, I beseech Thee, O Lord God of heaven, the great and terrible God, that keepeth covenant and mercy for them that love Him and observe His commandments:

Psalm 37:4

Delight thyself also in the Lord; and He shall give thee the desires of thine heart.

Psalm 91:14

Because he hath set his love upon Me, therefore will I deliver him: I will set him on high, because he hath known My name.

Psalm 145:20

The Lord preserveth all them that love Him: but all the wicked will He destroy.

Proverbs 8:17

I love them that love Me; and those that seek Me early shall find Me.

Proverbs 8:21

That I may cause those that love Me to inherit substance; and I will fill their treasures.

Mark 12:30, 32-33

And thou shalt love the Lord thy God with all thy heart, and with all thy soul, and with all thy mind, and with all thy strength: this is the first commandment.

. . . for there is one God; and there is none other but He:

And to love Him with all the heart, and with all the understanding, and with all the soul, and with all the strength, and to love his neighbor as himself, **is more than all whole burnt offerings and sacrifices.**

John 14:21

He that hath My commandments, and keepeth them, **he it is that loveth Me: and he that loveth Me shall be loved of My Father, and I will love Him, and will manifest Myself to him.**

John 16:27

For the Father Himself loveth you, **because ye have loved Me,** and have believed that I came out from God.

Romans 5:5

And hope maketh not ashamed; because **the love of God is shed abroad in our hearts** by the Holy Ghost which is given unto us.

Romans 7:4

Wherefore, my brethren, ye also are become dead to the law by the body of Christ: **that ye should be married to another, even to Him Who is raised from the dead,** that we should bring forth fruit unto God.

Romans 8:28

And we know that all things work together for good to them that love God, to them who are the called according to His purpose.

I Corinthians 2:9

But as it is written, Eye hath not seen, nor ear heard, neither have entered into the heart of man, **the things which God hath prepared for them that love Him.**

I Corinthians 8:3

But if any man love God, the same is known of him.

But if one loves God truly [with affectionate reverence, prompt obedience, and grateful recognition of His blessing], he is known by God [recognized as worthy of His intimacy and love, and he is owned by Him]. [AMP]

I Corinthians 13:13

And so faith, hope, love abide [faith - conviction and belief respecting man's relation to God and divine things; hope - joyful and confident expectation of eternal salvation; ***love - true affection for God and man, growing out of God's love for and in us],*** *these three;* ***but the greatest of these is love.*** *[AMP]*

Ephesians 3:17-19

That Christ may dwell in your hearts by faith; **that ye, being rooted and grounded in love,**

May be able to comprehend with all saints what is the breadth, and length, and depth, and height;

And to know the love of Christ, which passeth knowledge, that ye might be filled with all the fulness of God.

Ephesians 6:24

Grace be with all them that love our Lord Jesus Christ in sincerity. Amen.

II Thessalonians 3:5

And the Lord direct your hearts into the love of God, and into the patient waiting for Christ.

James 1:12

Blessed is the man that endureth temptation: for when he is tried, he shall receive the crown of life, **which the Lord hath promised to them that love Him.**

James 2:5

Hearken, my beloved brethren, Hath not God chosen the poor of this world rich in faith, **and heirs of the kingdom which He hath promised to them that love Him?**

I John 4:19

We love Him, because He first loved us.

Jude 21

Keep yourselves in the love of God, looking for the mercy of our Lord Jesus Christ unto eternal life.

C. Walking in Love Toward Our Brethren

Psalm 133:1-2

Behold, how good and how pleasant it is for brethren to dwell together in unity!

It is like the precious ointment upon the head, that ran down upon the beard, even Aaron's beard: that went down to the skirts of his garments;

Proverbs 10:12

Hatred stirreth up strifes: but **love covereth all sins**.

Matthew 5:44

But I say unto you, **Love your enemies, bless them that curse you, do good to them that hate you, and pray for them which despitefully use you, and persecute you;**

Matthew 7:12

Therefore all things whatsoever ye would that men should do to you, do ye even so to them: for this is the law and the prophets.

Mark 12:31

And the second is like, namely this, Thou shalt love thy neighbour as thyself. There is none other commandment greater than these.

John 13:34-35

A new commandment I give unto you, That ye love one another; as I have loved you, that ye also love one another.

By this shall all men know that ye are My disciples, if ye have love one to another.

John 15:12-14

This is My commandment, That ye love one another, as I have loved you.

Greater love hath no man than this, that a man lay down his life for his friends.

Ye are My friends, if ye do whatsoever I command you.

John 15:17

These things I command you, that ye love one another.

Romans 5:5

. . . because **the love of God is shed abroad in our hearts** by the Holy Ghost which is given unto us.

Romans 12:9-10

Let love be without dissimulation. Abhor that which is evil; cleave to that which is good.

Be kindly affectioned one to another with brotherly love; in honour preferring one another;

Romans 12:20-21

Therefore if thine enemy hunger, feed him; if he thirst, give him drink: for in so doing thou shalt heap coals of fire on his head.

Be not overcome of evil, but overcome evil with good.

Romans 13:8-10

Owe no man any thing, but to love one another: **for he that loveth another hath fulfilled the law.**

For this, Thou shalt not commit adultery, Thou shalt not kill, Thou shalt not steal, Thou shalt not bear false witness, Thou shalt not covet; and if there be any other commandment, it is briefly comprehended in this saying, namely, **Thou shalt love thy neighbour as thyself.**

Love worketh no ill to his neighbour: therefore love is the fulfilling of the law.

I Corinthians 8:13

Wherefore, if meat make my brother to offend, I will eat no flesh while the world standeth, lest I make my brother to offend.

I Corinthians 13:1-8

Though I speak with the tongues of men and of angels, and have not charity, I am become as sounding brass, or a tinkling cymbal.

And though I have the gift of prophecy, and understand all mysteries, and all knowledge; and though I have all faith, so that I could remove mountains, and have not charity, **I**

am nothing.

And though I bestow all my goods to feed the poor, and though I give my body to be burned, and have not charity, **it profiteth me nothing.**

Charity suffereth long, and is kind; charity envieth not; charity vaunteth not itself, is not puffed up,

Doth not behave itself unseemly, seeketh not her own, is not easily provoked, thinketh no evil;

Rejoiceth not in iniquity, but rejoiceth in the truth;

Beareth all things, believeth all things, hopeth all things, endureth all things.

Charity never faileth: . . .

<u>**I Corinthians 13:4-8**</u>

Love endures long and is patient and kind; *love never is envious nor boils over with jealousy, is not boastful or vainglorious, does not display itself haughtily.*

It is not conceited (arrogant and inflated with pride); it is not rude (unmannerly) and does not act unbecomingly. ***Love (God's love in us) does not insist on its own rights or its own way, for it is not self-seeking; it is not touchy or fretful or resentful; it takes no account of the evil done to it [it pays no attention to a suffered wrong].***

It does not rejoice at injustice and unrighteousness, but rejoices when right and truth prevail.

Love bears up under anything and everything that comes, is ever ready to believe the best of every person, its hopes are fadeless under all circumstances, and it endures everything [without weakening].

Love never fails [never fades out or becomes obsolete or comes to an end]. *. . . [AMP]*

<u>**I Corinthians 13:13**</u>

And so faith, hope, love abide [faith - conviction and belief respecting man's relation to God and divine things; hope - joyful and confident expectation of eternal salvation; ***love - true affection for God and man, growing out of God's love for and in us],*** *these three;* ***but the greatest of these is love.*** *[AMP]*

<u>**I Corinthians 14:1**</u>

Follow after charity, and desire spiritual gifts, . . .

<u>**Galatians 5:13-15**</u>

For brethren, ye have been called unto liberty; only use not liberty for an occasion to the flesh, **but by love serve one another.**

For all the law is fulfilled in one word, even in this; Thou shalt love thy neighbour as thyself.

But if ye bite and devour one another, take heed that ye be not consumed one of another.

<u>**Ephesians 4:32**</u>

And be ye kind one to another, tenderhearted, forgiving one another, even as God for Christ's sake hath forgiven you.

Ephesians 5:1-2

Be ye therefore followers of God, as dear children;

And walk in love, as Christ also hath loved us, and hath given Himself for us an offering and a sacrifice to God for a sweetsmelling savour.

Colossians 2:2

That their hearts might be comforted, **being knit together in love, . . .**

Colossians 3:13-14

Forbearing one another, and forgiving one another, if any man have a quarrel against any: even as Christ forgave you, so also do ye.

And above all these things, put on charity, which is the bond of perfectness.

Be gentle and forbearing with one another and, if one has a difference (a grievance or complaint) against another, readily pardoning each other; even as the Lord has [freely] forgiven you, so must you also [forgive].

And above all these [put on] love and enfold yourselves with the bond of perfectness [which binds everything together completely in ideal harmony]. *[AMP]*

I Thessalonians 3:12

And the Lord make you to increase and abound **in love one toward another**, and toward all men, even as we do toward you:

I Thessalonians 4:9

But as touching brotherly love ye need not that I write unto you: **for ye yourselves are taught of God to love one another.**

I Thessalonians 5:12-13

. . . know them which labour among you, and are over you in the Lord, and admonish you;

And to esteem them very highly in love for their work's sake. And be at peace among yourselves.

I Timothy 1:5

Now the end of the commandment is charity out of a pure heart, and of a good conscience, and of faith unfeigned:

II Timothy 1:7

For God hath not given us the spirit of fear; but of power, **and of love,** and of a sound mind.

Hebrews 6:10

For God is not unrighteous to forget your work and **labour of love,** which ye have shewed toward His name, **in that ye have ministered to the saints, and do minister.**

Hebrews 13:16

Do not forget or neglect to do kindness and good, to be generous and distribute and contribute to the needy [of the church as embodiment and proof of fellowship], for such sacrifices are pleasing to God. [AMP]

I Peter 1:22

Seeing ye have purified your souls **in obeying the truth through the Spirit unto unfeigned love of the brethren, see that ye love one another with a pure heart fervently:**

I Peter 3:8-9

Finally, be ye all of one mind, having compassion one of another, **love as brethren,** be pitiful, be courteous:

Not rendering evil for evil, or railing for railing: but contrariwise blessing; knowing that ye are thereunto called, that ye should inherit a blessing.

I Peter 4:8

And above all things have fervent charity among yourselves: **for charity shall cover the multitude of sins.**

Above all things have intense and unfailing love for one another, ***for love covers a multitude of sins*** *[forgives and disregards the offenses of others]. [AMP]*

I John 2:10

He that loveth his brother abideth in the light, and there is none occasion of stumbling in him.

I John 3:11-12

For this is the message that ye heard from the beginning, **that we should love one another.**

Not as Cain, who was of that wicked one, and slew his brother. And wherefore slew he him? Because his own works were evil, and his brother's righteous.

I John 3:14

We know that we have passed from death unto life, because we love the brethren. **He that loveth not his brother abideth in death.**

I John 3:16-18

Hereby perceive we the love of God, because He laid down His life for us: **and we ought to lay down our lives for the brethren.**

But whoso hath this world's good, and seeth his brother have need, and shutteth up his bowels of compassion from him, how dwelleth the love of God in him?

My little children, let us not love in word, neither in tongue; but in deed and in truth.

I John 3:23

And this is His commandment, That we should believe on the name of His Son Jesus

Christ, and **love one another**, as He gave us commandment.

<u>**I John 4:7-8**</u>

Beloved, let us love one another: for love is of God; and every one that loveth is born of God, and knoweth God.

He that loveth not knoweth not God; for God is love.

<u>**I John 4:11-12**</u>

Beloved, if God so loved us, we ought also to love one another.

No man hath seen God at any time. **If we love one another, God dwelleth in us, and His love is perfected in us.**

<u>**I John 4:16**</u>

And we have known and believed the love that God hath to us. **God is love; and he that dwelleth in love dwelleth in God, and God in him.**

<u>**I John 4:18**</u>

There is no fear in love; but perfect love casteth out fear: . . .

<u>**I John 4:20-21**</u>

If a man say, I love God and hateth his brother, he is a liar: for he that loveth not his brother whom he hath seen, how can he love God Whom he hath not seen?

And this commandment have we from Him, **That he who loveth God love his brother also.**

Part III

Our Daily Walk as Believers

Chapter 20

Developing a Relationship with the Lord

Genesis 5:22-24 *(Enoch)*

***Enoch walked [in habitual fellowship] with God** after the birth of Methuselah 300 years and had other sons and daughters.*

So all the days of Enoch were 365 years.

***And Enoch walked [in habitual fellowship] with God**; and he was not, for God took him [home with Him]. [AMP]*

Genesis 6:9 *(Noah)*

*This is the history of the generations of Noah. **Noah was a just and righteous man, blameless in his [evil] generation; Noah walked [in habitual fellowship] with God.** [AMP]*

Genesis 28:15 *(Jacob)*

And, **behold, I am with thee, and will keep thee** in all places whither thou goest, and will bring thee again into this land; **for I will not leave thee,** until I have done that which I have spoken to thee of.

Exodus 25:22 *(Moses)*

And there I will meet with thee, and I will commune with thee from above the mercy seat, from between the two cherubims which are upon the ark of the testimony, of all things which I will give thee in commandment unto the children of Israel.

Exodus 33:9-14 *(Moses)*

And it came to pass, as Moses entered into the tabernacle, the cloudy pillar descended, and stood at the door of the tabernacle, **and the Lord talked with Moses.**

And all the people saw the cloudy pillar stand at the tabernacle door: and all the people rose up and worshipped, every man in his tent door.

And the Lord spake unto Moses face to face, as a man speaketh unto his friend. And he turned again into the camp: but his servant Joshua, the son of Nun, a young man, departed not out of the tabernacle.

And Moses said unto the Lord, See, Thou sayest unto me, Bring up this people: and Thou hast not let me know whom Thou wilt send with me. **Yet Thou hast said, I know thee by name, and thou hast also found grace in My sight.**

Now therefore, I pray Thee, if I have found grace in Thy sight, **shew me now Thy way, that I may know Thee, that I may find grace in Thy sight**: and consider that this nation is Thy people.

And He said, **My Presence shall go with thee, and I will give thee rest.**

Deuteronomy 4:29

But if from thence thou shalt seek the Lord thy God, **thou shalt find Him**, if thou seek Him with all thy heart and with all thy soul.

Deuteronomy 6:5

And thou shalt love the Lord thy God with all thine heart, and with all thy soul, and with all thy might.

Psalm 16:8

I have set the Lord always before me: because He is at my right hand, I shall not be moved.

Psalm 73:28

But it is good for me to draw near to God: I have put my trust in the Lord God, that I may declare all Thy works.

Psalm 119:2

Blessed are they that keep His testimonies, and that seek Him with the whole heart.

Psalm 145:18

The Lord is nigh unto all them that call upon Him, to all that call upon Him in truth.

Isaiah 28:9-10

Whom shall He teach knowledge? and whom shall He make to understand doctrine? them that are weaned from the milk, and drawn from the breasts.

For precept must be upon precept, precept upon precept; line upon line, line upon line; here a little, and there a little:

Isaiah 43:2

When thou passest though the waters, I will be with thee; and through the rivers, they shall not overflow thee: when thou walkest through the fire, thou shalt not be burned; neither shall the flame kindle upon thee.

<u>Isaiah 46:3-4</u>

Hearken unto Me, O house of Jacob, and all the remnant of the house of Israel, **which are borne by Me from the belly, which are carried from the womb:**

And even to your old age I am He; and even to hoar hairs will I carry you: **I have made, and I will bear; even I will carry, and will deliver you.**

<u>Isaiah 54:5</u>

For thy Maker is thine Husband; the Lord of hosts is His name; and thy Redeemer the Holy One of Israel; The God of the whole earth shall He be called.

<u>Jeremiah 23:23</u>

Am I a God at hand, saith the Lord, and not a God afar off?

<u>Jeremiah 29:11-13</u>

For I know the thoughts that I think toward you, saith the Lord, thoughts of peace, and not of evil, to give you an expected end.

Then shall ye call upon Me, and ye shall go and pray unto Me, and I will hearken unto you.

And ye shall seek Me, and find Me, when ye shall search for Me with all your heart.

<u>Ezekiel 36:27</u>

And I will put My Spirit within you, and **cause you** to walk in My statutes, and ye shall keep My judgments, and do them.

<u>Ezekiel 37:27</u>

My tabernacle or dwelling place also shall be with them; ***and I will be their God, and they shall be My people. [AMP]***

<u>Hosea 2:19-20</u>

And I will betroth you to Me forever; yes, I will betroth you to Me in righteousness and justice, in steadfast love, and in mercy.

I will even betroth you to Me in stability and in faithfulness, and you shall know (recognize, be acquainted with, appreciate, give heed to, and cherish) the Lord. [AMP]

<u>Hosea 6:3</u>

Yes, let us know (recognize, be acquainted with, and understand) Him; let us be zealous to know the Lord [to appreciate, give heed to, and cherish Him]. *His going forth is prepared and certain as the dawn, and He will come to us as the [heavy] rain, as the latter rain that waters the earth. [AMP]*

<u>Malachi 2:6 (Levi)</u>

The law of truth was in his mouth, and iniquity was not found in his lips: **he walked with Me in peace and equity,** and did turn many away from iniquity.

<u>**Matthew 11:28-30**</u>

Come unto Me, all ye that labour and are heavy laden, **and I will give you rest.**

Take My yoke upon you, and learn of Me; for I am meek and lowly in heart: and ye shall find rest unto your souls.

For My yoke is easy, and My burden is light.

<u>**Matthew 12:48-50**</u>

. . . Who is My mother? and who are My brethren?

And He stretched forth His hand toward His disciples, and said, **Behold My mother and My brethren!**

For whosoever shall do the will of My Father which is in heaven, the same is my brother, and sister, and mother.

<u>**Matthew 18:20**</u>

For where two or three are gathered together in My name, **there am I in the midst of them.**

<u>**Matthew 28:20**</u>

Teaching them to observe all things whatsoever I have commanded you: and, **lo, I am with you alway, even unto the end of the world.** Amen.

<u>**John 15:4-7**</u>

Abide in Me, and I in you. As the branch cannot bear fruit of itself, except it abide in the vine; no more can ye, except ye abide in Me.

I am the vine, ye are the branches. He that abideth in Me, and I in him, the same bringeth forth much fruit: **for without Me ye can do nothing.**

If a man abide not in Me, he is cast forth as a branch, and is withered; and men gather them, and cast them into the fire, and they are burned.

If ye abide in Me, and My words abide in you, ye shall ask what ye will, and it shall be done unto you.

<u>**John 15:10**</u>

If ye keep My commandments, ye shall abide in My love; even as I have kept My Father's commandments, and abide in His love.

<u>**John 15:14**</u>

Ye are My friends, if ye do whatsoever I command you.

<u>**Acts 17:27**</u>

That they should seek the Lord, if haply they might feel after Him, and find Him, **though He be not far from every one of us:**

<u>**Romans 7:4**</u>

Wherefore, my brethren, ye also are become dead to the law by the body of Christ; **that ye should be married to another, even to Him Who is raised from the dead,** that we should bring forth fruit unto God.

Romans 9:26

And it shall come to pass, that in the place where it was said unto them, Ye are not My people; **there shall they be called the children of the living God.**

I Corinthians 1:9

God is faithful, **by Whom ye were called unto the fellowship of His Son Jesus Christ our Lord.**

Ephesians 2:19

Now therefore ye are no more strangers and foreigners**, but fellowcitizens with the saints, and of the household of God;**

Ephesians 3:14-15

For this cause I bow my knees unto the Father of our Lord Jesus Christ,
Of Whom **the whole family in heaven and earth** is named,

Hebrews 2:11

For both He that sanctifieth and they who are sanctified are all of one: **for which cause He is not ashamed to call them brethren,**

Hebrews 7:19

For the law made nothing perfect, but the bringing in of a better hope did; **by the which we draw nigh unto God.**

Hebrews 10:22

Let us draw near with a true heart in full assurance of faith, having our hearts sprinkled from an evil conscience, and our bodies washed with pure water.

James 2:23

. . . Abraham believed God, and it was imputed unto him for righteousness: **and he was called the Friend of God.**

James 4:8

Draw nigh to God, and He will draw nigh to you. Cleanse your hands, ye sinners; and purify your hearts, ye double-minded.

I John 1:3

That which we have seen and heard declare we unto you, that ye also may have fellowship with us: **and truly our fellowship is with the Father, and with His Son Jesus Christ.**

I John 2:5-6

But whoso keepeth His word, in Him verily is the love of God perfected: hereby know we that we are in Him.

He that saith he abideth in Him ought himself also so to walk, even as He walked.

<u>I John 2:28</u>

And now, little children, **abide in Him; that, when He shall appear, we may have confidence, and not be ashamed before Him at His coming.**

<u>I John 3:2</u>

Beloved, now are we the sons of God, and it doth not yet appear what we shall be: **but we know that, when He shall appear, we shall be like Him;** for we shall see Him as He is.

<u>I John 3:6</u>

Whosoever abideth in Him sinneth not: whosoever sinneth hath not seen Him, neither known Him.

<u>I John 3:24</u>

And he that keepeth His commandments dwelleth in Him, and He in him. And hereby we know that He abideth in us, by the Spirit Which He hath given us.

<u>II John 9</u>

Whosoever transgresseth, and abideth not in the doctrine of Christ, hath not God. **He that abideth in the doctrine of Christ, He hath both the Father and the Son.**

<u>Revelation 3:20</u>

Behold, I stand at the door, and knock: **if any man hear My voice, and open the door, I will come in to him, and will sup with him, and he with Me.**

<u>Revelation 21:2-3</u>

And I saw the holy city, the new Jerusalem, descending out of heaven from God, all arrayed like a bride beautified and adorned for her husband;

*Then I heard a mighty voice from the throne and I perceived its distinct words, saying, See! **The abode of God is with men**, and He will live (encamp, tent) among them; and they shall be His people, and God shall personally be with them and be their God. [AMP]*

Chapter 21

Commitment to God's Will

<u>Deuteronomy 30:19-20</u>

I call heaven and earth to record this day against you, that I have set before you life and death, blessing and cursing: **therefore choose life, that both thou and thy seed may live:**

That thou mayest love the Lord thy God, and that thou mayest obey His voice, and that thou mayest cleave unto Him: for He is thy life, and the length of thy days: that thou mayest dwell in the land which the Lord sware unto thy fathers, to Abraham, to Isaac, and to Jacob, to give them.

<u>Psalm 40:7-8</u>

Then said I, Lo, I come: in the volume of the book it is written of me,

I delight to do Thy will, O my God: yea, Thy law is within my heart.

<u>Psalm 143:10</u>

Teach me to do Thy will; for Thou art my God: Thy Spirit is good; lead me into the land of uprightness.

<u>Matthew 7:21</u>

Not every one that saith unto Me, Lord, Lord, shall enter into the kingdom of heaven; **but he that doeth the will of My Father Which is in heaven.**

<u>Matthew 10:37-39</u>

He that loveth father or mother more than Me is not worthy of Me: and He that loveth son or daughter more than Me is not worthy of Me.

And he that taketh not his cross, and followeth after Me, is not worthy of Me.

He that findeth his life shall lose it: and he that loseth his life for My sake shall find it.

He who loves [and takes more pleasure in] father or mother more than [in] Me is not worthy of Me; and he who loves [and takes more pleasure in] son or daughter more than [in]

Me is not worthy of Me;

And he who does not take up his cross and follow Me [cleave steadfastly to Me, conforming wholly to My example in living and, if need be, in dying also] is not worthy of Me.

Whoever finds his [lower] life will lose it [the higher life], and whoever loses his [lower] life on My account will find it [the higher life]. [AMP]

Matthew 12:50

For whosoever shall do the will of My Father Which is in heaven, the same is My brother, and sister, and mother.

Matthew 26:39

. . . O My Father, if it be possible, let this cup pass from Me: **nevertheless not as I will, but as Thou wilt.**

Matthew 26:42

. . . O My Father, if this cup may not pass away from Me, except I drink it, **Thy will be done**.

Mark 8:34-37

And when He had called the people unto Him with His disciples also, He said unto them, **Whosoever will come after Me, let him deny himself, and take up his cross, and follow Me.**

For whosoever will save his life shall lose it; but whosoever shall lose his life for My sake and the Gospel's, the same shall save it.

For what shall it profit a man, if he shall gain the whole world, and lose his own soul?

Or what shall a man give in exchange for his soul?

And Jesus called [to Him] the throng with His disciples, and said to them, ***If anyone intends to come after Me, let him deny himself [forget, ignore, disown, and lose sight of himself and his own interests] and take up his cross, and [joining Me as a disciple and siding with My party] follow with Me [continually, cleaving steadfastly to Me].***

For whoever wants to save his [higher, spiritual, eternal] life, will lose it [the lower, natural, temporal life which is lived only on earth]; and whoever gives up his life [which is lived only on earth] for My sake and the Gospel's will save it [his higher, spiritual life in the eternal kingdom of God].

For what does it profit a man to gain the whole world, and forfeit his life [in the eternal kingdom of God]?

For what can a man give as an exchange (a compensation, a ransom, in return) for his [blessed] life [in the eternal kingdom of God]? [AMP]

Mark 10:28-30

Then Peter began to say unto Him, **Lo, we have left all, and have followed Thee.**

And Jesus answered and said, Verily I say unto you, There is no man that hath left house, or brethren, or sisters, or father, or mother, or wife, or children, or lands, for My sake, and the Gospel's,

But he shall receive **an hundredfold now in this time**, houses, and brethren, and sisters, and mothers, and children, and lands, with persecutions; **and in the world to come eternal life.**

Mark 14:36

And He said, Abba, Father, all things are possible unto Thee; take away this cup from Me: **nevertheless not what I will, but what Thou wilt.**

Luke 1:38

And Mary said, **Behold the handmaid of the Lord; be it unto me according to Thy word.** And the angel departed from her.

Luke 9:23-25

. . . If any man will come after Me, let him deny himself, and take up his cross daily, and follow Me.

For whosoever will save his life shall lose it: but whosoever will lose his life for My sake, the same shall save it.

For what is a man advantaged, if he gain the whole world, and lose himself, or be cast away?

. . . If any person wills to come after Me, let him deny himself [disown himself, forget, lose sight of himself and his own interests, refuse and give up himself] and take up his cross daily, and follow Me [cleave steadfastly to Me, conform wholly to My example in living and, if need be, in dying also].

For whoever would preserve his life and save it will lose and destroy it, but whoever loses his life for My sake, he will preserve and save it [from the penalty of eternal death].

For what does it profit a man, if he gains the whole world and ruins or forfeits (loses) himself? [AMP]

Luke 12:47-48

And that servant, which knew his Lord's will, and prepared not himself, neither did according to His will, shall be beaten with many stripes.

But he that knew not, and did commit things worthy of stripes, shall be beaten with few stripes. For unto whomsoever much is given, of him shall be much required: and to whom men have committed much, of him they will ask the more.

Luke 14:26-27

If any man come to Me, and hate not his father, and mother, and wife, and children, and brethren, and sisters, yea, and his own life also, he cannot be My disciple.

And whosoever doth not bear his cross, and come after Me, cannot be My disciple.

If anyone comes to Me and does not hate his [own] father and mother [in the sense of indifference to or relative disregard for them in comparison with his attitude toward God] and [likewise] his wife and children and brothers and sisters - [yes] and even his own life also - he cannot be My disciple.

Whoever does not persevere and carry his own cross and come after (follow) Me cannot be My disciple. [AMP]

Luke 14:33

So likewise, whosoever he be of you that forsaketh not all that he hath, he cannot be My disciple.

So then, any of you who does not forsake (renounce, surrender claim to, give up, say good-bye to) all that he has cannot be My disciple. [AMP]

Luke 22:42

. . . Father, if Thou be willing, remove this cup from Me: **nevertheless not My will, but Thine, be done.**

John 4:34

Jesus saith unto them, My meat is to do the will of Him that sent Me, and to finish His work.

John 5:30

I can of Mine own self do nothing: as I hear, I judge: and My judgment is just; **because I seek not Mine own will, but the will of the Father Which hath sent Me.**

I am able to do nothing from Myself [independently, of My own accord - but only as I am taught by God and as I get His orders]. Even as I hear, I judge [I decide as I am bidden to decide. As the voice comes to Me, so I give a decision], and My judgment is right (just, righteous), ***because I do not seek or consult My own will [I have no desire to do what is pleasing to Myself, My own aim, My own purpose] but only the will and pleasure of the Father Who sent Me. [AMP]***

John 6:38

For I came down from heaven, **not to do Mine own will, but the will of Him that sent Me.**

John 7:17

If any man will do His will, He shall know of the doctrine, whether it be of God, or whether I speak of Myself.

John 18:11

Then said Jesus unto Peter, Put up thy sword into the sheath: **the cup which My Father hath given Me, shall I not drink it?**

Acts 21:14

And when he *(Paul)* would not be persuaded, we ceased, saying, **The will of the Lord be done.**

I Corinthians 6:19-20

What? know ye not that your body is the temple of the Holy Ghost Which is in you, Which ye have of God, and **ye are not your own?**

For ye are bought with a price: therefore glorify God in your body, and in your spirit, which are God's.

I Corinthians 9:16

For though I preach the Gospel, I have nothing to glory of: for necessity is laid upon me; yea, woe is unto me, if I preach not the Gospel!

I Corinthians 9:24-27

Know ye not that they which run in a race run all, but one receiveth the prize? So run, that ye may obtain.

And every man that striveth for the mastery is temperate in all things. Now they do it to obtain a corruptible crown; but we an incorruptible.

I therefore so run, not as uncertainly; so fight I, not as one that beateth the air:

But I keep under my body, and bring it into subjection: lest that by any means, when I have preached to others, I myself should be a castaway.

Do you not know that in a race all the runners compete, but [only] one receives the prize? So run [your race] that you may lay hold [of the prize] and make it yours.

Now every athlete who goes into training conducts himself temperately and restricts himself in all things. They do it to win a wreath that will soon wither, but we [do it to receive a crown of eternal blessedness] that cannot wither.

Therefore I do not run uncertainly (without definite aim). I do not box like one beating the air and striking without an adversary.

But [like a boxer] I buffet my body [handle it roughly, discipline it by hardships] and subdue it, for fear that after proclaiming to others the Gospel and things pertaining to it, I myself should become unfit [not stand the test, be unapproved and rejected as a counterfeit]. [AMP]

Ephesians 5:17

Wherefore be ye not unwise, but understanding what the will of the Lord is.

Ephesians 6:6

Not with eyeservice, as menpleasers; but as the servants of Christ, **doing the will of God from the heart;**

Philippians 3:7-11

But what things were gain to me, those I counted loss for Christ.

Yea doubtless, and I count all things but loss for the excellency of the knowledge of Christ Jesus my Lord: for Whom I have suffered the loss of all things, and do count them but dung, that I may win Christ,

And be found in Him, not having mine own righteousness, which is of the law, but that which is through the faith of Christ, the righteousness which is of God by faith:

That I may know Him, and the power of His resurrection, and the fellowship of His sufferings, being made conformable unto His death;

If by any means I might attain unto the resurrection of the dead.

Philippians 3:13-14

Brethren, I count not myself to have apprehended: but this one thing I do, **forgetting those things which are behind, and reaching forth unto those things which are before,**

I press toward the mark for the prize of the high calling of God in Christ Jesus.

Colossians 1:9

. . . that ye might be filled with the knowledge of His will in all wisdom and spiritual understanding;

Colossians 3:3

For ye are dead, and your life is hid with Christ in God.

II Timothy 1:9

Who hath saved us, and **called us with an holy calling, not according to our works, but according to His own purpose and grace**, which was given us in Christ Jesus before the world began,

[For it is He] Who delivered and saved us and called us with a calling in itself holy and leading to holiness [to a life of consecration, a vocation of holiness]; ***[He did it] not because of anything of merit that we have done, but because of and to further His own purpose and grace (unmerited favor)*** *which was given us in Christ Jesus before the world began [eternal ages ago]. [AMP]*

Hebrews 10:9

Then said He, **Lo, I come to do Thy will, O God** . . .

I John 2:15-17

Love not the world, neither the things that are in the world. If any man love the world, the love of the Father is not in him.

For all that is in the world, the lust of the flesh, and the lust of the eyes, and the pride of life, is not of the Father, but is of the world.

And the world passeth away, and the lust thereof: **but he that doeth the will of God abideth for ever.**

Chapter 22

Guidance & Direction from the Lord

Exodus 33:14 *(to Moses)*

And He said, **My Presence shall go with thee,** and I will give thee rest.

Numbers 9:16-18 *(to the children of Israel in the desert)*

So it was alway: **the cloud covered it by day, and the appearance of fire by night.**

And when the cloud was taken up from the tabernacle, then after that the children of Israel journeyed: and in the place where the cloud abode, there the children of Israel pitched their tents.

At the commandment of the Lord the children of Israel journeyed, and at the commandment of the Lord they pitched: as long as the cloud abode upon the tabernacle they rested in their tents.

Deuteronomy 8:2 *(to the children of Israel)*

And thou shalt remember **all the way which the Lord thy God led thee** these forty years in the wilderness, to humble thee, and to prove thee, to know what was in thine heart, whether thou wouldest keep His commandments, or no.

Deuteronomy 31:6 *(to the children of Israel)*

Be strong and of a good courage, fear not, nor be afraid of them: **for the Lord thy God, He it is that doth go with thee**; He will not fail thee, nor forsake thee.

Deuteronomy 32:10-12 *(to the children of Israel)*

He found him in a desert land, and in the waste howling wilderness; **He led him about, He instructed him, He kept him as the apple of His eye.**

As an eagle stirreth up her nest, fluttereth over her young, spreadeth abroad her wings, taketh them, beareth them on her wings:

So the Lord alone did lead him, and there was no strange god with him,

I Kings 19:11-12 *(to Elijah)*

. . . and a great and strong wind rent the mountains, and brake in pieces the rocks before the Lord; but the Lord was not in the wind: and after the wind an earthquake; but the Lord was not in the earthquake:

And after the earthquake a fire; but the Lord was not in the fire: **and after the fire a still small voice.**

Nehemiah 9:20 *(to the children of Israel)*

Thou gavest also Thy good Spirit to instruct them, . . .

Psalm 5:8 *(to David)*

Lead me, O Lord, in Thy righteousness because of mine enemies; make Thy way straight before my face.

Psalm 16:11 *(to David)*

Thou wilt shew me the path of life: in Thy presence is fulness of joy; at Thy right hand there are pleasures for evermore.

Psalm 23:2-3 *(to David)*

He maketh me to lie down in green pastures: He leadeth me beside the still waters.

He restoreth my soul: He leadeth me in the paths of righteousness for His name's sake.

Psalm 25:5,9 *(to David)*

Lead me in Thy truth, and teach me: for Thou art the God of My salvation; on Thee do I wait all the day.

The meek will He guide in judgment: and the meek will He teach His way.

Psalm 27:11 *(to David)*

Teach me Thy way, O Lord, and lead me in a plain path, because of mine enemies.

Psalm 31:3 *(to David)*

For Thou art my Rock and my Fortress; therefore for Thy name's sake lead me, and guide me.

Psalm 32:8 *(to David)*

I will instruct thee and teach thee in the way which thou shalt go: I will guide thee with Mine eye.

Psalm 37:23-24 *(to David)*

The steps of a good man are ordered by the Lord: and He delighteth in his way.

Though he fall, he shall not be utterly cast down: for the Lord upholdeth him with His hand.

The steps of a [good] man are directed and established by the Lord when He delights in his way [and He busies Himself with his every step].

Though he falls, he shall not be utterly cast down, for the Lord grasps his hand in support and upholds him. [AMP]

Psalm 48:14 *(to the sons of Korah)*

For this God is our God for ever and ever: He will be our guide even unto death.

Psalm 73:23-24 *(to Asaph)*

Nevertheless I am continually with Thee: Thou hast holden me by my right hand.

Thou shalt guide me with Thy counsel, and afterward receive me to glory.

Psalm 121:8

The Lord shall preserve thy going out and thy coming in from this time forth, and even for evermore.

Psalm 139:9-10 *(to David)*

If I take the wings of the morning, and dwell in the uttermost parts of the sea;

Even there shall Thy hand lead me, and Thy right hand shall hold me.

Psalm 143:10 *(to David)*

Teach me to do Thy will; for Thou art my God: Thy Spirit is good; lead me into the land of uprightness.

Proverbs 2:8

He keepeth the paths of judgment, and preserveth the way of His saints.

Proverbs 3:5-6

Trust in the Lord with all thine heart; and lean not unto thine own understanding.

In all thy ways acknowledge Him, and He shall direct thy paths.

Proverbs 6:22-23 *(God's word)*

When thou goest, it shall lead thee; when thou sleepest, it shall keep thee; and when thou awakest, it shall talk with thee.

For the commandment is a lamp; and the law is light; and reproofs of instruction are the way of life:

Proverbs 8:14 *(wisdom from God)*

Counsel is mine, and sound wisdom: I am understanding; I have strength.

Proverbs 16:9

A man's heart deviseth his way: but the Lord directeth his steps.

Proverbs 24:6

For by wise counsel thou shalt make thy war: and in the multitude of counsellors there is safety.

Isaiah 28:9-10

Whom shall He teach knowledge? and whom shall He make to understand doctrine? them that are weaned from the milk, and drawn from the breasts.

For precept must be upon precept, precept upon precept; line upon line, line upon line; here a little, and there a little:

Isaiah 28:26

For his God doth instruct him to discretion, and doth teach him.

Isaiah 30:21

And thine ears shall hear a word behind thee, saying, This is the way, walk ye in it, when ye turn to the right hand, and when ye turn to the left.

Isaiah 40:11

He shall feed His flock like a shepherd: He shall gather the lambs with His arm, and carry them in His bosom, and shall gently lead those that are with young.

Isaiah 42:16

And I will bring the blind by a way that they knew not; I will lead them in paths that they have not known: I will make darkness light before them, and crooked things straight. These things will I do unto them, and not forsake them.

Isaiah 45:2

I will go before thee, and make the crooked places straight: I will break in pieces the gates of brass, and cut in sunder the bars of iron:

Isaiah 48:17

Thus said the Lord, thy Redeemer, the Holy One of Israel; I am the Lord thy God Which teacheth thee to profit, Which leadeth thee by the way that thou shouldest go.

Isaiah 50:10

Who is among you that feareth the Lord, that obeyeth the voice of His servant, that walketh in darkness, and hath no light? **let him trust in the name of the Lord, and stay upon his God.**

Isaiah 52:12

For ye shall not go out with haste, nor go by flight: **for the Lord will go before you;** and the God of Israel will be your rereward.

Isaiah 57:18

I have seen his ways, and will heal him: **I will lead him also,** and restore comforts unto him and to his mourners.

Isaiah 58:11

And the Lord shall guide thee continually, and satisfy thy soul in drought, and make fat thy bones: and thou shalt be like a watered garden, and like a spring of water, whose waters fail not.

Isaiah 61:8

For I the Lord love judgment, I hate robbery for burnt offering; and **I will direct their work in truth,** and I will make an everlasting covenant with them.

Ezekiel 36:27

And I will put My Spirit within you, and cause you to walk in My statutes, and ye shall keep My judgments, and do them.

Amos 3:7

Surely the Lord God will do nothing, but He revealeth His secret unto His servants the prophets.

Luke 1:79

To give light to them that sit in darkness and in the shadow of death, **to guide our feet into the way of peace.**

Luke 12:12

For the Holy Ghost shall teach you in the same hour what ye ought to say.

John 10:27 *(to God's sheep)*

My sheep hear My voice, and I know them, and they follow Me:

John 14:26

But the Comforter, Which is the Holy Ghost, Whom the Father will send in My name, He shall teach you all things, and bring all things to your remembrance, whatsoever I have said unto you.

John 16:13

Howbeit when He, the Spirit of truth, is come, He will guide you into all truth: for He shall not speak of Himself; but whatsoever He shall hear, that shall He speak: and He will shew you things to come.

John 18:37

. . . Every one that is of the truth heareth My voice.

Acts 13:2 *(to the early Church)*

As they ministered to the Lord, and fasted, the Holy Ghost said, Separate Me Barnabas and Saul for the work whereunto I have called them.

Acts 16:6

Now when they had gone throughout Phrygia and the region of Galatia, **and were forbidden of the Holy Ghost to preach the word in Asia,**

Romans 8:14

For as many as are led by the Spirit of God, they are the sons of God.

Galatians 5:18

But if ye be led of the Spirit, ye are not under the law.

II Thessalonians 3:5

And the Lord direct your hearts into the love of God, and into the patient waiting for Christ.

James 1:5

If any of you lack wisdom, let him ask of God, that giveth to all men liberally, and upbraideth not; **and it shall be given him.**

Revelations 3:8

I know thy works: **behold, I have set before thee an open door, and no man can shut it:** for thou hast a little strength, and hast kept My word, and hast not denied My name.

Chapter 23

Waiting on God

<u>Genesis 49:18</u>

I have waited for Thy salvation, O Lord.

<u>Psalm 25:3-5</u>

Yea, let none that wait on Thee be ashamed: let them be ashamed which transgress without cause.

Shew me Thy ways, O Lord; teach me Thy paths.

Lead me in Thy truth, and teach me: for Thou art the God of my salvation; on Thee do I wait all the day.

<u>Psalm 25:21</u>

Let integrity and uprightness preserve me; **for I wait on Thee**.

<u>Psalm 27:14</u>

Wait and hope for and expect the Lord; *be brave and of good courage and let your heart be stout and enduring.* ***Yes, wait for and hope for and expect the Lord.*** *[AMP]*

<u>Psalm 31:24</u>

Be of good courage, and He shall strengthen your heart, all ye that hope in the Lord.

<u>Psalm 33:20-22</u>

Our soul waiteth for the Lord: He is our Help and our Shield.

For our heart shall rejoice in Him, because we have trusted in His holy name.

Let Thy mercy, O Lord, be upon us, according as we hope in Thee.

<u>Psalm 37:7,9</u>

Rest in the Lord, and wait patiently for Him: fret not thyself because of him who prospereth in his way, because of the man who bringeth wicked devices to pass.

For evildoers shall be cut off: **but those that wait upon the Lord, they shall inherit the earth.**

Psalm 37:34

Wait on the Lord, and keep His way, and He shall exalt thee to inherit the land: when the wicked are cut off, thou shalt see it.

Psalm 39:7-8

And now, Lord, **what wait I for?** my hope is in Thee.
Deliver me from all my transgressions: make me not the reproach of the foolish.

Psalm 40:1-3

I waited patiently for the Lord; and He inclined unto Me, and heard my cry.
He brought me up also out of an horrible pit, out of the miry clay, and set my feet upon a rock, and established my goings.
And He hath put a new song in my mouth, even praise unto our God: many shall see it, and fear, and shall trust in the Lord.

Psalm 62:1

Truly my soul waiteth upon God: from Him cometh my salvation.

Psalm 62:5-6

My soul, wait thou only upon God; for my expectation is from Him.
He only is my rock and my salvation: He is my defence; I shall not be moved.

Psalm 104:27-28

These wait all upon Thee; that Thou mayest give them their meat in due season.
That Thou givest them they gather: Thou openest Thine hand, they are filled with good.

Psalm 106:13-15

They soon forgat His works; **they waited not for His counsel:**
But lusted exceedingly in the wilderness, and tempted God in the desert.
And He gave them their request; but sent leanness into their soul.

Psalm 123:2

Behold, as the eyes of servants look unto the hand of their masters, and as the eyes of a maiden unto the hand of her mistress; **so our eyes wait upon the Lord our God, until that He have mercy upon us.**

Psalm 130:5-6

I wait for the Lord, my soul doth wait, and in His word do I hope.
My soul waiteth for the Lord more than they that watch for the morning: I say, more than they that watch for the morning.

Psalm 145:15-16

The eyes of all wait for You [looking, watching, and expecting] and You give them their food in due season.

You open Your hand and satisfy every living thing with favor. [AMP]

Proverbs 20:22

Say not thou, I will recompense evil; but wait on the Lord, and He shall save thee.

Isaiah 8:17

And I will wait upon the Lord, that hideth His face from the house of Jacob, and I will look for Him.

Isaiah 25:9

And it shall be said in the day, **Lo, this is our God; we have waited for Him, and He will save us: this is the Lord; we have waited for Him, we will be glad and rejoice in His salvation.**

Isaiah 26:8-9

Yea, in the way of Thy judgments, O Lord, have we waited for Thee; the desire of our soul is to Thy name, and to the remembrance of Thee.

With my soul have I desired Thee in the night; yea, with my spirit within me will I seek Thee early: for when Thy judgments are in the earth, the inhabitants of the world will learn righteousness.

Isaiah 30:18

And therefore will the Lord wait, that He may be gracious unto you, and therefore will He be exalted, that He may have mercy upon you: for the Lord is a God of judgment: **blessed are all they that wait for Him.**

Isaiah 33:2

O Lord, be gracious unto us; **we have waited for Thee:** be Thou their arm every morning, our salvation also in the time of trouble.

Isaiah 40:31

But they that wait upon the Lord shall renew their strength; they shall mount up with wings as eagles; they shall run, and not be weary; and they shall walk, and not faint.

But those who wait for the Lord [who expect, look for, and hope in Him] shall change and renew their strength and power; *they shall lift their wings and mount up [close to God] as eagles [mount up to the sun]; they shall run and not be weary, they shall walk and not faint or become tired. [AMP]*

Isaiah 49:23

. . . for they shall not be ashamed that wait for Me.

Isaiah 50:10

Who is among you that feareth the Lord, that obeyeth the voice of His servant, that walketh in darkness, and hath no light? let him trust in the name of the Lord, **and stay upon his God.**

Isaiah 64:4

For since the beginning of the world men have not heard, nor perceived by the ear, neither hath the eye seen, O God, beside Thee, what He hath prepared for him that waiteth for Him.

Lamentations 3:25-26

The Lord is good unto them that wait for Him, to the soul that seeketh Him.

It is good that a man should both hope and quietly wait for the salvation of the Lord.

Hosea 12:6

Therefore return to your God! Hold fast to love and mercy, to righteousness and justice, and wait [expectantly] for your God continually! [AMP]

Micah 7:7

But as for me, I will look to the Lord and confident in Him I will keep watch; ***I will wait with hope and expectancy for the God of my salvation;*** *my God will hear me. [AMP]*

Habakkuk 2:3

For the vision is yet for an appointed time, but at the end it shall speak, and not lie: **though it tarry, wait for it; because it will surely come, it will not tarry.**

Luke 2:25

And, behold, there was a man in Jerusalem, whose name was Simeon; and the same man was just and devout, **waiting for the consolation of Israel**: and the Holy Ghost was upon him.

Luke 2:37-38 *(Anna the prophetess)*

And she was a widow of about fourscore and four years, **which departed not from the temple, but served God with fastings and prayers night and day.**

And she coming in that instant gave thanks likewise unto the Lord, and spake of Him to all them that looked for redemption in Jerusalem.

Luke 24:49

And, behold, I send the promise of my Father upon you: but **tarry ye** in the city of Jerusalem, until ye be endued with power from on high.

Acts 1:4

And, being assembled together with them, commanded them that they should not depart from Jerusalem, **but wait for the promise of the Father,** which, saith He, ye have heard of Me.

II Thessalonians 3:5

And the Lord direct your hearts into the love of God, and into the patient waiting for Christ.

James 5:7

Be patient therefore, brethren, unto the coming of the Lord. **Behold, the husbandman waiteth for the precious fruit of the earth, and hath long patience for it, until he receive the early and latter rain.**

Chapter 24

Developing Patience

__Psalm 37:7-9__

Rest in the Lord, and wait patiently for Him: fret not thyself because of him who prospereth in his way, because of the man who bringeth wicked devices to pass.

Cease from anger, and forsake wrath: fret not thyself in any wise to do evil.

For evildoers shall be cut off: but those that wait upon the Lord, they shall inherit the earth.

__Psalm 40:1__

I waited patiently for the Lord; and He inclined unto me, and heard my cry.

__Proverbs 16:32__

He that is slow to anger is better than the mighty; and he that ruleth his spirit than he that taketh a city.

__Eccelesiastes 7:8__

Better is the end of a thing than the beginning thereof: **and the patient in spirit is better than the proud in spirit.**

__Eccelesiastes 11:1__

Cast thy bread upon the waters: **for thou shalt find it after many days.**

__Isaiah 30:15__

. . . In returning and rest shall ye be saved; in quietness and in confidence shall be your strength: . . .

__Lamentations 3:26__

It is good that a man should both hope and quietly wait for the salvation of the Lord.

Matthew 24:13

But he that shall endure unto the end, the same shall be saved.

Luke 8:15

But that on the good ground are they, which in an honest and good heart, having heard the word, keep it, and **bring forth fruit with patience.**

Luke 21:19

In your patience possess ye your souls.

Romans 2:7

To them who by **patient continuance in welldoing** seek for glory and honour and immortality, eternal life:

Romans 5:3-5

And not only so, but we glory in tribulations also: knowing that **tribulation worketh patience;**

And patience, experience; and experience, hope:

And hope maketh not ashamed; because the love of God is shed abroad in our hearts by the Holy Ghost Which is given unto us.

Romans 8:25

But if we hope for that we see not, **then do we with patience wait for it**.

Romans 12:12

Rejoicing in hope; **patient in tribulation**; continuing instant in prayer;

Romans 15:4-5

For whatsoever things were written aforetime were written for our learning, **that we through patience and comfort of the scriptures might have hope.**

Now **the God of patience and consolation** grant you to be likeminded one toward another according to Christ Jesus.

I Corinthians 13:4

Love is patient, *love is kind . . . [NIV]*

Galatians 5:22

But the fruit of the Spirit is love, joy, peace, ***patience*** *. . . [NIV]*

Galatians 6:9

And let us not be weary in well doing: for in due season we shall reap, if we faint not.

I Thessalonians 5:14-15

. . . be patient toward all men.

See that none render evil for evil unto any man; but ever follow that which is good, both among yourselves, and to all men.

Hebrews 6:12

That ye be not slothful, **but followers of them who through faith and patience inherit the promises**.

Hebrews 10:23

Let us hold fast the profession of our faith without wavering; (for He is faithful that promised;)

Hebrews 10:35-37

Cast not away therefore your confidence, which hath great recompence of reward.

For ye have need of patience, that, after ye have done the will of God, ye might receive the promise.

For yet a little while, and He that shall come will come, and will not tarry.

Hebrews 12:1

Wherefore seeing we also are compassed about with so great a cloud of witnesses, let us lay aside every weight, and the sin which doth so easily beset us, **and let us run with patience the race that is set before us,**

James 1:2-4

My brethren, count it all joy when ye fall into divers temptations;

Knowing this, **that the trying of your faith worketh patience.**

But let patience have her perfect work, that ye may be perfect and entire, wanting nothing.

James 5:7-8

Be patient therefore, brethren, unto the coming of the Lord. Behold, the husbandman waiteth for the precious fruit of the earth, and hath long patience for it, until he receive the early and latter rain.

Be ye also patient; stablish your hearts: for the coming of the Lord draweth nigh.

I Peter 2:20

For what glory is it, if, when ye be buffeted for your faults, ye shall take it patiently? but if, when ye do well, and suffer for it, ye take it patiently, this is acceptable with God.

Revelations 3:10

Because thou hast kept the word of My patience, I also will keep thee from the hour of temptation, which shall come upon all the world, to try them that dwell upon the earth.

Chapter 25

Trusting in the Lord

II Samuel 22:3

The God of my Rock; **in Him will I trust:** He is my Shield, and the Horn of my salvation, my High Tower, and my Refuge, my Saviour; Thou savest me from violence.

II Samuel 22:31

As for God, His way is perfect; the word of the Lord is tried: He is a Buckler to all them that trust in Him.

Job 13:15

Though He slay me, yet will I trust in Him: . . .

Psalm 4:5

Offer the sacrifices of righteousness, and put your trust in the Lord.

Psalm 7:1

O Lord my God, in Thee do I put my trust: save me from all them that persecute me, and deliver me:

Psalm 18:30

As for God, His way is perfect: the word of the Lord is tried: **He is a Buckler to all those that trust in Him.**

Psalm 20:7-8

Some trust in chariots, and some in horses: **but we will remember the name of the Lord our God.**

They are brought down and fallen: but we are risen, and stand upright.

Psalm 25:2

O my God, I trust in Thee: let me not be ashamed, let not mine enemies triumph over me.

Psalm 31:14-15

But I trusted in Thee, O Lord: I said, Thou art my God.

My times are in Thy hand: deliver me from the hand of mine enemies, and from them that persecute me.

Psalm 31:19

Oh how great is Thy goodness, which Thou hast laid up for them that fear Thee; **which Thou hast wrought for them that trust in Thee before the sons of men!**

Psalm 32:10

. . . but he that trusteth in the Lord, mercy shall compass him about.

Psalm 34:8

O taste and see that the Lord is good: **blessed is the man that trusteth in Him.**

Psalm 34:22

The Lord redeemeth the soul of His servants: and **none of them that trust in Him shall be desolate.**

Psalm 37:3-5

Trust in the Lord, and do good; so shalt thou dwell in the land, and verily thou shalt be fed.

Delight thyself also in the Lord; and He shall give thee the desires of thine heart.

Commit thy way unto the Lord; **trust also in Him;** and He shall bring it to pass.

Trust (lean on, rely on, and be confident) in the Lord and do good; so shall you dwell in the land and feed surely on His faithfulness, and truly you shall be fed.

Delight yourself also in the Lord, and He will give you the desires and secret petitions of your heart.

Commit your way to the Lord [roll and repose each care of your load on Him]; ***trust (lean on, rely on, and be confident) also in Him*** *and He will bring it to pass. [AMP]*

Psalm 37:39-40

But the salvation of the righteous is of the Lord: He is their strength in the time of trouble.

And the Lord shall help them, and deliver them: **He shall deliver them from the wicked, and save them, because they trust in Him.**

Psalm 40:4

Blessed is that man that maketh the Lord His trust, and respecteth not the proud, nor such as turn aside to lies.

Psalm 62:7-8

In God is my salvation and my glory: the Rock of my strength, and my refuge, is in God.

Trust in Him at all times; ye people, pour out your heart before Him: God is a refuge for us. Selah.

Psalm 73:28

But it is good for me to draw near to God: **I have put my trust in the Lord God, that I may declare all Thy works.**

Psalm 91:1-2, 4

He that dwelleth in the secret place of the Most High shall abide under the shadow of the Almighty.

I will say of the Lord, He is my Refuge and my Fortress: my God; **in Him will I trust.**

He shall cover thee with His feathers, and **under His wings shalt thou trust:** His truth shall be thy shield and buckler.

Psalm 115:9-11

O Israel, **trust thou in the Lord:** He is their Help and their Shield.

O house of Aaron, **trust in the Lord:** He is their Help and their Shield.

Ye that fear the Lord, trust in the Lord: He is their Help and their Shield.

Psalm 118:8-9

It is better to trust in the Lord than to put confidence in man.

It is better to trust in the Lord than to put confidence in princes.

Psalm 119:42

So shall I have wherewith to answer him that reproacheth me: for I trust in Thy word.

Psalm 125:1

They that trust in the Lord shall be as mount Zion, which cannot be removed, but abideth for ever.

Psalm 138:7

Though I walk in the midst of trouble, Thou wilt revive me: Thou shalt stretch forth Thine hand against the wrath of mine enemies, and Thy right hand shall save me.

Psalm 144:1-2

Blessed be the Lord, my Strength, Which teacheth my hands to war, and my fingers to fight:

My Goodness, and my Fortress; my High Tower, and my Deliverer: my Shield, and **He in Whom I trust;** Who subdueth my people under me.

Proverbs 3:5-6

Trust in the Lord with all thine heart; and lean not unto thine own understanding.

In all thy ways acknowledge Him, and He shall direct thy paths.

Lean on, trust in, and be confident in the Lord with all your heart and mind and do not rely on your own insight or understanding.

In all your ways know, recognize, and acknowledge Him, and He will direct and make straight and plain your paths. [AMP]

Proverbs 16:20

He that handleth a matter wisely shall find good: **and whoso trusteth in the Lord, happy is he.**

Proverbs 29:25

The fear of man bringeth a snare: but whoso putteth his trust in the Lord shall be safe.

Proverbs 30:5

Every word of God is pure: He is a shield unto them that put their trust in Him.

Isaiah 12:2

Behold, God is my salvation; **I will trust, and not be afraid:** for the Lord Jehovah is my strength and my song; He also is become my salvation.

Isaiah 26:3-4

Thou wilt keep him in perfect peace, whose mind is stayed on Thee, because he trusteth in Thee.

Trust ye in the Lord for ever: for in the Lord Jehovah is everlasting strength:

Isaiah 41:10

Fear thou not; for I am with thee: be not dismayed; for I am thy God: I will strengthen thee; yea, I will help thee; yea, I will uphold thee with the right hand of My righteousness.

Isaiah 43:2

When thou passest through the waters, I will be with thee; and through the rivers, they shall not overflow thee: when thou walkest through the fire, thou shalt not be burned; neither shall the flame kindle upon thee.

Isaiah 50:10

Who is among you that feareth the Lord, that obeyeth the voice of His servant, that walketh in darkness, and hath no light? **let him trust in the name of the Lord, and stay upon his God.**

Isaiah 54:10

For the mountains shall depart, and the hills be removed; but My kindness shall not depart from thee, neither shall the covenant of My peace be removed, saith the Lord that hath mercy on thee.

Jeremiah 17:7-8

Blessed is the man that trusteth in the Lord, and whose hope the Lord is.

For he shall be as a tree planted by the waters, and that spreadeth out her roots by the river, and shall not see when heat cometh, but her leaf shall be green; and shall not be careful in the year of drought, neither shall cease from yielding fruit.

Nahum 1:7

The Lord is good, a Strong hold in the day of trouble; and **He knoweth them that trust in Him.**

Matthew 6:34

Take therefore no thought for the morrow: for the morrow shall take thought for the things of itself. Sufficient unto the day is the evil thereof.

Matthew 18:4

*Whoever will humble himself therefore and become like this little child [**trusting**, lowly, loving, forgiving] is greatest in the kingdom of heaven. [AMP]*

John 14:1

Let not your heart be troubled: ye believe in God, believe also in Me.

Philippians 4:6-7

Be careful for nothing; but in every thing by prayer and supplication with thanksgiving let your requests be made known unto God.

And the peace of God, which passeth all understanding, shall keep your hearts and minds through Christ Jesus.

Colossians 3:15

And let the peace of God rule in your hearts, to the which also ye are called in one body; and be ye thankful.

I Timothy 4:10

For therefore we both labour and suffer reproach, **because we trust in the living God**, Who is the Saviour of all men, specially of those that believe.

I Timothy 6:17

Charge them that are rich in this world, that they be not highminded, nor **trust** in uncertain riches, **but in the living God,** Who giveth us richly all things to enjoy;

II Timothy 1:12

For the which cause I also suffer these things: nevertheless I am not ashamed: **for I know Whom I have believed, and am persuaded that He is able to keep that which I have committed unto Him against that day.**

I Peter 5:7

Casting all your care upon Him; for He careth for you.

Chapter 26

God's Proven Faithfulness

<u>Genesis 9:14-16</u>

And it shall come to pass, when I bring a cloud over the earth, that the bow shall be seen in the cloud:

And I will remember My covenant, which is between Me and you and every living creature of all flesh; and the waters shall no more become a flood to destroy all flesh.

And the bow shall be in the cloud; and I will look upon it, **that I may remember the everlasting covenant between God and every living creature of all flesh that is upon the earth.**

<u>Genesis 28:15</u>

And, behold, I am with thee, and will keep thee in all places whither thou goest, and will bring thee again into this land; **for I will not leave thee, until I have done that which I have spoken to thee of.**

<u>Numbers 23:19</u>

God is not a man, that He should lie; neither the son of man, that He should repent: hath He said, and shall He not do it? or hath He spoken, and shall He not make it good?

<u>Deuteronomy 7:8-9</u>

But because the Lord loveth you, and because He would keep the oath which He had sworn unto your fathers, hath the Lord brought you out with a mighty hand, and redeemed you out of the house of bondmen, from the hand of Pharaoh king of Egypt.

Know therefore that the Lord thy God, He is God, the faithful God, which keepeth covenant and mercy with them that love Him and keep His commandments to a thousand generations;

<u>Deuteronomy 9:5</u>

Not for thy righteousness, or for the uprightness of thine heart, dost thou go to possess their land: but for the wickedness of these nations the Lord thy God doth drive them out from before thee, and **that He may perform the word which the Lord sware unto thy fathers, Abraham, Isaac, and Jacob.**

Deuteronomy 31:7-8

And Moses called unto Joshua, and said unto him in the sight of all Israel, Be strong and of a good courage: for thou must go with this people unto the land which the Lord hath sworn unto their fathers to give them; and thou shalt cause them to inherit it.

And the Lord, He it is that doth go before thee; He will be with thee, He will not fail thee, neither forsake thee: fear not, neither be dismayed.

Joshua 23:14

And, behold, this day I am going the way of all the earth: and ye know in all your hearts and in all your souls, **that not one thing hath failed of all the good things which the Lord your God spake concerning you;** all are come to pass unto you, and not one thing hath failed thereof.

I Samuel 15:29

And also the Strength of Israel will not lie nor repent: for He is not a man, that He should repent.

I Kings 8:56

Blessed be the Lord, that hath given rest unto His people Israel, according to all that He promised: **there hath not failed one word of all His good promise**, which He promised by the hand of Moses His servant.

Psalm 36:5

Thy mercy, O Lord, is in the heavens; and **Thy faithfulness reacheth unto the clouds.**

Psalm 89:1-2

I will sing of the mercies of the Lord for ever: **with my mouth will I make known Thy faithfulness to all generations.**

For I have said, Mercy shall be built up for ever: **Thy faithfulness shalt Thou establish in the very heavens.**

Psalm 89:33-34

Nevertheless My lovingkindness will I not utterly take from him, **nor suffer My faithfulness to fail.**

My covenant will I not break, nor alter the thing that is gone out of My lips.

Psalm 105:8

He hath remembered His covenant for ever, the word which He commanded to a thousand generations.

Psalm 119:89

For ever, O Lord, Thy word is settled in heaven.

Psalm 119:138

Thy testimonies that Thou hast commanded are righteous and very faithful.

Psalm 119:152

Concerning Thy testimonies, I have known of old that Thou hast founded them for ever.

Psalm 119:160

Thy word is true from the beginning: and every one of Thy righteous judgments endureth for ever.

Psalm 121:3-4

He will not suffer thy foot to be moved: He that keepeth thee will not slumber.
Behold, He that keepeth Israel shall neither slumber nor sleep.

Psalm 138:2

. . . for Thou hast magnified Thy word above all Thy name.

Isaiah 40:8

The grass withereth, the flower fadeth: but the word of our God shall stand for ever.

Isaiah 41:10

Fear thou not; for I am with thee: be not dismayed; for I am thy God: I will strengthen thee; yea, I will help thee; **yea, I will uphold thee with the right hand of My righteousness.**

Isaiah 54:9-10

For this is as the waters of Noah unto Me: for as I have sworn that the waters of Noah should no more go over the earth; **so have I sworn that I would not be wroth with thee, nor rebuke thee**.

For the mountains shall depart, and the hills be removed; **but My kindness shall not depart from thee, neither shall the covenant of My peace be removed, saith the Lord that hath mercy on thee.**

Isaiah 55:11

So shall My word be that goeth forth out of My mouth: it shall not return unto Me void, but it shall accomplish that which I please, and it shall prosper in the thing whereto I sent it.

Jeremiah 1:12

. . . for I will hasten My word to perform it.

Jeremiah 29:10,14

For thus saith the Lord, **That after seventy years be accomplished at Babylon I will visit you, and perform My good word toward you, in causing you to return to this place.**

. . . and **I will turn away your captivity, and I will gather you from all the nations, and from all the places whither I have driven you, saith the Lord; and I will bring you again into the place whence I caused you to be carried away captive.**

Jeremiah 33:20-21

Thus saith the Lord; **If ye can break My covenant of the day, and My covenant of the night, and that there should not be day and night in their season;**

Then may also My covenant be broken with David My servant, that he should not have a son to reign upon his throne; and with the Levites the priests, My ministers.

Lamentations 3:22-23

It is of the Lord's mercies that we are not consumed, because His compassions fail not.

They are new every morning: **great is Thy faithfulness.**

Ezekiel 24:14

I the Lord have spoken it: it shall come to pass, and I will do it; I will not go back, neither will I spare, neither will I repent; . . .

Habakkuk 2:3

For the vision is yet for an appointed time, but at the end it shall speak, and not lie: though it tarry, wait for it; because it will surely come, it will not tarry.

Matthew 24:35

Heaven and earth shall pass away, but My words shall not pass away.

Romans 4:20-21

He staggered not at the promise of God through unbelief; but was strong in faith, giving glory to God;

And being fully persuaded that, **what He had promised, He was able also to perform.**

Romans 11:29

For the gifts and calling of God are without repentance.

Romans 15:8

Now I say that Jesus Christ was a minister of the circumcision for the truth of God, **to confirm the promises made unto the fathers:**

I Corinthians 1:9

God is faithful, by Whom ye were called unto the fellowship of His Son Jesus Christ our Lord.

I Corinthians 10:13

There hath no temptation taken you but such as is common to man: **but God is faithful**, Who will not suffer you to be tempted above that ye are able; but will with the temptation also make a way to escape, that ye may be able to bear it.

II Corinthians 1:20

For all the promises of God in Him are yea, and in Him Amen, unto the glory of God by us.

For as many as are the promises of God, they all find their Yes [answer] in Him [Christ]. For this reason we also utter the Amen (so be it) to God through Him [in His Person and by His agency] to the glory of God. [AMP]

I Thessalonians 5:24

Faithful is He that calleth you, Who also will do it.

II Thessalonians 3:3

But the Lord is faithful, Who shall stablish you, and keep you from evil.

II Timothy 2:11-13

It is a faithful saying: For if we be dead with Him, we shall also live with Him:
If we suffer, we shall also reign with Him: if we deny Him, He also will deny us:
If we believe not, yet He abideth faithful: He cannot deny Himself.

Hebrews 2:17

Wherefore in all things it behoved Him to be made like unto His brethren, **that He might be a merciful and faithful High Priest in things pertaining to God,** to make reconciliation for the sins of the people.

Hebrews 6:18

That by two immutable things, **in which it was impossible for God to lie**, we might have a strong consolation, who have fled for refuge to lay hold upon the hope set before us:

Hebrews 10:23

Let us hold fast the profession of our faith without wavering; **(for He is faithful that promised;)**

James 1:17

Every good gift and every perfect gift is from above, and cometh down from the Father of lights, **with Whom is no variableness, neither shadow of turning.**

I Peter 1:25

But the word of the Lord endureth forever. . . .

I Peter 4:19

Wherefore let them that suffer according to the will of God commit the keeping of their souls to Him in welldoing, **as unto a faithful Creator**.

II Peter 3:9

The Lord is not slack concerning His promise, . . .

Revelations 1:5

And from Jesus Christ, **Who is the faithful Witness**, and the First begotten of the dead, and the Prince of the kings of the earth. Unto Him that loved us, and washed us from our sins in His own blood.

Revelations 19:11

And I saw heaven opened, and behold a white horse; a**nd He that sat upon him was called Faithful and True**, and in righteousness He doth judge and make war.

Chapter 27

Receiving Correction

Job 5:17-18

Behold, happy is the man whom God correcteth: therefore despise not thou the chastening of the Almighty:

For He maketh sore, and bindeth up: He woundeth, and His hands make whole.

Psalm 141:5

Let the righteous man smite and correct me - it is a kindness. Oil so choice let not my head refuse or discourage; . . . [AMP]

Proverbs 3:11-12

My son, **despise not** the chastening of the Lord; **neither be weary** of His correction:

For whom the Lord loveth He correcteth; even as a father the son in whom he delighteth.

Proverbs 9:7-9

He who rebukes a scorner heaps upon himself abuse, and he who reproves a wicked man gets for himself bruises.

Reprove not a scorner, lest he hate you; reprove a wise man, and he will love you.

Give instruction to a wise man and he will be yet wiser; teach a righteous man (one upright and in right standing with God) and he will increase in learning. [AMP]

Proverbs 10:17

He who heeds instruction and correction is [not only himself] in the way of life [but also] is a way of life for others. And he who neglects or refuses reproof [not only himself] goes astray [but also] causes to err and is a path toward ruin for others. [AMP]

Proverbs 12:1

Whoever loves instruction and correction loves knowledge, but he who hates reproof is like a brute beast, stupid and indiscriminating. [AMP]

Proverbs 13:1

A wise son heeds [and is the fruit of] his father's instruction and correction, but a scoffer listens not to rebuke. [AMP]

Proverbs 13:18

Poverty and shame shall be to him that refuseth instruction: but he that regardeth reproof shall be honoured.

Proverbs 13:24

He that spareth his rod hateth his son: but he that loveth him chasteneth him betimes.

Proverbs 15:5

A fool despiseth his father's instruction: but he that regardeth reproof is prudent.

Proverbs 15:10

There is severe discipline for him who forsakes God's way; and ***he who hates reproof will die [physically, morally and spiritually].*** *[AMP]*

Proverbs 15:31-32

The ear that listens to the reproof [that leads to or gives] life will remain among the wise.

He who refuses and ignores instruction and correction despises himself, but he who heeds reproof gets understanding. [AMP]

Proverbs 17:10

A reproof entereth more into a wise man than an hundred stripes into a fool.

Proverbs 19:20

Hear counsel, receive instruction, and accept correction, that you may be wise in the time to come. *[AMP]*

Proverbs 19:25

Strike a scoffer, and the simple will learn prudence; ***reprove a man of understanding, and he will increase in knowledge.*** *[AMP]*

Proverbs 19:27

Cease, my son, to hear instruction only to ignore it and stray from the words of knowledge. [AMP]

Proverbs 21:11

When the scorner is punished, the simple is made wise: and when the wise is instructed, he receiveth knowledge.

Proverbs 23:12 -14

Apply thine heart unto instruction, and thine ears to the words of knowledge.
Withhold not correction from the child: for if thou beatest him with the rod, he shall not die.
Thou shalt beat him with the rod, and shalt deliver his soul from hell.

Proverbs 25:12

As an earring of gold, and an ornament of fine gold, so is a wise reprover upon an obedient ear.

Proverbs 27:5

Open rebuke is better than secret love.

Proverbs 28:9

He who turns away his ear from hearing the law [of God and man], even his prayer is an abomination, hateful and revolting [to God]. [AMP]

Proverbs 28:23

He that rebuketh a man afterwards shall find more favour than he that flattereth with the tongue.

Proverbs 29:1

He, that being often reproved hardeneth his neck, shall suddenly be destroyed, and that without remedy.

Ecclesiastes 7:5

It is better to hear the rebuke of the wise, than for a man to hear the song of fools.

Zephaniah 3:7

I said, Surely thou wilt fear Me, **thou wilt receive instruction**; so their dwelling should not be cut off, . . .

John 15:1-3

I am the True Vine, and My Father is the husbandman.
Every branch in Me that beareth not fruit He taketh away: **and every branch that beareth fruit, He purgeth it, that it may bring forth more fruit.**
Now ye are clean through the word which I have spoken unto you.

Titus 2:9

Exhort servants to be obedient unto their own masters, and to please them well in all things; **not answering again;**

Hebrews 12:5-11

And ye have forgotten the exhortation which speaketh unto you as unto children, **My son, despise not thou the chastening of the Lord, nor faint when thou art rebuked of Him:**
For whom the Lord loveth He chasteneth, and scourgeth every son whom He receiveth.

If ye endure chastening, God dealeth with you as with sons; for what son is he whom the father chasteneth not?

But if ye be without chastisement, whereof all are partakers, then are ye bastards, and not sons.

Furthermore we have had fathers of our flesh which corrected us, and we gave them reverence: shall we not much rather be in subjection unto the Father of spirits, and live?

For they verily for a few days chastened us after their own pleasure; but He for our profit, that we might be partakers of His holiness.

Now no chastening for the present seemeth to be joyous, but grievous: nevertheless afterward it yieldeth the peaceable fruit of righteousness unto them which are exercised thereby.

James 3:17

But the wisdom that is from above is first pure, then peaceable, gentle, and **easy to be intreated**, full of mercy and good fruits, without partiality, and without hypocrisy.

James 5:19-20

[My] brethren, if anyone among you strays from the Truth and falls into error and another [person] brings him back [to God],

Let the [latter] one be sure that whoever turns a sinner from his evil course will save [that one's] soul from death and will cover a multitude of sins [procure the pardon of the many sins committed by the convert]. *[AMP]*

Chapter 28

Repentance

<u>Job 13:23</u>

How many are mine iniquities and sins? make me to know my transgression and my sin.

<u>Psalm 34:18</u>

The Lord is nigh unto them that are of a broken heart; and saveth such as be of a contrite spirit.

<u>Psalm 38:18</u>

For I will declare mine iniquity; I will be sorry for my sin.

<u>Psalm 51:1-12</u>

Have mercy upon me, O God, according to Thy lovingkindness: according unto the multitude of Thy tender mercies blot out my transgressions.

Wash me throughly from mine iniquity, and cleanse me from my sin.

For I acknowledge my transgressions: and my sin is ever before me.

Against Thee, Thee only, have I sinned, and done this evil in Thy sight: that Thou mightest be justified when Thou speakest, and be clear when Thou judgest.

Behold, I was shapen in iniquity; and in sin did my mother conceive me.

Behold, Thou desirest truth in the inward parts: and in the hidden part Thou shalt make me to know wisdom.

Purge me with hyssop, and I shall be clean: wash me, and I shall be whiter than snow.

Make me to hear joy and gladness; that the bones which Thou hast broken may rejoice.

Hide Thy face from my sins, and blot out all mine iniquities.

Create in me a clean heart, O God; and renew a right spirit within me.

Cast me not away from Thy presence; and take not Thy Holy Spirit from me.

Restore unto me the joy of Thy salvation; and uphold Me with Thy free Spirit.

Psalm 51:16-17

For Thou desirest not sacrifice; else would I give it: Thou delightest not in burnt offering.

The sacrifices of God are a broken spirit: a broken and a contrite heart, O God, Thou wilt not despise.

Psalm 78:34-35

When He slew them, **then they sought Him: and they returned and enquired early after God.**

And they remembered that God was their Rock, and the High God their Redeemer.

Psalm 86:5

For Thou, Lord, art good, and ready to forgive; and plenteous in mercy unto all them that call upon Thee.

Psalm 130:3-4

If Thou, Lord, shouldest mark iniquities, O Lord, who shall stand?

But there is forgiveness with Thee, that Thou mayest be feared.

Proverbs 28:13

He that covereth his sins shall not prosper: but whoso confesseth and forsaketh them shall have mercy.

Ecclesiastes 7:3

Sorrow is better than laughter: **for by the sadness of the countenance the heart is made better.**

Isaiah 66:2

. . . but to this man will I look, **even to him that is poor and of a contrite spirit,** and trembleth at My word.

Jeremiah 4:4

Circumcise yourselves to the Lord, and take away the foreskins of your heart, ye men of Judah and inhabitants of Jerusalem: lest My fury come forth like fire, and burn that none can quench it, because of the evil of your doings.

Jeremiah 7:3

Thus saith the Lord of hosts, the God of Israel, **Amend your ways and your doings,** and I will cause you to dwell in this place.

Jeremiah 17:9-10

The heart is deceitful above all things, and desperately wicked: who can know it?

I the Lord search the heart, I try the reins, even to give every man according to his ways, and according to the fruit of his doings.

Jeremiah 35:15

I have sent also unto you all My servants the prophets, rising up early and sending them, saying, **Return ye now every man from his evil way, and amend your doings, and go not after other gods to serve them,** and ye shall dwell in the land which I have given to you and to your fathers: . . .

Lamentations 1:20

Behold, O Lord; for I am in distress: my bowels are troubled; **mine heart is turned within me; for I have grievously rebelled:** abroad the sword bereaveth, at home there is as death.

Lamentations 3:40-41

Let us search and try our ways, and turn again to the Lord.

Let us lift up our heart with our hands unto God in the heavens.

Ezekiel 33:11

. . . As I live, saith the Lord God, **I have no pleasure in the death of the wicked; but that the wicked turn from his way and live:** turn ye, turn ye from your evil ways; for why will ye die, O house of Israel?

Ezekiel 33:14-16

Again, when I say unto the wicked, Thou shalt surely die; if he turn from his sin, and do that which is lawful and right;

If the wicked restore the pledge, give again that he had robbed, walk in the statutes of life, without committing iniquity; he shall surely live, he shall not die.

None of his sins that he hath committed shall be mentioned unto him: he hath done that which is lawful and right; he shall surely live.

Hosea 2:6-7

Therefore, behold, I will hedge up thy way with thorns, and make a wall, that she shall not find her paths.

And she shall follow after her lovers, but she shall not overtake them; and she shall seek them, but shall not find them: **then shall she say, I will go and return to my first husband** *(The Lord God)*; **for then was it better with me than now.**

Hosea 10:12

Sow to yourselves in righteousness, reap in mercy; break up your fallow ground: for it is time to seek the Lord, till He come and rain righteousness upon you.

Joel 2:12-13

Therefore also now, saith the Lord, turn ye even to Me with all your heart, and with fasting, and with weeping, and with mourning:

And rend your heart, and not your garments, and turn unto the Lord your God: for He is gracious and merciful, slow to anger, and of great kindness, and repenteth Him of the evil.

Amos 5:14

Seek good, and not evil, that ye may live: and so the Lord, the God of hosts, shall be with you, as ye have spoken.

Jonah 2:8

They that observe lying vanities forsake their own mercy.

Haggai 1:5-7,9

Now therefore thus saith the Lord of hosts; **Consider your ways.**

Ye have sown much, and bring in little; ye eat, but ye have not enough; ye drink, but ye are not filled with drink; ye clothe you, but there is none warm; and he that earneth wages earneth wages to put it into a bag with holes.

Thus saith the Lord of hosts; **Consider your ways**.

Ye looked for much, and, low, it came to little; and when ye brought it home, I did blow upon it. Why? saith the Lord of hosts. **Because of Mine house that is waste, and ye run every man unto his own house.**

Malachi 1:6

A son honoureth his father, and a servant his master: if then I be a Father, where is Mine honour? and if I be a Master, where is My fear? . . .

Matthew 5:4

Blessed are they that mourn: for they shall be comforted.

Matthew 23:25-28

Woe unto you, scribes and Pharisees, hypocrites! for ye make clean the outside of the cup and of the platter, but within they are full of extortion and excess.

Thou blind Pharisee, cleanse first that which is within the cup and platter, that the outside of them may be clean also.

Woe unto you, scribes and Pharisees, hypocrites! for ye are like unto whited sepulchres, which indeed appear beautiful outward, but are within full of dead men's bones, and of all uncleanness.

Even so ye also outwardly appear righteous unto men, but within ye are full of hypocrisy and iniquity.

Mark 2:17

. . . They that are whole have no need of the physician, but they that are sick: **I came not to call the righteous, but sinners to repentance.**

Luke 6:46

And why call ye Me, Lord, Lord, and do not the things which I say?

Luke 15:4-7

What man of you, having an hundred sheep, if he lose one of them, doth not leave the ninety and nine in the wilderness, and go after that which is lost, until he find it?

And when he hath found it, he layeth it on his shoulders, rejoicing.

And when he cometh home, he calleth together his friends and neighbours, saying unto them, Rejoice with me; for I have found my sheep which was lost.

I say unto you, that likewise joy shall be in heaven over one sinner that repenteth, more than over ninety and nine just persons, which need no repentance.

Luke 18:13-14

And the publican, standing afar off, would not lift up so much as his eyes unto heaven, but smote upon his breast, saying, **God be merciful to me a sinner.**

I tell you, this man went down to his house justified rather than the other: for every one that exalteth himself shall be abased; and he that humbleth himself shall be exalted.

Acts 2:37

Now when they heard this, **they were pricked in their heart,** and said unto Peter and to the rest of the apostles, Men and brethren, what shall we do?

Acts 3:19

Repent ye therefore, and be converted, that your sins may be blotted out, when the times of refreshing shall come from the presence of the Lord;

Romans 2:4

Or despisest thou the riches of His goodness and forbearance and longsuffering; **not knowing that the goodness of God leadeth thee to repentance?**

Romans 14:10-13

But why dost thou judge thy brother? or why dost thou set at nought thy brother? **for we shall all stand before the judgment seat of Christ.**

For it is written, As I live, saith the Lord, every knee shall bow to Me, and every tongue shall confess to God.

So then every one of us shall give account of himself to God.

Let us not therefore judge one another any more: but judge this rather, that no man put a stumblingblock or an occasion to fall in his brother's way.

II Corinthians 5:10-11

For we must all appear before the judgment seat of Christ; that every one may receive the things done in his body, according to that he hath done, whether it be good or bad.

Knowing therefore the terror of the Lord, we persuade men; . . .

II Corinthians 5:20

. . . we pray you in Christ's stead, **be ye reconciled to God.**

II Corinthians 7:1

Having therefore these promises, dearly beloved, **let us cleanse ourselves from all filthiness of the flesh and spirit, perfecting holiness in the fear of God.**

II Corinthians 7:9-10

Now I rejoice, not that ye were made sorry, but that ye sorrowed to repentance: for ye were made sorry after a godly manner, that ye might receive damage by us in nothing.

For godly sorrow worketh repentance to salvation not to be repented of: but the sorrow of the world worketh death.

Philippians 3:13-15

Brethren, I count not myself to have apprehended: but this one thing I do, **forgetting those things which are behind, and reaching forth unto those things which are before,**

I press toward the mark for the prize of the high calling of God in Christ Jesus.

Let us therefore, as many as be perfect, be thus minded: **and if in any thing ye be otherwise minded, God shall reveal even this unto you.**

Hebrews 10:30-31

For we know Him that hath said, Vengeance belongeth unto Me, I will recompense, saith the Lord. And again, The Lord shall judge His people.

It is a fearful thing to fall into the hands of the living God.

Hebrews 10:38-39

Now the just shall live by faith: **but if any man draw back, My soul shall have no pleasure in him.**

But we are not of them who draw back unto perdition; but of them that believe to the saving of the soul.

James 4:6-10

. . . God sets Himself against the proud and haughty, but gives grace [continually] to the lowly (those who are humble enough to receive it).

So be subject to God. Resist the devil [stand firm against him], and he will flee from you.

Come close to God and He will come close to you. [Recognize that you are] sinners, get your soiled hands clean; [realize that you have been disloyal] wavering individuals with divided interests, and purify your hearts [of your spiritual adultery].

[As you draw near to God] be deeply penitent and grieve, even weep [over your disloyalty]. Let your laughter be turned to grief and your mirth to dejection and heartfelt shame [for your sins].

Humble yourselves [feeling very insignificant] in the presence of the Lord, and He will exalt you [He will lift you up and make your lives significant]. [AMP]

James 5:16

Confess to one another therefore your faults (your slips, your false steps, your offenses, your sins) and pray [also] for one another, that you may be healed and restored [to a spiritual tone of mind and heart]. The earnest (heartfelt, continued) prayer of a righteous man makes tremendous power available [dynamic in its working]. [AMP]

II Peter 3:9

The Lord is not slack concerning His promise, as some men count slackness; but is longsuffering to us-ward, **not willing that any should perish, but that all should come to repentance.**

I John 1:8-9

If we say that we have no sin, we deceive ourselves, and the truth is not in us.

If we confess our sins, He is faithful and just to forgive us our sins, and to cleanse us from all unrighteousness.

Jude 22-23

And of some have compassion, making a difference:

And others save with fear, pulling them out of the fire; hating even the garment spotted by the flesh.

Revelation 2:4-5

Nevertheless I have somewhat against thee, because thou hast left thy first love.

Remember therefore from whence thou art fallen, and repent, and do the first works; or else I will come unto thee quickly, and will remove thy candlestick out of his place, except thou repent.

Revelation 2:23

. . . I am He which searcheth the reins and hearts: and I will give unto every one of you according to your works.

Revelation 3:1-3

. . . I know thy works, that thou hast a name that thou livest, and art dead.

Be watchful, and strengthen the things which remain, that are ready to die: for I have not found thy works perfect before God.

Remember therefore how thou hast received and heard, and hold fast, and repent. If therefore thou shalt not watch, I will come on thee as a thief, and thou shalt not know what hour I will come upon thee.

Revelation 3:15-20

I know thy works, that thou art neither cold nor hot: I would thou wert cold or hot.

So then because thou art lukewarm, and neither cold nor hot, I will spue thee out of My mouth.

Because thou sayest, I am rich, and increased with goods, and have need of nothing; and knowest not that thou art wretched, and miserable, and poor, and blind, and naked:

I counsel thee to buy of Me gold tried in the fire, that thou mayest be rich; and white raiment, that thou mayest be clothed, and that the shame of thy nakedness do not appear; and anoint thine eyes with eye-salve, that thou mayest see.

As many as I love, I rebuke and chasten: be zealous therefore, and repent.

Behold, I stand at the door, and knock: if any man hear My voice, and open the door, I will come in to him, and will sup with him, and he with Me.

Chapter 29

Victory Over Sins of the Flesh

A. General References to Overcoming our Flesh

<u>Numbers 15:39</u>
. . . Remember all the commands of the Lord, that you may observe them and not prostitute yourselves by going after the lusts of your own hearts and eyes. [NIV]

<u>Psalm 119:133</u>
Order my steps in Thy word: and let not any iniquity have dominion over me.

<u>Proverbs 25:28</u>
He that hath no rule over his own spirit is like a city that is broken down, and without walls.

<u>Matthew 26:41</u>
Watch and pray, that ye enter not into temptation: the spirit indeed is willing, but the flesh is weak.

<u>Luke 21:34</u>
But take heed to yourselves and be on your guard, lest your hearts be overburdened and depressed (weighed down) with the giddiness and headache and nausea of self-indulgence, drunkenness, and worldly worries and cares pertaining to [the business of] this life, and [lest] that day come upon you suddenly like a trap or a noose; [AMP]

<u>John 8:31-36</u>
Then said Jesus to those Jews which believed on Him, **If ye continue in My word, then are ye My disciples indeed;**
And ye shall know the truth, and the truth shall make you free.

They answered Him, We be Abraham's seed, and were never in bondage to any man: how sayest Thou, Ye shall be made free?

Jesus answered them, Verily, verily, I say unto you, **Whosoever committeth sin is the servant of sin.**

And the servant abideth not in the house for ever: but the Son abideth ever.

If the Son therefore shall make you free, ye shall be free indeed.

Romans 1:21-22,24

Because that, when they knew God, **they glorified Him not as God, neither were thankful**; but became vain in their imaginations, and their foolish heart was darkened.

Professing themselves to be wise, they became fools.

Wherefore God also gave them up to uncleanness through the lusts of their own hearts, to dishonor their own bodies between themselves:

Romans 6:11-16

Likewise reckon ye also yourselves to be dead indeed unto sin, but alive unto God, through Jesus Christ our Lord.

Let not sin therefore reign in your mortal body, that ye should obey it in the lusts thereof.

Neither yield ye your members as instruments of unrighteousness unto sin: but yield yourselves unto God, as those that are alive from the dead, and your members as instruments of righteousness unto God.

For sin shall not have dominion over you: for ye are not under the law, but under grace.

What then? shall we sin, because we are not under the law, but under grace? God forbid.

Know ye not, that to whom ye yield yourselves servants to obey, his servants ye are to whom ye obey; whether of sin unto death, or of obedience unto righteousness?

Romans 8:5-8

For they that are after the flesh do mind the things of the flesh; but they that are after the Spirit the things of the Spirit.

For to be carnally minded is death; but to be spiritually minded is life and peace.

Because the carnal mind is enmity against God: for it is not subject to the law of God, neither indeed can be.

So then they that are in the flesh cannot please God.

Romans 8:12-13

Therefore, brethren, we are debtors, not to the flesh, to live after the flesh.

For if ye live after the flesh, ye shall die: but if ye through the Spirit do mortify the deeds of the body, ye shall live.

So then, brethren, we are debtors, but not to the flesh [we are not obligated to our carnal nature], to live [a life ruled by the standards set up by the dictates] of the flesh.

For if you live according to [the dictates of] the flesh, you will surely die. But if through the power of the [Holy] Spirit you are [habitually] putting to death (making extinct, deadening) the [evil] deeds prompted by the body, you shall [really and genuinely] live forever. [AMP]

Romans 12:1-2

I beseech you therefore, brethren, by the mercies of God, **that ye present your bodies a living sacrifice,** holy, acceptable unto God, which is your reasonable service.

And be not conformed to this world: but be ye transformed by the renewing of your mind, that ye may prove what is that good, and acceptable, and perfect, will of God.

Romans 13:14

But put ye on the Lord Jesus Christ, and make not provision for the flesh, to fulfill the lusts thereof.

But clothe yourself with the Lord Jesus Christ (the Messiah) and make no provision for [indulging] the flesh [put a stop to thinking about the evil cravings of your physical nature] to [gratify its] desires (lusts). [AMP]

I Corinthians 6:19-20

What? know ye not that your body is the temple of the Holy Ghost which is in you, which ye have of God, and ye are not your own?

For ye are bought with a price: therefore glorify God in your body, and in your spirit, which are God's.

I Corinthians 9:27

But I keep under my body, and bring it into subjection: lest that by any means, when I have preached to others, I myself should be a castaway.

But [like a boxer] I buffet my body [handle it roughly, discipline it by hardships] and subdue it, for fear that after proclaiming to others the Gospel and things pertaining to it, I myself should become unfit [not stand the test, be unapproved and rejected as a counterfeit]. [AMP]

I Corinthians 10:13

There hath no temptation taken you but such as is common to man: but God is faithful, Who will not suffer you to be tempted above that ye are able; but will with the temptation also make a way to escape, that ye may be able to bear it.

Galatians 2:20

I am crucified with Christ: nevertheless I live; yet not I, but Christ liveth in me: and the life which I now live in the flesh I live by the faith of the Son of God, Who loved me, and gave Himself for me.

Galatians 5:16-17

This I say then, **Walk in the Spirit, and ye shall not fulfil the lust of the flesh.**

For the flesh lusteth against the Spirit, and the Spirit against the flesh: and these are contrary the one to the other: so that ye cannot do the things that ye would.

But I say, walk and live [habitually] in the [Holy] Spirit [responsive to and controlled and guided by the Spirit]; then you will certainly not gratify the cravings and desires of the flesh (of human nature without God).

For the desires of the flesh are opposed to the [Holy] Spirit, and the [desires of the] Spirit are opposed to the flesh (godless human nature); for these are antagonistic to each other [continually withstanding and in conflict with each other], so that you are not free but are prevented from doing what you desire to do. [AMP]

<u>Galatians 5:19-21</u>

Now the works of the flesh are manifest, which are these; Adultery, fornication, uncleanness, lasciviousness,

Idolatry, witchcraft, hatred, variance, emulations, wrath, strife, seditions, heresies,

Envyings, murders, drunkenness, revellings, and such like: **of the which I tell you before, as I have also told you in time past, that they which do such things shall not inherit the kingdom of God.**

<u>Galatians 5:24</u>

And they that are Christ's have crucified the flesh with the affections and lusts.

And those who belong to Christ Jesus (the Messiah) have crucified the flesh (the godless human nature) with its passions and appetites and desires. [AMP]

<u>Galatians 6:7-8</u>

Be not deceived; God is not mocked: **for whatsoever a man soweth, that shall he also reap.**

For he that soweth to his flesh shall of the flesh reap corruption; but he that soweth to the Spirit shall of the Spirit reap life everlasting.

Do not be deceived and deluded and misled; God will not allow Himself to be sneered at (scorned, disdained, or mocked by mere pretensions or professions, or by His precepts being set aside). [He inevitably deludes himself who attempts to delude God.] ***For whatever a man sows, that and that only is what he will reap.***

For he who sows to his own flesh (lower nature, sensuality) will from the flesh reap decay and ruin and destruction, but he who sows to the Spirit will from the Spirit reap eternal life. [AMP]

<u>Ephesians 5:3-8</u>

But fornication, and all uncleanness, or covetousness, **let it not be once named among you,** as becometh saints;

Neither filthiness, nor foolish talking, nor jesting, which are not convenient: but rather giving of thanks.

For this ye know, that no whoremonger, nor unclean person, nor covetous man, who is an idolater, hath any inheritance in the kingdom of Christ and of God.

Let no man deceive you with vain words: for because of these things cometh the wrath of God upon the children of disobedience.

Be not ye therefore partakers with them.

For ye were sometimes darkness, but now are ye light in the Lord: walk as children of light:

But immorality (sexual vice) and all impurity [of lustful, rich, wasteful living] or greediness must not even be named among you, as is fitting and proper among saints (God's consecrated people).

Let there be no filthiness (obscenity, indecency) nor foolish and sinful (silly and corrupt) talk, nor coarse jesting, which are not fitting or becoming; but instead voice your thankfulness [to God].

For be sure of this: that no person practicing sexual vice or impurity in thought or in life, or one who is covetous [who has lustful desire for the property of others and is greedy for gain] - for he [in effect] is an idolater - has any inheritance in the kingdom of Christ and of God.

Let no one delude and deceive you with empty excuses and groundless arguments [for these sins], for through these things the wrath of God comes upon the sons of rebellion and disobedience.

So do not associate or be sharers with them.

For once you were darkness, but now you are light in the Lord; walk as children of Light [lead the lives of those native-born to the Light]. [AMP]

<u>Philippians 4:8</u>

Finally, brethren, whatsoever things are **true**, whatsoever things are **honest**, whatsoever things are **just**, whatsoever things are **pure**, whatsoever things are **lovely**, whatsoever things are **of good report;** if there be **any virtue**, and if there be **any praise**, think on these things.

<u>Colossians 3:2</u>

Set your affection on things above, not on things on the earth.

<u>Colossians 3:5-6</u>

Mortify therefore your members which are upon the earth; fornication, uncleanness, inordinate affection, evil concupiscence, and covetousness, which is idolatry:

For which things' sake the wrath of God cometh on the children of disobedience:

So kill (deaden, deprive of power) the evil desire lurking in your members [those animal impulses and all that is earthly in you that is employed in sin]; *sexual vice, impurity, sensual appetites, unholy desires, and all greed and covetousness, for that is idolatry (the deifying of self and other created things instead of God).*

It is on account of these [very sins] that the [holy] anger of God is ever coming upon the sons of disobedience (those who are obstinately opposed to the divine will), [AMP]

<u>Colossians 3:9-10</u>

Lie not one to another, **seeing that ye have put off the old man with his deeds.**

And have put on the new man, which is renewed in knowledge after the image of Him that created him:

Hebrews 2:18

For because He Himself [in His humanity] has suffered in being tempted (tested and tried), He is able [immediately] to run to the cry of (assist, relieve) those who are being tempted and tested and tried [and who therefore are being exposed to suffering]. [AMP]

Hebrews 4:15

For we have not an High Priest which cannot be touched with the feeling of our infirmities; but was in all points tempted like as we are, yet without sin.

James 1:12-15

Blessed is the man that endureth temptation: for when he is tried, he shall receive the crown of life, which the Lord hath promised to them that love him.

Let no man say when he is tempted, I am tempted of God: for God cannot be tempted with evil, neither tempted he any man:

But every man is tempted, when he is drawn away of his own lust, and enticed.

Then when **lust** hath conceived, it bringeth forth **sin**: and sin, when it is finished, bringeth forth **death**.

James 4:4

Ye adulterers and adulteresses, know ye not that the friendship of the world is enmity with God? **whosoever therefore will be a friend of the world is the enemy of God.**

I Peter 1:15-16

But as He which hath called you is holy, so be ye holy in all manner of conversation;
Because it is written, Be ye holy; for I am holy.

I Peter 2:11

Dearly beloved, I beseech you as strangers and pilgrims, **abstain from fleshly lusts, which war against the soul;**

Beloved, I implore you as aliens and strangers and exiles [in this world] ***to abstain from the sensual urges (the evil desires, the passions of the flesh, your lower nature) that wage war against the soul.*** *[AMP]*

I Peter 4:1-2

Forasmuch then as Christ hath suffered for us in the flesh, arm yourselves likewise with the same mind: **for he that hath suffered in the flesh hath ceased from sin;**

That he no longer should live the rest of his time in the flesh to the lusts of men, but to the will of God.

II Peter 2:9

The Lord knoweth how to deliver the godly out of temptations, . . .

II Peter 2:19

While they promise them liberty, they themselves are the servants of corruption: **for of**

whom a man is overcome, of the same is he brought in bondage.

I John 2:15-17

Love not the world, neither the things that are in the world. If any man love the world, the love of the Father is not in him.

For all that is in the world, the **lust of the flesh**, and the **lust of the eyes**, and the **pride of life**, is not of the Father, but is of the world.

And the world passeth away, and the lust thereof: but he that doeth the will of God abideth for ever.

I John 2:28-29

And now, little children, abide in Him; that, when He shall appear, we may have confidence, and not be ashamed before Him at His coming.

If ye know that He is righteous, **ye know that every one that doeth righteousness is born of Him.**

I John 3:3

And every man that hath this hope in Him purifieth himself, even as He is pure.

B. Overcoming Adultery & Fornication

Exodus 20:14

Thou shalt not commit adultery.

Exodus 20:17

. . . thou shalt not covet thy neighbour's wife . . .

Leviticus 20:10

The man who commits adultery with another's wife, even his neighbor's wife, the adulterer and the adulteress shall surely be put to death. [AMP]

Proverbs 5:15-23

Drink waters out of thine own cistern, and running waters out of thine own well.

Let thy fountains be dispersed abroad, and rivers of waters in the streets.

Let them be only thine own, and not strangers' with thee.

Let thy fountain be blessed: and rejoice with the wife of thy youth.

Let her be as the loving hind and pleasant roe; let her breasts satisfy thee at all times; and be thou ravished always with her love.

And why wilt thou, my son, be ravished with a strange woman, and embrace the bosom of a stranger?

For the ways of man are before the eyes of the Lord, and He pondereth all his goings.

His own iniquities shall take the wicked himself, **and he shall be holden with the cords of his sins.**

He shall die without instruction; and in the greatness of his folly he shall go astray.

Proverbs 6:23-29

For the commandment is a lamp; and the law is light; and reproofs of instruction are the way of life:

To keep thee from the evil woman, from the flattery of the tongue of a strange woman.

Lust not after her beauty in thine heart; neither let her take thee with her eyelids.

For by means of a whorish woman a man is brought to a piece of bread: and the adulteress will hunt for the precious life.

Can a man take fire in his bosom, and his clothes not be burned?

Can one go upon hot coals, and his feet not be burned?

So he that goeth in to his neighbour's wife; whosoever toucheth her shall not be innocent.

Proverbs 6:32-35

But whoso committeth adultery with a woman lacketh understanding: he that doeth it destroyeth his own soul.

A wound and dishonour shall he get; and his reproach shall not be wiped away.

For jealousy is the rage of a man: therefore he will not spare in the day of vengeance.

He will not regard any ransom; neither will he rest content, though thou givest many gifts.

Proverbs 7:6-23

For at the window of my house I looked through my casement,

And beheld among the simple ones, **I discerned among the youths, a young man void of understanding,**

Passing through the street near her corner; and he went the way to her house,

In the **twilight,** in the **evening**, in the **black and dark night:**

And, behold, **there met him a woman with the attire of an harlot, and subtil of heart.**

(She is loud and stubborn; her feet abide not in her house:

Now is she without, now in the streets, and lieth in wait at every corner.)

So she caught him, and kissed him, and with an impudent face said unto him,

I have peace offerings with me; this day have I payed my vows.

Therefore came I forth to meet thee, diligently to seek thy face, and I have found thee.

I have decked my bed with coverings of tapestry, with carved works, with fine linen of Egypt.

I have perfumed my bed with myrrh, aloes, and cinnamon.

Come, let us take our fill of love until the morning: let us solace ourselves with loves.

For the goodman is not at home, he is gone a long journey:

He hath taken a bag of money with him, and will come home at the day appointed.

With her much fair speech she caused him to yield, with the flattering of her lips she forced him.

He goeth after her straightway, as an ox goeth to the slaughter, or as a fool to the correction of the stocks;

Till a dart strike through his liver; as a bird hasteth to the snare, and knoweth not that it is for his life.

<u>**Proverbs 7:24-27**</u>

Hearken unto me now therefore, O ye children, and attend to the words of my mouth.

Let not thine heart decline to her ways, go not astray in her paths.

For she hath cast down many wounded: yea, many strong men have been slain by her.

Her house is the way to hell, going down to the chambers of death.

<u>**Jeremiah 5:7-9**</u>

How shall I pardon thee for this? thy children have forsaken Me, and sworn by them that are no gods: **when I had fed them to the full, they then committed adultery, and assembled themselves by troops in the harlots' houses.**

They were as fed horses in the morning: every one neighed after his neighbour's wife.

Shall I not visit for these things? saith the Lord: and shall not My soul be avenged on such a nation as this?

<u>**Hosea 4:10-11**</u>

For they shall eat and not have enough; ***they shall play the harlot and beget no increase, because they have forsaken the Lord for harlotry:***

Harlotry and wine and new wine take away the heart and the mind and the spiritual understanding. [AMP]

<u>**Matthew 5:27-30**</u>

Ye have heard that it was said by them of old time, **Thou shalt not commit adultery**:

But I say unto you, **That whosoever looketh on a woman to lust after her hath committed adultery with her already in his heart.**

And if thy right eye offend thee, pluck it out, and cast it from thee: for it is profitable for thee that one of thy members should perish, and not that thy whole body should be cast into hell.

And if thy right hand offend thee, cut it off, and cast it from thee: for it is profitable for thee that one of thy members should perish, and not that thy whole body should be cast into hell.

<u>**John 8:3-5,7,10-11**</u>

And the scribes and Pharisees brought unto Him a woman taken in adultery; and when they had set her in the midst,

They say unto Him, **Master, this woman was taken in adultery, in the very act.**

Now Moses in the law commanded us, that such should be stoned: but what sayest Thou?

So when they continued asking Him, He lifted up Himself, and said unto them, **He that is without sin among you, let him first cast a stone at her.**

When Jesus had lifted up Himself, and saw none but the woman, He said unto her, Woman, where are those thine accusers? hath no man condemned thee?

She said, No man, Lord. And Jesus said unto her, **Neither do I condemn thee: go, and sin no more.**

<u>**Romans 1:24-25**</u>

Wherefore God also gave them up to uncleanness through the lusts of their own hearts, to dishonour their own bodies between themselves:

Who changed the truth of God into a lie, and worshipped and served the creature more than the Creator, Who is blessed for ever. Amen.

<u>**I Corinthians 6:9-10**</u>

Know ye not that the unrighteous shall not inherit the kingdom of God? Be not deceived: neither **fornicators**, nor idolaters, nor **adulterers**, nor effeminate, nor abusers of themselves with mankind,

Nor thieves, nor covetous, nor drunkards, nor revilers, nor extortioners, shall inherit the kingdom of God.

<u>**I Corinthians 6:13**</u>

. . . **Now the body is not for fornication, but for the Lord;** and the Lord for the body.

<u>**I Corinthians 6:15-20**</u>

Know ye not that your bodies are the members of Christ? shall I then take the members of Christ, and make them the members of an harlot? God forbid.

What? know ye not that he which is joined to an harlot is one body? for two, saith He, shall be one flesh.

But he that is joined unto the Lord is one spirit.

Flee fornication. Every sin that a man doeth is without the body; **but he that committeth fornication sinneth against his own body.**

What? know ye not that your body is the temple of the Holy Ghost which is in you, which ye have of God, and **ye are not your own?**

For ye are bought with a price: therefore glorify God in your body, and in your spirit, which are God's.

<u>**I Corinthians 6:18-20**</u>

Shun immorality and all sexual looseness [flee from impurity in thought, word, or deed]. *Any other sin which a man commits is one outside the body,* ***but he who commits sexual immorality sins against his own body.***

Do you not know that your body is the temple (the very sanctuary) of the Holy Spirit Who lives within you, Whom you have received [as a Gift] from God? ***You are not your own,***

You were bought with a price [purchased with a preciousness and paid for, made His own]. So then, honor God and bring glory to Him in your body. *[AMP]*

<u>**I Corinthians 7:1-2**</u>

. . . It is good for a man not to touch a woman.

Nevertheless, **to avoid fornication,** let every man have his own wife, and let every woman have her own husband.

<u>**Galatians 5:19-21**</u>

Now the works of the flesh are manifest, which are these; **Adultery, fornication**, uncleanness, lasciviousness,

Idolatry, witchcraft, hatred, variance, emulations, wrath, strife, seditions, heresies,

Envyings, murders, drunkenness, revellings, and such like: **of the which I tell you before, as I have also told you in time past, that they which do such things shall not inherit the kingdom of God.**

Ephesians 5:3-5

But **fornication**, and all uncleanness, or covetousness, **let it not be once named among you, as becometh saints;**

Neither filthiness, nor foolish talking, nor jesting, which are not convenient: but rather giving of thanks.

For this ye know, that **no whoremonger,** nor unclean person, nor covetous man, who is an idolater, **hath any inheritance in the kingdom of Christ and of God**.

*But **immorality (sexual vice)** and all impurity [of lustful, rich, wasteful living] or greediness must not even be named among you, as is fitting and proper among saints (God's consecrated people).*

Let there be no filthiness (obscenity, indecency) nor foolish and sinful (silly and corrupt) talk, nor coarse jesting, which are not fitting or becoming; but instead voice your thankfulness [to God].

*For be sure of this: **that no person practicing sexual vice or impurity in thought or in life,** or one who is covetous [who has lustful desire for the property of others and is greedy for gain] – for he [in effect] is an idolater – **has any inheritance in the kingdom of Christ and of God.** [AMP]*

Colossians 3:5-6

Mortify therefore your members which are upon the earth; **fornication,** uncleanness, inordinate affection, evil concupiscence, and covetousness, which is idolatry:

For which things' sake the wrath of God cometh on the children of disobedience:

*So kill (deaden, deprive of power) the evil desire lurking in your members [those animal impulses and all that is earthly in you that is employed in sin]; **sexual vice, impurity, sensual appetites,** unholy desires, and all greed and covetousness, for that is idolatry (the deifying of self and other created things instead of God).*

It is on account of these [very sins] that the [holy] anger of God is ever coming upon the sons of disobedience (those who are obstinately opposed to the divine will), [AMP]

I Thessalonians 4:3-7

For this is the will of God, even your sanctification, **that ye should abstain from fornication**:

That every one of you should know how to possess his vessel in sanctification and honour;

Not in the lust of concupiscence, even as the Gentiles which know not God:

That no man go beyond and defraud his brother in any matter: because that the Lord is the avenger of all such, as we also have forewarned you and testified.

For God hath not called us unto uncleanness, but unto holiness.

*For this is the will of God, that you should be consecrated (separated and set apart for pure and holy living): **that you should abstain and shrink from all sexual vice,***

That each one of you should know how to possess (control, manage) his own body in consecration (purity, separated from things profane) and honor,

***Not [to be used] in the passion of lust like the heathen,** who are ignorant of the true God and have no knowledge of His will,*

***That no man transgress and overreach his brother and defraud him in this matter** or defraud his brother in business. For the Lord is an avenger in all these things, as we have already warned you solemnly and told you plainly.*

For God has not called us to impurity but to consecration [to dedicate ourselves to the most thorough purity]. [AMP]

I Timothy 5:1-2

Rebuke not an elder, but intreat him as a father; and the younger men as brethren;

The elder women as mothers; **the younger as sisters, with all purity.**

II Timothy 2:22

Flee also youthful lusts; but follow righteousness, faith, charity, peace, with them that call on the Lord out of a pure heart.

Hebrews 13:4

Marriage is honourable in all, and the bed undefiled: **but whoremongers and adulterers God will judge.**

I John 2:15-17

Love not the world, neither the things that are in the world. If any man love the world, the love of the Father is not in him.

For all that is in the world, **the lust of the flesh**, and the lust of the eyes, and the pride of life, **is not of the Father, but is of the world.**

And the world passeth away, and the lust thereof: but he that doeth the will of God abideth for ever.

Revelations 21:7-8

He that overcometh shall inherit all things; and I will be his God, and he shall be My son.

But the fearful, and unbelieving, and the abominable, and murderers, and **whoremongers,** and sorcerers, and idolaters, and all liars, shall have their part in the lake which burneth with fire and brimstone: which is the second death.

C. Overcoming Overeating & Gluttony

<u>**Numbers 11:4-6, 18-20**</u>

And the mixed multitude that was among them fell a-lusting: and the children of Israel also wept again, and said, **Who shall give us flesh to eat?**

We remember the fish, which we did eat in Egypt freely; the cucumbers, and the melons, and the leeks, and the onions, and the garlick:

But now our soul is dried away: there is nothing at all, beside this manna, before our eyes.

And say thou unto the people, Sanctify yourselves against to morrow, and ye shall eat flesh: for ye have wept in the ears of the Lord, saying, **Who shall give us flesh to eat? for it was well with us in Egypt:** therefore the Lord will give you flesh, and ye shall eat.

Ye shall not eat one day, nor two days, nor five days, neither ten days, nor twenty days;

But even a whole month, until it come out at your nostrils, and it be loathsome unto you: because that ye have despised the Lord Which is among you, and have wept before Him, saying, Why came we forth out of Egypt?

<u>**Psalm 141:4**</u>

Incline not my heart to any evil thing, to practise wicked works with men that work iniquity: **and let me not eat of their dainties.**

<u>**Proverbs 16:26**</u>

He that laboureth laboureth for himself; **for his mouth craveth it of him**.

<u>**Proverbs 23:1-3**</u>

When thou sittest to eat with a ruler, consider diligently what is before thee:

And put a knife to thy throat, if thou be a man given to appetite.

Be not desirous of his dainties: **for they are deceitful meat.**

<u>**Proverbs 23:20-21**</u>

Be not among winebibbers**; among riotous eaters of flesh:**

For the drunkard and **the glutton shall come to poverty**: and drowsiness shall clothe a man with rags.

<u>**Proverbs 25:16**</u>

Hast thou found honey? **eat so much as is sufficient for thee,** lest thou be filled therewith, and vomit it.

<u>**Proverbs 25:27**</u>

It is not good to eat much honey: . . .

<u>**Ecclesiastes 6:7**</u>

All the labour of man is for his mouth, **and yet the appetite is not filled.**

Luke 12:22-24

And He said unto His disciples, Therefore I say unto you, **Take no thought for your life, what ye shall eat;** neither for the body, what ye shall put on.

The life is more than meat, and the body is more than raiment.

Consider the ravens: for they neither sow nor reap; which neither have storehouse nor barn; and **God feedeth them**: how much more are ye better than the fowls?

Luke 12:29-31

And seek not ye what ye shall eat, or what ye shall drink, neither be ye of doubtful mind.

For all these things do the nations of the world seek after: and your Father knoweth that ye have need of these things.

But rather seek ye the kingdom of God; and all these things shall be added unto you.

Luke 21:34

And take heed to yourselves, **lest at any time your hearts be overcharged with surfeiting, and drunkenness, and cares of this life,** and so that day come upon you unawares.

John 6:26-27

Jesus answered them and said, Verily, verily, I say unto you, **Ye seek Me, not because ye saw the miracles, but because ye did eat of the loaves, and were filled.**

Labour not for the meat which perisheth, but for that meat which endureth unto everlasting life, which the Son of Man shall give unto you: for Him hath God the Father sealed.

John 6:35

And Jesus said unto them, **I am the Bread of Life: he that cometh to Me shall never hunger;** and he that believeth on Me shall never thirst.

Romans 14:17

For the kingdom of God is not meat and drink; but righteousness, and peace, and joy in the Holy Ghost.

I Corinthians 10:31

Whether therefore ye eat, or drink, or whatsoever ye do, **do all to the glory of God.**

Philippians 3:19

Whose end is destruction, **whose God is their belly**, and whose glory is in their shame, who mind earthly things.)

I John 2:15-17

Love not the world, neither the things that are in the world. If any man love the world, the love of the Father is not in him.

For all that is in the world, the **lust of the flesh**, and the lust of the eyes, and the pride of life, **is not of the Father, but is of the world.**

And the world passeth away, and the lust thereof: but he that doeth the will of God abideth for ever.

D. Overcoming Alcohol & Drug Abuse

<u>Leviticus 19:26</u>

. . . neither shall ye use enchantment *(pharmakeia)*, nor observe times.

<u>Proverbs 20:1</u>

Wine is a mocker, strong drink is raging: and whosoever is deceived thereby is not wise.

<u>Proverbs 21:17</u>

He that loveth pleasure shall be a poor man: **he that loveth wine and oil shall not be rich.**

<u>Proverbs 23:20-21</u>

Be not among winebibbers; among riotous eaters of flesh:

For the drunkard and the glutton shall come to poverty: . . .

<u>Proverbs 23:29-35</u>

Who hath woe? who hath sorrow? who hath contentions? who hath babbling? who hath wounds without cause? who hath redness of eyes?

They that tarry long at the wine; they that go to seek mixed wine.

Look not thou upon the wine when it is red, when it giveth his colour in the cup, when it moveth itself aright.

At the last it biteth like a serpent, and stingeth like an adder.

Thine eyes shall behold strange women, and thine heart shall utter perverse things.

Yea, thou shalt be as he that lieth down in the midst of the sea, or as he that lieth upon the top of a mast.

They have stricken me, shalt thou say, and I was not sick; they have beaten me, and I felt it not: when shall I awake? I will seek it yet again.

<u>Proverbs 31:4-5</u>

It is not for kings, O Lemuel, **it is not for kings to drink wine; nor for princes strong drink**:

Lest they drink, and forget the law, and pervert the judgment of any of the afflicted.

<u>Isaiah 5:11-12</u>

Woe unto them that rise up early in the morning, that they may follow strong drink; that continue until night, till wine inflame them!

And the harp, and the viol, the tabret, and pipe, **and wine,** are in their feasts: **but they regard not the work of the Lord, neither consider the operation of His hands.**

Isaiah 5:22

Woe unto them that are mighty to drink wine, and men of strength to mingle strong drink:

Isaiah 28:1

Woe to the crown of pride, **to the drunkards of Ephraim**, whose glorious beauty is a fading flower, which are on the head of the fat valleys **of them that are overcome with wine!**

Isaiah 28:7

But they also have erred through wine, and through strong drink are out of the way; the priest and the prophet have erred through strong drink, they are swallowed up of wine, they are out of the way through strong drink; they err in vision, they stumble in judgment.

Hosea 4:11

*Harlotry and **wine** and **new wine take away the heart and the mind and the spiritual understanding. [AMP]***

Habakkuk 2:5

Yea also, **because he transgresseth by wine,** he is a proud man, neither keepeth at home, who enlargeth his desire as hell, and is as death, and cannot be satisfied . . .

Habakkuk 2:15-16

Woe to him who gives his neighbors drink, who pours out your bottle to them and adds to it your poisonous and blighting wrath and also makes them drunk, that you may look on their stripped condition and pour out foul shame [on their glory]!

*You [yourself] will be filled with shame and contempt instead of glory. **Drink also and be like an uncircumcised [heathen]!** The cup [of wrath] in the Lord's right hand will come around to you [O destroyer], and foul shame shall be upon your own glory! [AMP]*

Luke 21:34

And take heed to yourselves, lest at any time your hearts be overcharged with surfeiting, and drunkenness, and cares of this life, and so that day come upon you unawares.

Romans 13:13-14

Let us walk honestly, as in the day; **not in rioting and drunkenness,** not in chambering and wantonness, not in strife and envying.

But put ye on the Lord Jesus Christ, and make not provision for the flesh, to fulfil the lusts thereof.

I Corinthians 6:10

Nor thieves, nor covetous, **nor drunkards**, nor revilers, nor extortioners, **shall inherit the kingdom of God.**

Galatians 5:19-21

Now the works of the flesh are manifest, which are these; Adultery, fornication, unclean-

ness, lasciviousness,
Idolatry, witchcraft, hatred, variance, emulations, wrath, strife, seditions, heresies,
Envyings, murders, **drunkenness**, revellings, and such like: of the which I tell you before, as I have also told you in time past**, that they which do such things shall not inherit the kingdom of God.**

<u>**Ephesians 5:18**</u>
And be not drunk with wine, wherein is excess; but be filled with the Spirit;

<u>**Revelations 21:7-8**</u>
He that overcometh shall inherit all things; and I will be his God, and he shall be My son.
But the fearful, and unbelieving, and the abominable, and murderers, and whoremongers, and **sorcerers *(pharmakeia)***, and idolaters, and all liars, shall have their part in the lake which burneth with fire and brimstone: which is the second death.

E. Overcoming the Lust for Wealth & Material Possessions

<u>**Exodus 20:17**</u>
Thou shalt not covet thy neighbour's house, thou shalt not covet thy neighbour's wife, nor his manservant, nor his maidservant, nor his ox, nor his ass, nor any thing that is thy neighbour's.

<u>**Psalm 37:16**</u>
A little that a righteous man hath is better than the riches of many wicked.

<u>**Psalm 62:10**</u>
Trust not in oppression, and become not vain in robbery: **if riches increase, set not your heart upon them.**

<u>**Proverbs 11:4**</u>
Riches profit not in the day of wrath: but righteousness delivereth from death.

<u>**Proverbs 11:28**</u>
He that trusteth in his riches shall fall: but the righteous shall flourish as a branch.

<u>**Proverbs 13:7**</u>
There is that maketh himself rich, yet hath nothing: there is that maketh himself poor, yet hath great riches.

<u>**Proverbs 15:27**</u>
He that is greedy of gain troubleth his own house; . . .

Proverbs 23:4-5

Labour not to be rich: cease from thine own wisdom.

Wilt thou set thine eyes upon that which is not? **for riches certainly make themselves wings; they fly away as an eagle toward heaven.**

Proverbs 27:20

Hell and destruction are never full; **so the eyes of man are never satisfied.**

Ecclesiastes 5:10-17

He that loveth silver shall not be satisfied with silver; nor he that loveth abundance with increase: this is also vanity.

When goods increase, they are increased that eat them: **and what good is there to the owners thereof, saving the beholding of them with their eyes?**

The sleep of a labouring man is sweet, whether he eat little or much: **but the abundance of the rich will not suffer him to sleep.**

There is a sore evil which I have seen under the sun, namely, riches kept for the owners thereof to their hurt.

But those riches perish by evil travail: and he begetteth a son, and there is nothing in his hand.

As he came forth of his mother's womb, naked shall he return to go as he came, and shall take nothing of his labour, which he may carry away in his hand.

And this also is a sore evil, that in all points as he came, so shall he go: and what profit hath he that hath laboured for the wind?

All his days also he eateth in darkness, and he hath much sorrow and wrath with his sickness.

Jeremiah 9:23-24

Thus saith the Lord, Let not the wise man glory in his wisdom, neither let the mighty man glory in his might, **let not the rich man glory in his riches:**

But let him that glorieth glory in this, that he understandeth and knoweth Me, that I am the Lord which exercise lovingkindness, judgment, and righteousness, in the earth: for in these things I delight, saith the Lord.

Ezekiel 33:31

And they come unto thee as the people cometh, and they sit before thee as My people, and they hear thy words, but they will not do them: for with their mouth they shew much love, **but their heart goeth after their covetousness.**

Matthew 6:19-21

Lay not up for yourselves treasures upon earth, where moth and rust doth corrupt, and where thieves break through and steal:

But lay up for yourselves treasures in heaven, where neither moth nor rust doth corrupt, and where thieves do not break through nor steal:

For where your treasure is, there will your heart be also.

<u>**Matthew 6:24-25**</u>

No man can serve two masters: for either he will hate the one, and love the other; or else he will hold to the one, and despise the other. **Ye cannot serve God and mammon.**

Therefore I say unto you, **Take no thought for your life,** what ye shall eat, or what ye shall drink; nor yet for your body, what ye shall put on. **Is not the life more than meat, and the body than raiment?**

<u>**Matthew 16:26**</u>

For what is a man profited, if he shall gain the whole world, and lose his own soul? or what shall a man give in exchange for his soul?

<u>**Matthew 19:21-24**</u> *(the rich young ruler)*

Jesus said unto him, **If thou wilt be perfect, go and sell that thou hast, and give to the poor, and thou shalt have treasure in heaven: and come and follow Me.**

But when the young man heard that saying, he went away sorrowful: for he had great possessions.

Then said Jesus unto His disciples, Verily I say unto you, **That a rich man shall hardly enter into the kingdom of heaven.**

And again I say unto you, **It is easier for a camel to go through the eye of a needle, than for a rich man to enter into the kingdom of God.**

<u>**Matthew 26:14-15**</u>

Then one of the twelve, called Judas Iscariot, went unto the chief priests,

And said unto them, **What will ye give me, and I will deliver Him unto you? And they covenanted with him for thirty pieces of silver.**

<u>**Mark 4:18-19**</u>

And these are they which are sown among thorns; such as hear the word,

And the cares of this world, and **the deceitfulness of riches**, and **the lusts of other things entering in,** choke the word, and it becometh unfruitful.

<u>**Luke 12:15-21**</u>

And He said unto them, **Take heed, and beware of covetousness: for a man's life consisteth not in the abundance of the things which he possesseth.**

And He spake a parable unto them saying, The ground of a certain rich man brought forth plentifully:

And he thought within himself, saying, What shall I do, because I have no room where to bestow my fruits?

And he said, This will I do: I will pull down my barns, and build greater; and there will I bestow all my fruits and my goods.

And I will say to my soul, Soul, thou hast much goods laid up for many years; take thine ease, eat, drink, and be merry.

But God said unto him, Thou fool, this night thy soul shall be required of thee: then whose shall those things be, which thou hast provided?

So is he that layeth up treasure for himself, and is not rich toward God.

Luke 12:22-23

And He said unto His disciples, Therefore I say unto you, **Take no thought for your life, what ye shall eat; neither for the body, what ye shall put on.**

The life is more than meat, and the body is more than raiment.

Luke 12:33-34

Sell that ye have, and give alms; provide yourselves bags which wax not old, a treasure in the heavens that faileth not, where no thief approacheth, neither moth corrupteth.

For where your treasure is, there will your heart be also.

Acts 5:3-4 *(Ananias & Sapphira)*

But Peter said, **Ananias, why hath Satan filled thine heart to lie to the Holy Ghost, and to keep back part of the price of the land?**

Whiles it remained, was it not thine own? and after it was sold, was it not in thine own power? why hast thou conceived this thing in thine heart? thou hast not lied unto men, but unto God.

Ephesians 5:3,5

But immorality (sexual vice) and ***all impurity [of lustful, rich, wasteful living] or greediness must not even be named among you****, as is fitting and proper among saints (God's consecrated people).*

For be sure of this: that no person practicing sexual vice or impurity in thought or in life, ***or one who is covetous [who has lustful desire for the property of others and is greedy for gain] - for he [in effect] is an idolater*** *- has any inheritance in the kingdom of Christ and of God. [AMP]*

Colossians 3:5

Mortify therefore your members which are upon the earth; fornication, uncleanness, inordinate affection, evil concupiscence, **and covetousness, which is idolatry**:

So kill (deaden, deprive of power) the evil desire lurking in your members [those animal impulses and all that is earthly in you that is employed in sin]: sexual vice, impurity, sensual appetites, unholy desires, and ***all greed and covetousness, for that is idolatry (the deifying of self and other created things instead of God).*** *[AMP]*

I Timothy 6:5-11

Perverse disputings of men of corrupt minds, and destitute of the truth, **supposing that gain is godliness**: from such withdraw thyself.

But godliness with contentment is great gain.

For we brought nothing into this world, and it is certain we can carry nothing out.

And having food and raiment let us be therewith content.

But they that will be rich fall into temptation and a snare, and into many foolish and hurtful lusts, which drown men in destruction and perdition.

For the love of money is the root of all evil: which while some coveted after, they have erred from the faith, and pierced themselves through with many sorrows.

But thou, O man of God, flee these things; and follow after righteousness, godliness, faith, love, patience, meekness.

I Timothy 6:17

Charge them that are rich in this world, that they be not highminded, nor trust in uncertain riches, but in the living God, Who giveth us richly all things to enjoy;

James 4:1-3

What leads to strife (discord and feuds) and how do conflicts (quarrels and fightings) originate among you? Do they not arise from your sensual desires that are ever warring in your bodily members?

You are jealous and covet [what others have] and your desires go unfilfilled; *[so] you become murderers. [To hate is to murder as far as your hearts are concerned.] You burn with envy and anger and are not able to obtain [the gratification, the contentment, and the happiness that you seek], so you fight and war. You do not have, because you do not ask.*

[Or] you do ask [God for them] and yet fail to receive, because you ask with wrong purpose and evil, selfish motives. Your intention is [when you get what you desire] to spend it in sensual pleasures. *[AMP]*

James 5:1-3

Go to now, ye rich men, weep and howl for your miseries that shall come upon you.

Your riches are corrupted, and your garments are moth-eaten.

Your gold and silver is cankered; and the rust of them shall be a witness against you, and shall eat your flesh as it were fire. Ye have heaped treasure together for the last days.

II Peter 2:15

Which have forsaken the right way, and are gone astray, following the way of Balaam the son of Bosor, **who loved the wages of unrighteousness**;

I John 2:15-17

Love not the world, neither the things that are in the world. If any man love the world, the love of the Father is not in him.

For all that is in the world, the lust of the flesh, and **the lust of the eyes**, and the pride of life, **is not of the Father, but is of the world.**

And the world passeth away, and the lust thereof: but he that doeth the will of God abideth for ever.

Revelations 21:7-8

He that overcometh shall inherit all things; and I will be his God, and he shall be My son.

But the fearful, and unbelieving, and the abominable, and murderers, and whoremongers, and sorcerers, and **idolaters,** and all liars, shall have their part in the lake which burneth with fire and brimstone: which is the second death.

F. Overcoming Slothfulness

Proverbs 6:6-11

Go to the ant, thou sluggard; consider her ways, and be wise:
Which having no guide, overseer, or ruler,
Provideth her meat in the summer, and gathereth her food in the harvest.
How long wilt thou sleep, O sluggard? when wilt thou arise out of thy sleep?
Yet a little sleep, a little slumber, a little folding of the hands to sleep:
So shall thy poverty come as one that travelleth, and thy want as an armed man.

Proverbs 10:4-5

He becometh poor that dealeth with a slack hand: but the hand of the diligent maketh rich.

He that gathereth in summer is a wise son: **but he that sleepeth in harvest is a son that causeth shame.**

Proverbs 13:4

The soul of the sluggard desireth, and hath nothing: but the soul of the diligent shall be made fat.

Proverbs 15:19

The way of the slothful man is as an hedge of thorns: but the way of the righteous is made plain.

Proverbs 18:9

He also that is slothful in his work is brother to him that is a great waster.

Proverbs 19:15

Slothfulness casteth into a deep sleep; and an idle soul shall suffer hunger.

Proverbs 19:24

A slothful man hideth his hand in his bosom, and will not so much as bring it to his mouth again.

Proverbs 20:4

The sluggard will not plow by reason of the cold; therefore shall he beg in harvest, and have nothing.

Proverbs 20:13

Love not sleep, lest thou come to poverty; open thine eyes, and thou shalt be satisfied with bread.

Proverbs 21:25

The desire of the slothful killeth him; for his hands refuse to labour.

Proverbs 22:13

The slothful man saith, **There is a lion without,** I shall be slain in the streets.

Proverbs 23:21

For the drunkard and the glutton shall come to poverty: **and drowsiness shall clothe a man with rags.**

Proverbs 24:30-34

I went by the field of the slothful, and by the vineyard of the man void of understanding;
And lo, it was all grown over with thorns, and nettles had covered the face thereof, and the stone wall thereof was broken down.
Then I saw, and considered it well: I looked upon it, and received instruction.
Yet a little sleep, a little slumber, a little folding of the hands to sleep:
So shall thy poverty come as one that travelleth; and thy want as an armed man.

Proverbs 26:13

The slothful man saith, There is a lion in the way; a lion is in the streets.

Proverbs 26:14

As the door turneth upon his hinges, so doth the slothful upon his bed.

Proverbs 26:15

The slothful hideth his hand in his bosom; it grieveth him to bring it again to his mouth.

Proverbs 26:16

The sluggard is wiser in his own conceit than seven men that can render a reason.

Ecclesiastes 10:18

By much slothfulness the building decayeth; and through idleness of the hands the house droppeth through.

Matthew 25:24-29

Then he which had received the one talent came and said, Lord, I knew thee that thou art an hard man, reaping where thou hast not sown, and gathering where thou hast not strawed:
And I was afraid, and went and hid thy talent in the earth: lo, there thou hast that is thine.
His lord answered and said unto him, **Thou wicked and slothful servant**, thou knewest that I reap where I sowed not, and gather where I have not strawed:
Thou oughtest therefore to have put my money to the exchangers, and then at my coming I should have received mine own with usury.
Take therefore the talent from him, and give it unto him which hath ten talents.
For unto every one that hath shall be given, and he shall have abundance: but from him that hath not shall be taken away even that which he hath.

Romans 12:11

Not slothful in business; fervent in spirit; serving the Lord;

Ephesians 5:14-16

Wherefore He saith, **Awake thou that sleepest,** and arise from the dead, and Christ shall give thee light.

See then that ye walk circumspectly, not as fools, but as wise,

Redeeming the time, because the days are evil.

II Thessalonians 3:10-12

For even when we were with you, this we commanded you, **that if any would not work, neither should he eat**.

For we hear that there are some which walk among you disorderly, **working not at all**, but are busybodies.

Now them that are such we command and exhort by our Lord Jesus Christ, **that with quietness they work, and eat their own bread.**

Hebrews 6:12

That ye be not slothful, but followers of them who through faith and patience inherit the promises.

Chapter 30

Victory Over Sins of the Heart

A. Overcoming Hypocrisy & Religious Pretense

<u>**Job 8:13**</u>

. . . **the hypocrite's hope shall perish:**

<u>**Job 27:8**</u>

For what is the hope of the hypocrite, though he hath gained, when God taketh away his soul?

<u>**Job 36:13-14**</u>

But the hypocrites in heart heap up wrath: they cry not when He bindeth them.

They die in youth, and their life is among the unclean.

<u>**Psalm 78:35-37**</u>

And they remembered that God was their Rock, and the High God their Redeemer.

Nevertheless they did flatter Him with their mouth, and they lied unto Him with their tongues.

For their heart was not right with Him, neither were they stedfast in His covenant.

<u>**Proverbs 11:9**</u>

An hypocrite with his mouth destroyeth his neighbour: but through knowledge shall the just be delivered.

<u>**Proverbs 26:23**</u>

Burning lips and a wicked heart are like **a potsherd covered with silver dross**.

Isaiah 29:13

Wherefore the Lord said, **Forasmuch as this people draw near Me with their mouth, and with their lips do honour Me, but have removed their heart far from Me, and their fear toward Me is taught by the precept of men:**

Isaiah 48:1

Hear ye this, O house of Jacob, which are called by the name of Israel, and are come forth out of the waters of Judah, **which swear by the name of the Lord, and make mention of the God of Israel, but not in truth, nor in righteousness.**

Isaiah 58:2

Yet they seek, inquire for, and require Me daily and delight [externally] to know My ways, *as [if they were in reality] a nation that did righteousness and forsook not the ordinance of their God. They ask of Me righteous judgments,* ***they delight to draw near to God [in visible ways].*** *[AMP]*

Isaiah 65:5

Which say, Stand by thyself, come not near to me; **for I am holier than thou**. . . .

Jeremiah 2:32-35

Can a maid forget her ornaments, or a bride her attire? yet My people have forgotten Me days without number.

Why trimmest thou thy way to seek love? therefore hast thou also taught the wicked ones thy ways.

Also in thy skirts is found the blood of the souls of the poor innocents: I have not found it by secret search, but upon all these.

Yet thou sayest, Because I am innocent, surely His anger shall turn from me. Behold, I will plead with thee, because thou sayest, I have not sinned.

Ezekiel 33:31-32

And they come unto thee as the people cometh, and they sit before thee as My people, and they hear thy words, but they will not do them: **for with their mouth they shew much love, but their heart goeth after their covetousness.**

And, lo, thou art unto them as a very lovely song of one that hath a pleasant voice, and can play well on an instrument: **for they hear thy words, but they do them not.**

Matthew 6:1-2

Take heed that ye do not your alms before men, to be seen of them: otherwise ye have no reward of your Father Which is in heaven.

Therefore when thou doest thine alms, do not sound a trumpet before thee, as the hypocrites do in the synagogues and in the streets, that they may have glory of men. Verily I say unto you, **They have their reward.**

Matthew 6:5

And when thou prayest, thou shalt not be as the hypocrites are: for they love to pray

standing in the synagogues and in the corners of the streets, that they may be seen of men. Verily I say unto you, They have their reward.

Matthew 6:16

Moreover when ye fast, be not, as the hypocrites, of a sad countenance: for they disfigure their faces, that they may appear unto men to fast. Verily I say unto you, They have their reward.

Matthew 7:3-5

And why beholdest thou the mote that is in thy brother's eye, but considerest not the beam that is in thine own eye?

Or how wilt thou say to thy brother, Let me pull out the mote out of thine eye; and, behold, a beam is in thine own eye?

Thou hypocrite, first cast out the beam out of thine own eye; and then shalt thou see clearly to cast out the mote out of thy brother's eye.

Matthew 7:21-23

Not every one that saith unto Me, Lord, Lord, shall enter into the kingdom of heaven; but he that doeth the will of My Father Which is in heaven.

Many will say to Me in that day, Lord, Lord, have we not prophesied in Thy name? and in Thy name have cast out devils? and in Thy name done many wonderful works?

And then will I profess unto them, **I never knew you: depart from Me, ye that work iniquity.**

Matthew 23:2-7

. . . The scribes and the Pharisees sit in Moses' seat:

All therefore whatsoever they bid you observe, that observe and do; **but do not ye after their works: for they say, and do not.**

For they bind heavy burdens and grievous to be borne, and lay them on men's shoulders; but they themselves will not move them with one of their fingers.

But all their works they do for to be seen of men: they make broad their phylacteries, and enlarge the borders of their garments,

And love the uppermost rooms at feasts, and the chief seats in the synagogues,

And greetings in the markets, and to be called of men, Rabbi, Rabbi.

Matthew 23:13-15

But woe unto you, scribes and Pharisees, **hypocrites**! for ye shut up the kingdom of heaven against men: for ye neither go in yourselves, neither suffer ye them that are entering to go in.

Woe unto you, scribes and Pharisees, **hypocrites**! **for ye devour widows' houses, and for a pretence make long prayer: therefore ye shall receive the greater damnation.**

Woe unto you, scribes and Pharisees, **hypocrites**! for ye compass sea and land to make one proselyte, and when he is made, ye make him twofold more the child of hell than yourselves.

<u>Matthew 23:23-28</u>

Woe unto you, scribes and Pharisees, hypocrites! **for ye pay tithe of mint and anise and cummin, and have omitted the weightier matters of the law, judgment, mercy, and faith:** these ought ye to have done, and not to leave the other undone.

Ye blind guides, which strain at a gnat, and swallow a camel.

Woe unto you, scribes and Pharisees, hypocrites! **for ye make clean the outside of the cup and of the platter, but within they are full of extortion and excess.**

Thou blind Pharisee, cleanse first that which is within the cup and platter, that the outside of them may be clean also.

Woe unto you, scribes and Pharisees, hypocrites! **for ye are like unto whited sepulchres, which indeed appear beautiful outward, but are within full of dead men's bones, and of all uncleanness.**

Even so ye also outwardly appear righteous unto men, but within ye are full of hypocrisy and iniquity.

<u>Mark 7:6-8</u>

. . . Well hath Esaias prophesied of you hypocrites, as it is written, **This people honoureth Me with their lips, but their heart is far from Me.**

Howbeit in vain do they worship Me, teaching for doctrines the commandments of men.

For laying aside the commandment of God, ye hold the tradition of men, as the washing of pots and cups: and many other such like things ye do.

<u>Luke 6:46</u>

And why call ye Me, Lord, Lord, and do not the things which I say?

<u>Luke 11:44</u>

Woe unto you, scribes and Pharisees, **hypocrites**! for ye are as graves which appear not, and the men that walk over them are not aware of them.

<u>Luke 12:1</u>

. . . Beware ye of the leaven of the Pharisees, which is hypocrisy.

For there is nothing covered, that shall not be revealed; neither hid, that shall not be known.

<u>John 7:23</u>

If a man on the sabbath day receive circumcision, that the law of Moses should not be broken; are ye angry at Me, because I have made a man every whit whole on the sabbath day?

<u>Romans 2:1</u>

Therefore thou art inexcusable, O man, whosoever thou art that judgest: for wherein thou judgest another, thou condemnest thyself; for thou that judgest doest the same things.

<u>Romans 2:21-24</u>

Thou therefore which teachest another, teachest thou not thyself? thou that preachest a man should not steal, doest thou steal?

Thou that sayest a man should not commit adultery, dost thou commit adultery? thou that abhorrest idols, dost thou commit sacrilege?

Thou that makest thy boast of the law, through breaking the law dishonourest thou God?

For the name of God is blasphemed among the Gentiles through you, as it is written.

Romans 2:28-29

For he is not a Jew, which is one outwardly; neither is that circumcision, which is outward in the flesh:

But he is a Jew, which is one inwardly; and circumcision is that of the heart, in the spirit, and not in the letter; whose praise is not of men, but of God.

Galatians 4:10-11

Ye observe days, and months, and times, and years.

I am afraid of you, lest I have bestowed upon you labour in vain.

Colossians 2:20-22

Wherefore if ye be dead with Christ from the rudiments of the world, why, as though living in the world, are ye subject to ordinances,

(Touch not; taste not; handle not;

Which all are to perish with the using;) after the commandments and doctrines of men?

II Timothy 3:5

Having a form of godliness, but denying the power thereof: . . .

Titus 1:16

They profess that they know God; but in works they deny Him, being abominable, and disobedient, and unto every good work reprobate.

James 2:15-16

If a brother or sister be naked, and destitute of daily food,

And one of you say unto them, Depart in peace, be ye warmed and filled; notwithstanding ye give them not those things which are needful to the body; what doth it profit?

James 3:17

But **the wisdom that is from above** is first pure, then peaceable, gentle, and easy to be intreated, full of mercy and good fruits, without partiality, and **without hypocrisy.**

I Peter 2:1-3

Wherefore laying aside all malice, and all guile, and hypocrisies, and envies, and all evil speakings,

As newborn babes, desire the sincere milk of the word, that ye may grow thereby:

If so be ye have tasted that the Lord is gracious.

I John 3:18

My little children, let us not love in word, neither in tongue; but in deed and in truth.

B. Overcoming Self-Righteousness

<u>Deuteronomy 9:4-6</u>

Speak not thou in thine heart, after that the Lord thy God hath cast them out from before thee, saying, For my righteousness the Lord hath brought me in to possess this land: but for the wickedness of these nations the Lord doth drive them out from before thee.

Not for thy righteousness, or for the uprightness of thine heart, dost thou go to possess their land: but for the wickedness of these nations the Lord thy God doth drive them out from before thee, and that He may perform the word which the Lord sware unto thy fathers, Abraham, Isaac, and Jacob.

Understand therefore, that the Lord thy God giveth thee not this good land to possess it for thy righteousness; for thou art a stiffnecked people.

<u>Job 9:20</u>

If I justify myself, mine own mouth shall condemn me: **if I say, I am perfect, it shall also prove me perverse.**

<u>Job 33:8-9</u>

Surely thou hast spoken in mine hearing, and I have heard the voice of thy words, saying, **I am clean without transgression, I am innocent; neither is there iniquity in me.**

<u>Job 35:2</u>

Thinkest thou this to be right, that thou saidst, **My righteousness is more than God's?**

<u>Proverbs 12:15</u>

The way of a fool is right in his own eyes: but he that hearkeneth unto counsel is wise.

<u>Proverbs 16:2</u>

All the ways of a man are clean in his own eyes; but the Lord weigheth the spirits.

<u>Proverbs 20:6</u>

Most men will proclaim every one his own goodness: but a faithful man who can find?

<u>Proverbs 21:2</u>

Every way of a man is right in his own eyes: but the Lord pondereth the hearts.

<u>Proverbs 30:12-13</u>

There is a generation that are pure in their own eyes, and yet is not washed from their filthiness.

There is a generation, O how lofty are their eyes! and their eyelids are lifted up.

<u>Isaiah 5:21</u>

Woe unto them that are wise in their own eyes, and prudent in their own sight!

<u>Jeremiah 2:35</u>

Yet thou sayest, Because **I am innocent**, surely His anger shall turn from me. Behold, I will plead with thee, because thou sayest, **I have not sinned**.

<u>Matthew 23:29-30</u>

Woe unto you, scribes and Pharisees, hypocrites! **because ye build the tombs of the prophets, and garnish the sepulchres of the righteous,**

And say, If we had been in the days of our fathers, we would not have been partakers with them in the blood of the prophets.

<u>Luke 18:9-14</u>

And He spake this parable unto certain which trusted in themselves that they were righteous, and despised others:

Two men went up into the temple to pray; the one a Pharisee, and the other a publican.

The Pharisee stood and prayed thus with himself, God, I thank Thee, that I am not as other men are, extortioners, unjust, adulterers, or even as this publican.

I fast twice in the week, I give tithes of all that I possess.

And the publican, standing afar off, would not lift up so much as his eyes unto heaven, but smote upon his breast, saying, God be merciful to me a sinner.

I tell you, this man went down to his house justified rather than the other: **for every one that exalteth himself shall be abased; and he that humbleth himself shall be exalted.**

<u>Romans 12:3</u>

For I say, through the grace given unto me, to every man that is among you, **not to think of himself more highly than he ought to think; but to think soberly,** according as God hath dealt to every man the measure of faith.

<u>II Corinthians 10:12</u>

For we dare not make ourselves of the number, or compare ourselves with some that commend themselves: but they measuring themselves by themselves, and comparing themselves among themselves, are not wise.

<u>Revelation 3:17-18</u>

Because thou sayest, I am rich, and increased with goods, and have need of nothing; and knowest not that thou art wretched, and miserable, and poor, and blind, and naked:

I counsel thee to buy of Me gold tried in the fire, that thou mayest be rich; and white raiment, that thou mayest be clothed, and that the shame of thy nakedness do not appear; and anoint thine eyes with eyesalve, that thou mayest see.

C. Overcoming Pride & Self-Exaltation

<u>**Psalm 10:4**</u>

The wicked, through the pride of his countenance, will not seek after God: God is not in all his thoughts.

<u>**Psalm 31:23**</u>

O love the Lord, all ye His saints: for the Lord preserveth the faithful, and **plentifully rewardeth the proud doer.**

<u>**Psalm 101:5**</u>

Whoso privily slandereth his neighbour, him will I cut off: **him that hath an high look and a proud heart will not I suffer.**

<u>**Psalm 131:1**</u>

Lord, my heart is not haughty, nor mine eyes lofty: neither do I exercise myself in great matters, or in things too high for me.

<u>**Proverbs 3:34**</u>

Surely He scorneth the scorners: but He giveth grace unto the lowly.

<u>**Proverbs 6:16-17**</u>

These six things the Lord hates, indeed, seven are an abomination to Him:

A proud look [the spirit that makes one overestimate himself and underestimate others], *. . . [AMP]*

<u>**Proverbs 8:13**</u>

The fear of the Lord is to hate evil: **pride, and arrogancy, and the evil way, and the froward mouth, do I hate.**

<u>**Proverbs 11:2**</u>

When pride cometh, then cometh shame: but with the lowly is wisdom.

<u>**Proverbs 13:10**</u>

Only by pride cometh contention: but with the well advised is wisdom.

<u>**Proverbs 14:3**</u>

In the mouth of the foolish is a rod of pride: but the lips of the wise shall preserve them.

<u>**Proverbs 15:25**</u>

The Lord will destroy the house of the proud: but He will establish the border of the widow.

Proverbs 16:5

Every one that is proud in heart is an abomination to the Lord: though hand join in hand, he shall not be unpunished.

Proverbs 16:18-19

Pride goeth before destruction, and an haughty spirit before a fall.

Better it is to be of an humble spirit with the lowly, than to divide the spoil with the proud.

Proverbs 21:4

An high look, and a proud heart, and the plowing of the wicked, is sin.

Proverbs 25:6-7

Put not forth thyself in the presence of the king, and stand not in the place of great men:

For better it is that it be said unto thee, Come up hither; than that thou shouldest be put lower in the presence of the prince whom thine eyes have seen.

Proverbs 27:2

Let another man praise thee, and not thine own mouth; a stranger, and not thine own lips.

Proverbs 28:25

He that is of a proud heart stirreth up strife: but he that putteth his trust in the Lord shall be made fat.

Proverbs 29:23

A man's pride shall bring him low: but honour shall uphold the humble in spirit.

Proverbs 30:32

If thou hast done foolishly in lifting up thyself, or if thou hast thought evil, **lay thine hand upon thy mouth.**

Ecclesiastes 7:8

Better is the end of a thing than the beginning thereof: and **the patient in spirit is better than the proud in spirit.**

Isaiah 2:11-12

The lofty looks of man shall be humbled, and the haughtiness of men shall be bowed down, and the Lord alone shall be exalted in that day.

For the day of the Lord of hosts shall be upon every one that is proud and lofty, and upon every one that is lifted up; and **he shall be brought low:**

Isaiah 10:33

. . . the haughty shall be humbled.

Isaiah 14:12-15 *(Lucifer)*

How art thou fallen from heaven, O Lucifer, son of the morning! how art thou cut down to the ground, which didst weaken the nations!

For thou hast said in thine heart, **I will** ascend into heaven, **I will** exalt my throne above the stars of God: **I will** sit also upon the mount of the congregation, in the sides of the north:

I will ascend above the heights of the clouds; **I will** be like the Most High.

Yet thou shalt be brought down to hell, to the sides of the pit.

Jeremiah 9:23-24

Thus saith the Lord, **Let not the wise man glory in his wisdom, neither let the mighty man glory in his might, let not the rich man glory in his riches:**

But let him that glorieth glory in this, that he understandeth and knoweth Me, that I am the Lord Which exercise lovingkindness, judgment, and righteousness, in the earth: for in these things I delight, saith the Lord.

Jeremiah 45:5

And seekest thou great things for thyself? seek them not: . . .

Ezekiel 28:17 *(Lucifer)*

Thine heart was lifted up because of thy beauty, thou hast corrupted thy wisdom by reason of thy brightness: I will cast thee to the ground, I will lay thee before kings, that they may behold thee.

Habakkuk 2:4

Behold, his soul which is lifted up is not upright in him: but the just shall live by his faith.

Zephaniah 3:11

In that day shalt thou not be ashamed for all thy doings, wherein thou hast transgressed against Me: **for then I will take away out of the midst of thee them that rejoice in thy pride, and thou shalt no more be haughty** because of My holy mountain.

Matthew 18:1-4

At the same time came the disciples unto Jesus, saying, **Who is the greatest in the kingdom of heaven?**

And Jesus called a little child unto Him, and set him in the midst of them,

And said, Verily I say unto you, Except ye be converted, and become as little children, ye shall not enter into the kingdom of heaven.

Whosoever therefore shall humble himself as this little child, the same is greatest in the kingdom of heaven.

Matthew 19:30

But many that are first shall be last; and the last shall be first.

<u>**Matthew 20:20-28**</u>

Then came to Him the mother of Zebedee's children with her sons, worshipping Him, and desiring a certain thing of Him.

And He said unto her, What wilt thou? She saith unto Him, **Grant that these my two sons may sit, the one on Thy right hand, and the other on the left, in Thy kingdom.**

But Jesus answered and said, Ye know not what ye ask. Are ye able to drink of the cup that I shall drink of, and to be baptized with the baptism that I am baptized with? They say unto Him, We are able.

And He saith unto them, Ye shall drink indeed of My cup, and be baptized with the baptism that I am baptized with: but to sit on My right hand, and on My left, is not Mine to give, but it shall be given to them for whom it is prepared of My Father.

And when the ten heard it, they were moved with indignation against the two brethren.

But Jesus called them unto Him, and said, **Ye know that the princes of the Gentiles exercise dominion over them, and they that are great exercise authority upon them.**

But it shall not be so among you: but whosoever will be great among you, let him be your minister;

And whosoever will be chief among you, let him be your servant:

Even as the Son of Man came not to be ministered unto, but to minister, and to give His life a ransom for many.

<u>**Matthew 20:26-28**</u>

Not so shall it be among you; ***but whoever wishes to be great among you must be your servant,***

And whoever desires to be first among you must be your slave -

Just as the Son of Man came not to be waited on but to serve, and to give His life as a ransom for many [the price paid to set them free]. [AMP]

<u>**Matthew 23:11-12**</u>

But he that is greatest among you shall be your servant.

And whosoever shall exalt himself shall be abased; and he that shall humble himself shall be exalted.

He who is greatest among you shall be your servant.

Whoever exalts himself [with haughtiness and empty pride] shall be humbled (brought low), and whoever humbles himself [whoever has a modest opinion of himself and behaves accordingly] shall be raised to honor. [AMP]

<u>**Luke 1:51-52**</u>

He hath shewed strength with His arm; **He hath scattered the proud in the imagination of their hearts.**

He hath put down the mighty from their seats, and exalted them of low degree.

<u>**Luke 14:7-11**</u>

And He put forth a parable to those which were bidden, when He marked how they chose out the chief rooms; saying unto them,

When thou art bidden of any man to a wedding, sit not down in the highest room; lest a more honourable man than thou be bidden of him;

And he that bade thee and him come and say to thee, Give this man place; and thou begin with shame to take the lowest room.

But when thou art bidden, go and sit down in the lowest room; that when he that bade thee cometh, he may say unto thee, Friend, go up higher: then shalt thou have worship in the presence of them that sit at meat with thee.

For whosoever exalteth himself shall be abased; and he that humbleth himself shall be exalted.

Luke 22:24-27

And there was also a strife among them, which of them should be accounted the greatest.

And He said unto them, The kings of the Gentiles exercise lordship over them; and they that exercise authority upon them are called benefactors.

But ye shall not be so: **but he that is greatest among you, let him be as the younger; and he that is chief, as he that doth serve.**

For whether is greater, he that sitteth at meat, or he that serveth? is not he that sitteth at meat? **but I am among you as He that serveth.**

John 8:50

And I seek not Mine own glory: there is One that seeketh and judgeth.

However, I am not in search of honor for Myself. [I do not seek and am not aiming for My own glory.] *There is One Who [looks after that; He] seeks [My glory], and He is the Judge. [AMP]*

Romans 11:18-20

Boast not against the branches. **But if thou boast, thou bearest not the root, but the root thee**.

Thou wilt say then, The branches were broken off, that I might be grafted in.

Well; because of unbelief they were broken off, and thou standest by faith. **Be not high-minded,** but fear:

Romans 12:16

Be of the same mind one toward another. **Mind not high things, but condescend to men of low estate. Be not wise in your own conceits.**

I Corinthians 3:18-21

Let no man deceive himself. **If any man among you seemeth to be wise in this world, let him become a fool, that he may be wise.**

For the wisdom of this world is foolishness with God. For it is written, He taketh the wise in their own craftiness.

And again, **The Lord knoweth the thoughts of the wise, that they are vain.**

Therefore let no man glory in men. For all things are yours;

<u>**I Corinthians 13:4-5**</u>

. . . charity vaunteth not itself, is not puffed up,
Doth not behave itself unseemly, seeketh not her own, . . .

. . . (Love) is not boastful or vainglorious, does not display itself haughtily.
It is not conceited (arrogant and inflated with pride); it is not rude (unmannerly) and does not act unbecomingly. Love (God's love in us) does not insist on its own rights or its own way, for it is not self-seeking; . . . [AMP]

<u>**II Corinthians 12:5-6**</u>

Of such an one will I glory: **yet of myself I will not glory, but in mine infirmities.**
For though I would desire to glory, I shall not be a fool; for I will say the truth: but now I forbear, lest any man should think of me above that which he seeth me to be, or that he heareth of me.

<u>**Galatians 5:26**</u>

Let us not be desirous of vain glory, provoking one another, envying one another.

<u>**Galatians 6:14**</u>

But God forbid that I should glory, save in the cross of our Lord Jesus Christ, by Whom the world is crucified unto me, and I unto the world.

<u>**Philippians 2:3**</u>

Let nothing be done through strife or vainglory; **but in lowliness of mind let each esteem other better than themselves.**

Do nothing from factional motives [through contentiousness, strife, selfishness, or for unworthy ends] or prompted by conceit and empty arrogance. ***Instead, in the true spirit of humility (lowliness of mind) let each regard the others as better than and superior to himself [thinking more highly of one another than you do of yourselves]. [AMP]***

<u>**James 3:1**</u>

My brethren, be not many masters, knowing that we shall receive the greater condemnation.

Not many [of you] should become teachers (self-constituted censors and reprovers of others), *my brethren, for you know that we [teachers] will be judged by a higher standard and with greater severity [than other people; thus we assume the greater accountability and the more condemnation]. [AMP]*

<u>**James 4:6**</u>

But He giveth more grace. Wherefore He saith, **God resisteth the proud, but giveth grace unto the humble.**

James 4:10

Humble yourselves in the sight of the Lord, and He shall lift you up.

I Peter 5:3

Neither as being lords over God's heritage, but being ensamples to the flock.

I Peter 5:5-6

Likewise, ye younger, submit yourselves unto the elder. Yea, all of you be subject one to another, and be clothed with humility**: for God resisteth the proud, and giveth grace to the humble.**

Humble yourselves therefore under the mighty hand of God, that He may exalt you in due time:

Likewise, you who are younger and of lesser rank, be subject to the elders (the ministers and spiritual guides of the church) - [giving them due respect and yielding to their counsel]. Clothe (apron) yourselves, all of you, with humility [as the garb of a servant, so that its covering cannot possibly be stripped from you, with freedom from pride and arrogance] toward one another. ***For God sets Himself against the proud (the insolent, the overbearing, the disdainful, the presumptuous, the boastful) - [and He opposes, frustrates, and defeats them],*** *but gives grace (favor, blessing) to the humble.*

Therefore humble yourselves [demote, lower yourselves in your own estimation] under the mighty hand of God, that in due time He may exalt you. [AMP]

I John 2:15-17

Love not the world, neither the things that are in the world. If any man love the world, the love of the Father is not in him.

For all that is in the world, the lust of the flesh, and the lust of the eyes, and **the pride of life,** is not of the Father, but is of the world.

And the world passeth away, and the lust thereof: but he that doeth the will of God abideth for ever.

D. Overcoming Guile & Deceit

Psalm 24:3-4

Who shall ascend into the hill of the Lord? or who shall stand in His holy place?

He that hath clean hands, and a pure heart; **who hath not lifted up his soul unto vanity, nor sworn deceitfully.**

Psalm 32:2

Blessed is the man unto whom the Lord imputeth not iniquity, **and in whose spirit there is no guile.**

Psalm 34:13

Keep thy tongue from evil, and thy lips from speaking guile.

Psalm 55:23

. . . deceitful men shall not live out half their days; . . .

Psalm 101:7

He that worketh deceit shall not dwell within my house: he that telleth lies shall not tarry in my sight.

Proverbs 11:1

A false balance is abomination to the Lord: but a just weight is His delight.

Proverbs 12:5

The thoughts of the righteous are right: **but the counsels of the wicked are deceit.**

Proverbs 12:20

Deceit is in the heart of them that imagine evil: but to the counsellors of peace is joy.

Proverbs 20:10

Divers weights, and divers measures, both of them are alike abomination to the Lord.

Proverbs 20:17

Food gained by deceit is sweet to a man, but afterward his mouth will be filled with gravel. [AMP]

Proverbs 21:6

The getting of treasures by a lying tongue is a vanity tossed to and fro of them that seek death.

Jeremiah 8:5

Why then is this people of Jerusalem slidden back by a perpetual backsliding? **they hold fast deceit,** they refuse to return.

Jeremiah 9:5-6

And they will deceive every one his neighbour, and will not speak the truth: they have taught their tongue to speak lies, and weary themselves to commit iniquity.

Thine habitation is in the midst of deceit; through deceit they refuse to know Me, saith the Lord.

Jeremiah 17:9-11

The heart is deceitful above all things, and desperately wicked: who can know it?

I the Lord search the heart, I try the reins, even to give every man according to his ways, and according to the fruit of his doings.

As the partridge sitteth on eggs, and hatcheth them not; **so he that getteth riches, and not**

by right, shall leave them in the midst of his days, and at his end shall be a fool.

Jeremiah 22:13

Woe unto him that buildeth his house by unrighteousness, and his chambers by wrong; that useth his neighbour's service without wages, and giveth him not for his work;

Micah 6:11

Shall I count them pure with the wicked balances, and with the bag of deceitful weights?

John 1:47

Jesus saw Nathanael coming to Him, and saith of Him, **Behold an Israelite indeed, in whom is no guile!**

II Corinthians 4:2

But have renounced the hidden things of dishonesty, not walking in craftiness, nor handling the word of God deceitfully; but by manifestation of the truth commending ourselves to every man's conscience in the sight of God.

Ephesians 4:22-25

That ye put off concerning the former conversation the old man, which is corrupt according to the deceitful lusts;

And be renewed in the spirit of your mind;

And that ye put on the new man, which after God is created in righteousness and true holiness.

Wherefore putting away lying, speak every man truth with his neighbour: for we are members one of another.

Colossians 2:8

Beware lest any man spoil you through philosophy and vain deceit, after the tradition of men, after the rudiments of the world, and not after Christ.

Titus 1:10

For there are many unruly and vain talkers and deceivers, specially they of the circumcision:

Whose mouths must be stopped, who subvert whole houses, teaching things which they ought not, for filthy lucre's sake.

I Peter 2:21-23

For even hereunto were ye called: because Christ also suffered for us, leaving us an example, that ye should follow His steps:

Who did no sin, **neither was guile found in His mouth:**

Who, when He was reviled, reviled not again; when He suffered, He threatened not; but committed Himself to Him that judgeth righteously:

I Peter 3:10

For he that will love life, and see good days, **let him refrain his tongue from evil, and his lips that they speak no guile.**

For let him who wants to enjoy life and see good days [good - whether apparent or not] ***keep his tongue free from evil and his lips from guile (treachery, deceit).*** *[AMP]*

Revelation 14:4-5 *(the 144,000)*

These are they which were not defiled with women; for they are virgins. These are they which follow the Lamb whithersoever He goeth. These were redeemed from among men, being the firstfruits unto God and to the Lamb.

And in their mouth was found no guile: for they are without fault before the throne of God.

E. Overcoming Man Pleasing & the Fear of Man

Deuteronomy 1:17 *(Moses to the wise men)*

Ye shall not respect persons in judgment; but ye shall hear the small as well as the great; **ye shall not be afraid of the face of man**; for the judgment is God's: . . .

Psalm 56:11

In God have I put my trust: **I will not be afraid what man can do unto me.**

Proverbs 29:25

The fear of man bringeth a snare: but whoso putteth his trust in the Lord shall be safe.

Isaiah 51:7-8

Hearken unto Me, ye that know righteousness, the people in whose heart is My law; **fear ye not the reproach of men, neither be ye afraid of their revilings.**

For the moth shall eat them up like a garment, and the worm shall eat them like wool: but My righteousness shall be for ever, and My salvation from generation to generation.

Isaiah 51:12-13

I, even I, am He that comforteth you: **who art thou, that thou shouldest be afraid of a man that shall die, and of the son of man which shall be made as grass.**

And forgettest the Lord thy Maker, that hath stretched forth the heavens, and laid the foundations of the earth; and hast feared continually every day because of the fury of the oppressor, as if he were ready to destroy? and where is the fury of the oppressor?

Jeremiah 1:7-8

But the Lord said unto me, Say not, I am a child: for thou shalt go to all that I shall send thee, and whatsoever I command thee thou shalt speak.

Be not afraid of their faces: for I am with thee to deliver thee, saith the Lord.

<u>**Jeremiah 1:17**</u>

Thou therefore gird up thy loins, and arise, and speak unto them all that I command thee: **be not dismayed at their faces,** lest I confound thee before them.

<u>**Luke 12:4-5**</u>

And I say unto you My friends, **Be not afraid of them that kill the body, and after that have no more that they can do.**

But I will forewarn you Whom ye shall fear: Fear Him, Which after He hath killed hath power to cast into hell; yea, I say unto you, Fear Him.

<u>**John 7:13**</u>

Howbeit no man spake openly of Him for fear of the Jews.

<u>**John 12:42-43**</u>

Nevertheless among the chief rulers also many believed on Him; but because of the Pharisees they did not confess Him, lest they should be put out of the synagogue:

For they loved the praise of men more than the praise of God.

<u>**John 12:43**</u>

For they loved the approval and the praise and the glory that come from men [instead of and] more than the glory that comes from God. [They valued their credit with men more than their credit with God]. [AMP]

<u>**John 19:38**</u>

And after this Joseph of Arimathaea, **being a disciple of Jesus, but secretly for fear of the Jews,** besought Pilate that he might take away the body of Jesus: and Pilate gave him leave....

<u>**Acts 12:1-3**</u>

Now about that time Herod the king stretched forth his hands to vex certain of the church.

And he killed James the brother of John with the sword.

And because he saw it pleased the Jews, he proceeded further to take Peter also. . . .

<u>**Acts 24:27**</u>

But after two years Porcius Festus came into Felix' room: **and Felix, willing to shew the Jews a pleasure, left Paul bound.**

<u>**Acts 25:9**</u>

But Festus, willing to do the Jews a pleasure, answered Paul, and said, Wilt thou go up to Jerusalem, and there be judged of these things before me?

<u>**Galatians 1:10**</u>

For do I now persuade men, or God? or do I seek to please men? **for if I yet pleased men, I should not be the servant of Christ.**

<u>Galatians 2:12</u>
For before that certain came from James, he did eat with the Gentiles: **but when they were come, he withdrew and separated himself, fearing them which were of the circumcision.**

<u>Colossians 3:22</u>
Servants, obey in all things your masters according to the flesh; **not with eyeservice, as menpleasers; but in singleness of heart, fearing God:**

<u>Hebrews 13:6</u>
So that we may boldly say, **The Lord is my Helper, and I will not fear what man shall do unto me.**

So we take comfort and are encouraged and confidently and boldly say, ***The Lord is my Helper; I will not be seized with alarm [I will not fear or dread or be terrified]. What can man do to me? [AMP]***

F. Overcoming Prejudice & Hatred

<u>Genesis 43:32</u> *(Joseph, his Hebrew brothers, and the Egyptians)*
And they set on for him by himself, and for them by themselves, and for the Egyptians, which did eat with him, by themselves: **because the Egyptians might not eat bread with the Hebrews; for that is an abomination unto the Egyptians.**

<u>Leviticus 19:17</u>
Thou shalt not hate thy brother in thine heart: . . .

<u>Numbers 12:1, 10-11</u> *(Moses' interracial marriage)*
And Miriam and Aaron spake against Moses because of the Ethiopian woman whom he had married: for he had married an Ethiopian woman.

And the cloud departed from off the tabernacle; and, behold, Miriam became leprous, white as snow: and Aaron looked upon Miriam, and, behold, she was leprous.
And Aaron said unto Moses, Alas, my lord, I beseech thee, lay not the sin upon us, wherein we have done foolishly, and wherein we have sinned.

<u>Luke 4:24</u> *(familiarity breeds disrespect)*
And He said, Verily I say unto you, No prophet is accepted in his own country.

<u>Luke 9:51-53</u> *(The Samaritans refuse to receive Jesus, a Jew)*
And it came to pass, when the time was come that He should be received up, He stedfastly set His face to go to Jerusalem,
And sent messengers before His face: and they went, and entered into a village of the

Samaritans, to make ready for Him.

And they did not receive Him, because His face was as though He would go to Jerusalem.

<u>**John 1:46**</u> *(regional prejudice)*

And Nathanael said unto him, **Can there any good thing come out of Nazareth?** Philip saith unto him, Come and see.

<u>**John 4:9**</u> *(Jesus and the woman of Samaria)*

Then saith the woman of Samaria unto Him, How is it that Thou, being a Jew, askest drink of me, which am a woman of Samaria? **for the Jews have no dealings with the Samaritans.**

<u>**Acts 6:1**</u> *(the Grecian and Hebrew believers)*

And in those days, when the number of the disciples was multiplied, **there arose a murmuring of the Grecians against the Hebrews, because their widows were neglected in the daily ministration.**

<u>**Acts 10:28**</u> *(Peter and Cornelius)*

And he said unto them, Ye know how that it is an unlawful thing for a man that is a Jew to keep company, or come unto one of another nation; **but God hath shewed me that I should not call any man common or unclean.**

<u>**Acts 11:2-3**</u> *(Peter accused for going to the Gentiles)*

And when Peter was come up to Jerusalem, they that were of the circumcision **contended with him,**

Saying, Thou wentest in to men uncircumcised, and didst eat with them.

<u>**Acts 19:34**</u> *(The Jews and the Ephesians)*

But when they knew that he was a Jew, all with one voice about the space of two hours cried out, Great is Diana of the Ephesians.

<u>**Acts 26:10-11**</u> *(The Jewish leader, Saul, against the early Christian believers)*

. . . many of the saints did I shut up in prison, having received authority from the chief priests; and when they were put to death, I gave my voice against them.

And I punished them oft in every synagogue, and compelled them to blaspheme; and being exceedingly mad against them, I persecuted them even unto strange cities.

<u>**Galatians 2:11-13**</u> *(Peter separating himself from the Gentile believers)*

But when Peter was come to Antioch, I withstood him to the face, because he was to be blamed.

For before that certain came from James, he did eat with the Gentiles: **but when they were come, he withdrew and separated himself, fearing them which were of the circumcision.**

And the other Jews dissembled likewise with him; insomuch that Barnabas also was carried away with their dissimulation.

<u>**I John 2:9-11**</u>

He that saith he is in the light, and hateth his brother, is in darkness even until now.

He that loveth his brother abideth in the light, and there is none occasion of stumbling in him.

But he that hateth his brother is in darkness, and walketh in darkness, and knoweth not whither he goeth, because that darkness hath blinded his eyes.

<u>**I John 3:14-15**</u>

. . . He that loveth not his brother abideth in death.

Whosoever hateth his brother is a murderer: and ye know that no murderer hath eternal life abiding in him.

<u>**I John 4:20**</u>

If a man say, I love God, and hateth his brother, he is a liar: for he that loveth not his brother whom he hath seen, how can he love God Whom he hath not seen?

G. Overcoming Murmuring Against God & Spiritual Leaders

<u>**Exodus 14:10-12**</u>

And when Pharaoh drew nigh, the children of Israel lifted up their eyes, and behold, the Egyptians marched after them; and they were sore afraid: and the children of Israel cried out unto the Lord.

And they said unto Moses, Because there were no graves in Egypt, hast thou taken us away to die in the wilderness? wherefore hast thou taken us away to die in the wilderness? wherefore hast thou dealt thus with us, to carry us forth out of Egypt?

Is not this the word that we did tell thee in Egypt, saying, Let us alone, that we may serve the Egyptians? For it had been better for us to serve the Egyptians, than that we should die in the wilderness.

<u>**Exodus 15:23-24**</u>

And when they came to Marah, they could not drink of the waters of Marah, for they were bitter: therefore the name of it was called Marah.

And the people murmured against Moses, saying What shall we drink?

<u>**Exodus 16:2-3**</u>

And the whole congregation of the children of Israel murmured against Moses and Aaron in the wilderness:

And the children of Israel said unto them, **Would to God we had died by the hand of the Lord in the land of Egypt, when we sat by the flesh pots, and when we did eat bread to the full; for ye have brought us forth into this wilderness, to kill this whole assembly with hunger.**

Exodus 16:7-8

And in the morning, then ye shall see the glory of the Lord; for that He heareth your murmurings against the Lord: and what are we, that ye murmur against us?

And Moses said, This shall be, when the Lord shall give you in the evening flesh to eat, and in the morning bread to the full; **for that the Lord heareth your murmurings which ye murmur against Him: and what are we? your murmurings are not against us, but against the Lord.**

Exodus 17:1-3

And all the congregation of the children of Israel journeyed from the wilderness of Sin, after their journeys, according to the commandment of the Lord, and pitched in Rephidim: and there was no water for the people to drink.

Wherefore the people did chide with Moses, and said, Give us water that we may drink. **And Moses said unto them, Why chide ye with me? wherefore do ye tempt the Lord?**

And the people thirsted there for water; **and the people murmured against Moses, and said, Wherefore is this that thou hast brought us up out of Egypt, to kill us and our children and our cattle with thirst?**

Numbers 11:1-2

And when the people complained, it displeased the Lord: and the Lord heard it; and His anger was kindled; and the fire of the Lord burnt among them, and consumed them that were in the uttermost parts of the camp.

And the people cried unto Moses; and when Moses prayed unto the Lord, the fire was quenched.

Numbers 11:4-6, 10, 18-20

And the mixt multitude that was among them fell a lusting: and the children of Israel also wept again, and said, Who shall give us flesh to eat?

We remember the fish, which we did eat in Egypt freely; the cucumbers, and the melons, and the leeks, and the onions, and the garlick:

But now our soul is dried away: there is nothing at all, beside this manna, before our eyes.

Then Moses heard the people weep throughout their families, every man in the door of his tent: **and the anger of the Lord was kindled greatly;** Moses also was displeased.

And say thou unto the people, Sanctify yourselves against to morrow, and ye shall eat flesh: for ye have wept in the ears of the Lord, saying, Who shall give us flesh to eat? for it was well with us in Egypt: therefore the Lord will give you flesh, and ye shall eat.

Ye shall not eat one day, nor two days, nor five days, neither ten days, nor twenty days;

But even a whole month, until it come out at your nostrils, and it be loathsome unto you: **because that ye have despised the Lord which is among you, and have wept before Him, saying, Why came we forth out of Egypt?**

Numbers 14:1-3, 26-34

And all the congregation lifted up their voice, and cried; and the people wept that night.

And all the children of Israel murmured against Moses and against Aaron: and the whole congregation said unto them, Would God that we had died in the land of Egypt! or would God we had died in this wilderness!

And wherefore hath the Lord brought us unto this land, to fall by the sword, that our wives and our children should be a prey? were it not better for us to return into Egypt?

And the Lord spake unto Moses and unto Aaron, saying,

How long shall I bear with this evil congregation, which murmur against Me? I have heard the murmurings of the children of Israel, which they murmur against Me.

Say unto them, As truly as I live, saith the Lord, as ye have spoken in Mine ears, so will I do to you:

Your carcases shall fall in this wilderness; and all that were numbered of you, according to your whole number, from twenty years old and upward, which have murmured against Me,

Doubtless ye shall not come into the land, concerning which I sware to make you dwell therein, save Caleb the son of Jephunneh, and Joshua the son of Nun.

But your little ones, which ye said should be a prey, them will I bring in, and they shall know the land which ye have despised.

But as for you, your carcases, they shall fall in this wilderness.

And your children shall wander in the wilderness forty years, and bear your whoredoms, until your carcases be wasted in the wilderness.

After the number of days in which ye searched the land, even forty days, each day for a year, shall ye bear your iniquities, even forty years, and ye shall know my breach of promise.

<u>Numbers 20:2-5</u>

And there was no water for the congregation: and they gathered themselves together against Moses and against Aaron.

And the people chode with Moses, and spake, saying, Would God that we had died when our brethren died before the Lord!

And why have ye brought up the congregation of the Lord into this wilderness, that we and our cattle should die there?

And wherefore have ye made us to come up out of Egypt, to bring us in unto this evil place? it is no place of seed, or of figs, or of vines, or of pomegranates; neither is there any water to drink.

<u>Numbers 21:5-7</u>

And the people spake against God, and against Moses, Wherefore have ye brought us up out of Egypt to die in the wilderness? for there is no bread, neither is there any water; and our soul loatheth this light bread.

And the Lord sent fiery serpents among the people, and they bit the people; and much people of Israel died.

Therefore the people came to Moses, and said, We have sinned, for we have spoken against the Lord, and against thee; pray unto the Lord, that He take away the serpents from us. And Moses prayed for the people.

<u>Deuteronomy 1:26-27</u>

Notwithstanding ye would not go up, but rebelled against the commandment of the Lord your God:

And ye murmured in your tents, and said, Because the Lord hated us, He hath brought us forth out of the land of Egypt, to deliver us into the hand of the Amorites, to destroy us.

Joshua 9:18-19

And the children of Israel smote them *(the Gibeonites)* not, because the princes of the congregation had sworn unto them by the Lord God of Israel. **And all the congregation murmured against the princes.**

But all the princes said unto all the congregation, We have sworn unto them by the Lord God of Israel: now therefore we may not touch them.

Psalm 106:24-25

Yea, they despised the pleasant land, they believed not His word:

But murmured in their tents, and hearkened not unto the voice of the Lord.

Proverbs 19:3

The foolishness of man perverteth his way: **and his heart fretteth against the Lord.**

Matthew 9:10-11

And it came to pass, as Jesus sat at meat in the house, behold, many publicans and sinners came and sat down with Him and His disciples.

And when the Pharisees saw it, they said unto His disciples, **Why eateth your Master with publicans and sinners?**

Matthew 12:1-2

At that time Jesus went on the sabbath day through the corn; and His disciples were an hungred, and began to pluck the ears of corn, and to eat.

But when the Pharisees saw it, they said unto Him, **Behold, Thy disciples do that which is not lawful to do upon the sabbath day.**

Matthew 15:1-2

Then came to Jesus scribes and Pharisees, which were of Jerusalem, saying,

Why do Thy disciples transgress the tradition of the elders? for they wash not their hands when they eat bread.

Mark 2:3-7

And they come unto Him, bringing one sick of the palsy, which was borne of four.

And when they could not come nigh unto Him for the press, they uncovered the roof where He was: and when they had broken it up, they let down the bed wherein the sick of the palsy lay.

When Jesus saw their faith, He said unto the sick of the palsy, Son, thy sins be forgiven thee.

But there were certain of the scribes sitting there, and reasoning in their hearts,

Why doth this Man thus speak blasphemies? Who can forgive sins but God only?

<u>Mark 2:16</u>

And when the scribes and Pharisees saw Him eat with publicans and sinners, **they said unto His disciples, How is it that He eateth and drinketh with publicans and sinners?**

<u>Mark 7:1-2</u>

Then came together unto Him the Pharisees, and certain of the scribes, which came from Jerusalem.

And when they saw some of His disciples eat bread with defiled, that is to say, with unwashen, hands, **they found fault.**

<u>Luke 15:1-2</u>

Then drew near unto Him all the publicans and sinners for to hear Him.

And the Pharisees and scribes murmured, saying, This man receiveth sinners, and eateth with them.

<u>Luke 19:7</u>

And when they saw it, they all murmured, saying, That He was gone to be guest with a man that is a sinner *(Zacchaeus).*

<u>John 6:41-44</u>

The Jews then murmured at Him, because He said, I am the Bread Which came down from heaven.

And they said, Is not this Jesus, the Son of Joseph, Whose father and mother we know? how is it then that He saith, I came down from heaven?

Jesus therefore answered and said unto them, Murmur not among yourselves.

No man can come to Me, except the Father Which hath sent Me draw him: and I will raise him up at the last day.

<u>Acts 25:7</u>

And when he was come, the Jews which came down from Jerusalem stood round about, **and laid many and grievous complaints against Paul, which they could not prove.**

<u>I Corinthians 10:10</u>

Neither murmur ye, as some of them also murmured, and were destroyed of the destroyer.

Nor discontentedly complain as some of them did - and were put out of the way entirely by the destroyer (death). [AMP]

<u>Philippians 2:14</u>

Do all things without murmurings and disputings:

<u>Philippians 2:14</u>

Do all things without grumbling and faultfinding and complaining [against God] and questioning and doubting [among yourselves]. [AMP]

Jude 16

These are murmurers, complainers, walking after their own lusts; and their mouth speaketh great swelling words, having men's persons in admiration because of advantage.

Chapter 31

Victory Over Strongholds in our Emotions

A. Overcoming Anger

Job 5:2
For wrath killeth the foolish man, and envy slayeth the silly one.

Psalm 37:8
Cease from anger, and forsake wrath: fret not thyself in any wise to do evil.

Proverbs 12:16
A fool's wrath is presently known: but a prudent man covereth shame.

Proverbs 14:16-17
A wise man feareth, and departeth from evil: **but the fool rageth, and is confident.**
He that is soon angry dealeth foolishly: and a man of wicked devices is hated.

Proverbs 14:29
He that is slow to wrath is of great understanding: but he that is hasty of spirit exalteth folly.

Proverbs 15:1
A soft answer turneth away wrath: but grievous words stir up anger.

Proverbs 15:18
A wrathful man stirreth up strife: but he that is slow to anger appeaseth strife.

Proverbs 16:32

He that is slow to anger is better than the mighty; and he that ruleth his spirit than he that taketh a city.

Proverbs 19:11

The discretion of a man deferreth his anger; and it is his glory to pass over a transgression.

Proverbs 21:14

A gift in secret pacifieth anger: and a reward in the bosom strong wrath.

Proverbs 21:19

It is better to dwell in the wilderness, than with a contentious and an angry woman.

Proverbs 22:24-25

Make no friendship with an angry man; and with a furious man thou shalt not go:
Lest thou learn his ways, and get a snare to thy soul.

Proverbs 25:28

He that hath no rule over his own spirit is like a city that is broken down, and without walls.

Proverbs 27:4

Wrath is cruel, and anger is outrageous; but who is able to stand before envy?

Proverbs 29:8

Scornful men bring a city into a snare: **but wise men turn away wrath.**

Proverbs 29:11

A fool gives full vent to his anger, *but a wise man keeps himself under control. [NIV]*

Proverbs 29:22

An angry man stirreth up strife, and a furious man aboundeth in transgression.

Proverbs 30:33

Surely the churning of milk bringeth forth butter, and the wringing of the nose bringeth forth blood: **so the forcing of wrath bringeth forth strife.**

Ecclesiastes 7:9

Be not hasty in thy spirit to be angry: for anger resteth in the bosom of fools.

Matthew 5:21-22

Ye have heard that it was said by them of old time, Thou shalt not kill; and whosoever shall kill shall be in danger of the judgment:

But I say unto you, **That whosoever is angry with his brother without a cause shall be in danger of the judgment:** and whosoever shall say to his brother, Raca, shall be in danger of the council: but whosoever shall say, Thou fool, shall be in danger of hell fire.

Romans 12:19-21

Dearly beloved, avenge not yourselves, but rather give place unto wrath: for it is written, Vengeance is Mine; I will repay, saith the Lord.

Therefore if thine enemy hunger, feed him; if he thirst, give him drink: for in so doing thou shalt heap coals of fire on his head.

Be not overcome of evil, but overcome evil with good.

Ephesians 4:26-27

Be ye angry and sin not: let not the sun go down upon your wrath:

Neither give place to the devil.

Ephesians 4:31-32

Let all bitterness, and wrath, and anger, and clamour, and evil speaking, be put away from you, with all malice:

And be ye kind one to another, tenderhearted, forgiving one another, even as God for Christ's sake hath forgiven you.

Let all bitterness and ***indignation*** *and* ***wrath (passion, rage, bad temper)*** *and* ***resentment (anger, animosity)*** *and quarreling (brawling, clamor, contention) and slander (evil-speaking, abusive or blasphemous language) be banished from you, with all malice (spite, ill will, or baseness of any kind).*

And become useful and helpful and kind to one another, tenderhearted (compassionate, understanding, loving-hearted), forgiving one another [readily and freely], as God in Christ forgave you. [AMP]

Colossians 3:8

But now ye also put off all these; **anger, wrath,** malice, blasphemy, filthy communication out of your mouth.

But now put away and rid yourselves [completely] of all these things: anger, rage, bad feeling toward others, curses and slander, and foulmouthed abuse and shameful utterances from your lips! [AMP]

Hebrews 10:30

For we know Him that hath said, **Vengeance belongeth unto Me**, I will recompense, saith the Lord. And again, The Lord shall judge His people.

James 1:19-20

Wherefore, my beloved brethren, let every man be swift to hear, slow to speak, **slow to wrath:**

For the wrath of man worketh not the righteousness of God.

B. Overcoming Fear

Genesis 15:1

. . . **Fear not,** Abram: I am thy shield, and thy exceeding great reward.

Deuteronomy 31:7-8

. . . Be strong and of a good courage: for thou must go with this people unto the land which the Lord hath sworn unto their fathers to give them; and thou shalt cause them to inherit it.

And the Lord, He it is that doth go before thee; He will be with thee, He will not fail thee, neither forsake thee: **fear not, neither be dismayed.**

I Samuel 12:20-22

And Samuel said unto the people, **Fear not:** ye have done all this wickedness: yet turn not aside from following the Lord, but serve the Lord with all your heart;

And turn ye not aside: for then should ye go after vain things, which cannot profit nor deliver; for they are vain.

For the Lord will not forsake His people for His great name's sake: because it hath pleased the Lord to make you His people.

II Kings 6:15-17 *(Elisha)*

And when the servant of the man of God was risen early, and gone forth, behold, an host compassed the city both with horses and chariots. And his servant said unto him, Alas, my master! how shall we do?

And he answered, **Fear not**: for they that be with us are more than they that be with them.

And Elisha prayed, and said, Lord, I pray Thee, open his eyes, that he may see. And the Lord opened the eyes of the young man; and he saw: and, behold, the mountain was full of horses and chariots of fire round about Elisha.

II Chronicles 32:7-8 *(Hezekiah)*

Be strong and courageous, be not afraid nor dismayed for the king of Assyria, nor for all the multitude that is with him: for there be more with us than with him:

With him is an arm of flesh; but with us is the Lord our God to help us, and to fight our battles. . . .

Job 5:21

Thou shalt be hid from the scourge of the tongue: **neither shalt thou be afraid of destruction when it cometh.**

Job 11:15

For then shalt thou lift up thy face without spot; yea, thou shalt be steadfast, and shalt not fear:

<u>**Job 11:19**</u>
Also thou shalt lie down, and none shall make thee afraid; . . .

<u>**Psalm 3:6**</u>
I will not be afraid of ten thousands of people, that have set themselves against me round about.

<u>**Psalm 23:4**</u>
Yea, though I walk through the valley of the shadow of death, **I will fear no evil: for Thou art with me;** Thy rod and Thy staff they comfort me.

<u>**Psalm 27:1-3**</u>
The Lord is my Light and my Salvation; whom shall I fear? the Lord is the Strength of my life; of whom shall I be afraid?
When the wicked, even mine enemies and my foes, came upon me to eat up my flesh, they stumbled and fell.
Though a host should encamp against me, **my heart shall not fear**: though war should rise against me, in this will I be confident.

<u>**Psalm 34:4**</u>
I sought the Lord, and He heard me, and delivered me from all my fears.

<u>**Psalm 46:1-3**</u>
God is our Refuge and Strength, a very present help in trouble.
Therefore will not we fear, though the earth be removed, and though the mountains be carried into the midst of the sea;
Though the waters thereof roar and be troubled, though the mountains shake with the swelling thereof. Selah.

<u>**Psalm 56:11**</u>
In God have I put my trust: **I will not be afraid what man can do unto me.**

<u>**Psalm 91:5-8**</u>
Thou shalt not be afraid for the terror by night; nor for the arrow that flieth by day;
Nor for the pestilence that walketh in darkness; nor for the destruction that wasteth at noonday.
A thousand shall fall at thy side, and ten thousand at thy right hand; but it shall not come nigh thee.
Only with thine eyes shalt thou behold and see the reward of the wicked.

<u>**Psalm 112:6-8**</u>
. . . the righteous shall be in everlasting remembrance.
He shall not be afraid of evil tidings: his heart is fixed, trusting in the Lord.
His heart is established, he shall not be afraid, until he see his desire upon his enemies.

<u>**Psalm 118:6**</u>
The Lord is on my side; I will not fear: what can man do unto me?

<u>**Proverbs 18:10**</u>
The name of the Lord is a strong tower: the righteous runneth into it, and is safe.

<u>**Proverbs 28:1**</u>
The wicked flee when no man pursueth: **but the righteous are bold as a lion.**

<u>**Proverbs 29:25**</u>
The fear of man bringeth a snare: but whoso putteth his trust in the Lord shall be safe.

<u>**Isaiah 8:12-13**</u>
. . . neither fear ye their fear, nor be afraid.
Sanctify the Lord of hosts Himself; and let Him be your fear, and let Him be your dread.

<u>**Isaiah 12:2**</u>
Behold, God is my salvation; **I will trust, and not be afraid:** for the Lord Jehovah is my strength and my song; He also is become my salvation.

<u>**Isaiah 41:10**</u>
Fear thou not; for I am with thee: be not dismayed; for I am thy God: I will strengthen thee; yea, I will help thee; yea, I will uphold thee with the right hand of My righteousness.

<u>**Isaiah 43:1-2**</u>
But now thus saith the Lord that created thee, O Jacob, and He that formed thee, O Israel, **Fear not: for I have redeemed thee, I have called thee by thy name; thou art Mine.**
When thou passest through the waters, I will be with thee; and through the rivers, they shall not overflow thee: when thou walkest through the fire, thou shalt not be burned; neither shall the flame kindle upon thee.

<u>**Matthew 8:25-26**</u>
And His disciples came to Him, and awoke Him, saying, Lord, save us: we perish.
And He saith unto them, **Why are ye fearful, O ye of little faith?** Then He arose, and rebuked the winds and the sea; and there was a great calm.

<u>**Matthew 14:28-31**</u> *(Peter walking on the water)*
And Peter answered Him and said, Lord, if it be Thou, bid me come unto Thee on the water.
And He said, Come. And when Peter was come down out of the ship, he walked on the water, to go to Jesus.
But when he saw the wind boisterous, he was afraid; and beginning to sink, he cried, saying, Lord, save me.
And immediately Jesus stretched forth His hand, and caught him, and said unto him, **O**

thou of little faith, wherefore didst thou doubt?

Matthew 28:20

. . . lo, I am with you alway, even unto the end of the world. Amen.

Luke 12:4-7

And I say unto you My friends, **Be not afraid of them that kill the body, and after that have no more that they can do.**

But I will forewarn you Whom ye shall fear: Fear Him, which after He hath killed hath power to cast into hell; yea, I say unto you, Fear Him.

Are not five sparrows sold for two farthings, and not one of them is forgotten before God?

But even the very hairs of your head are all numbered. **Fear not therefore: ye are of more value than many sparrows.**

John 14:27

Peace I leave with you, My peace I give unto you: not as the world giveth, give I unto you. **Let not your heart be troubled, neither let it be afraid.**

Romans 8:15

For ye have not received the spirit of bondage again to fear; but ye have received the Spirit of adoption, whereby we cry, Abba, Father.

Philippians 1:28

And in nothing terrified by your adversaries: which is to them an evident token of perdition, but to you of salvation, and that of God.

II Thessalonians 3:3

But the Lord is faithful, Who shall stablish you, and keep you from evil.

II Timothy 1:7

For God hath not given us the spirit of fear; but of power, and of love, and of a sound mind.

For God did not give us a spirit of timidity (of cowardice, of craven and cringing and fawning fear), but [He has given us a spirit] of power and of love and of calm and well-balanced mind and discipline and self-control. [AMP]

Hebrews 11:23

By faith Moses, when he was born, was hid three months of his parents, because they saw he was a proper child; **and they were not afraid of the king's commandment.**

Hebrews 13:6

So that we may boldly say, **The Lord is my helper, and I will not fear what man shall do unto me.**

I John 4:18

There is no fear in love; but perfect love casteth out fear: . . .

Revelations 21:7-8

He that overcometh shall inherit all things; and I will be his God, and he shall be My son. **But the fearful and unbelieving,** and the abominable, and murderers, and whoremongers, and sorcerers, and idolaters, and all liars, **shall have their part in the lake which burneth with fire and brimstone: which is the second death.**

C. Rising Above Discouragement

II Chronicles 16:9

For the eyes of the Lord run to and fro throughout the whole earth, to shew Himself strong in the behalf of them whose heart is perfect toward Him . . .

Nehemiah 8:10

Then he said unto them, Go your way, eat the fat, and drink the sweet, and send portions unto them for whom nothing is prepared: for this day is holy unto our Lord: **neither be ye sorry; for the joy of the Lord is your strength.**

Job 8:20

Behold, God will not cast away a perfect man, neither will He help the evil doers:

Psalm 4:3

But know that the Lord hath set apart him that is godly for Himself: the Lord will hear when I call unto Him.

Psalm 27:1

The Lord is my Light and my Salvation; whom shall I fear? the Lord is the Strength of my life; of whom shall I be afraid?

Psalm 30:5

For His anger endureth but a moment; in His favour is life: **weeping may endure for a night, but joy cometh in the morning.**

Psalm 37:4-5

Delight thyself also in the Lord; and He shall give thee the desires of thine heart.

Commit thy way unto the Lord; trust also in Him; and He shall bring it to pass.

Psalm 138:7

Though I walk in the midst of trouble, Thou wilt revive me: Thou shalt stretch forth Thine hand against the wrath of mine enemies, and Thy right hand shall save me.

Psalm 147:3

He healeth the broken in heart, and bindeth up their wounds.

Isaiah 40:31

But they that wait upon the Lord shall renew their strength; they shall mount up with wings as eagles; they shall run, and not be weary; and they shall walk, and not faint.

Isaiah 41:10

Fear thou not; for I am with thee: **be not dismayed; for I am thy God:** I will strengthen thee; yea, I will help thee; yea, I will uphold thee with the right hand of My righteousness.

Isaiah 43:1-2

But now thus saith the Lord that created thee, O Jacob, and He that formed thee, O Israel, Fear not: for I have redeemed thee, I have called thee by thy name; thou art Mine.

When thou passest through the waters, **I will be with thee;** and through the rivers, **they shall not overflow thee:** when thou walkest through the fire, **thou shalt not be burned; neither shall the flame kindle upon thee.**

Isaiah 49:15-16

Can a woman forget her sucking child, that she should not have compassion on the son of her womb? yea, they may forget, **yet will I not forget thee.**

Behold, I have graven thee upon the palms of My hands; thy walls are continually before Me.

Isaiah 51:11

Therefore the redeemed of the Lord shall return, and come with singing unto Zion; and everlasting joy shall be upon their head: they shall obtain gladness and joy; and sorrow and mourning shall flee away.

Isaiah 61:3

To appoint unto them that mourn in Zion, **to give unto them beauty for ashes, the oil of joy for mourning, the garment of praise for the spirit of heaviness;** that they might be called trees of righteousness, the planting of the Lord, that He might be glorified.

Jeremiah 17:7-8

Blessed is the man that trusteth in the Lord, and whose hope the Lord is.

For he shall be as a tree planted by the waters, and that spreadeth out her roots by the river, and shall not see when heat cometh, but her leaf shall be green; and shall not be careful in the year of drought, neither shall cease from yielding fruit.

Hosea 6:3

Then shall we know, if we follow on to know the Lord: His going forth is prepared as the morning; and He shall come unto us as the rain, as the latter and former rain unto the earth.

Joel 2:25

And I will restore to you the years that the locust hath eaten, . . .

Matthew 6:33

But seek ye first the kingdom of God, and His righteousness; and all these things shall be added unto you.

Matthew 11:28-30

Come unto Me, all ye that labour and are heavy laden, and I will give you rest.

Take My yoke upon you, and learn of Me; for I am meek and lowly in heart: and ye shall find rest unto your souls.

For My yoke is easy, and My burden is light.

Mark 10:29-31

And Jesus answered and said, Verily I say unto you, **There is no man that hath left house, or brethren, or sisters, or father, or mother, or wife, or children, or lands, for My sake, and the Gospel's,**

But He shall receive an hundredfold now in this time, houses, and brethren, and sisters, and mothers, and children, and lands, with persecutions; **and in the world to come eternal life.**

But many that are first shall be last; and the last first.

Luke 18:1

And He spake a parable unto them to this end, **that men ought always to pray, and not to faint;**

John 14:27

Peace, I leave with you, My peace I give unto you: **not as the world giveth, give I unto you**. Let not your heart be troubled, neither let it be afraid.

Romans 8:18

For I reckon that the sufferings of this present time are not worthy to be compared with the glory which shall be revealed in us.

Romans 8:38-39

For I am persuaded, that neither death, nor life, nor angels, nor principalities, nor powers, nor things present, nor things to come,

Nor height, nor depth, nor any other creature, shall be able to separate us from the love of God, which is in Christ Jesus our Lord.

I Corinthians 2:9

But as it is written, **Eye hath not seen, nor ear heard, neither have entered into the heart of man, the things which God hath prepared for them that love Him.**

II Corinthians 4:16-18

For which cause we faint not; but though our outward man perish, yet the inward man is renewed day by day.

For our light affliction, which is but for a moment, worketh for us a far more exceeding and eternal weight of glory;

While we look not at the things which are seen, but at the things which are not seen: **for the things which are seen are temporal; but the things which are not seen are eternal.**

Galatians 6:9

And let us not be weary in well doing: for in due season we shall reap, if we faint not.

Philippians 1:6

Being confident of this very thing, that **He which hath begun a good work in you will perform it until the day of Jesus Christ:**

Philippians 3:13-14

Brethren, I count not myself to have apprehended: but this one thing I do, **forgetting those things which are behind, and reaching forth unto those things which are before,**

I press toward the mark for the prize of the high calling of God in Christ Jesus.

Philippians 4:8

Finally, brethren, whatsoever things are **true**, whatsoever things are **honest**, whatsoever things are **just**, whatsoever things are **pure**, whatsoever things are **lovely**, whatsoever things are **of good report;** if there be any **virtue**, and if there be any **praise**, **think on these things.**

Hebrews 10:35-36

Cast not away therefore your confidence, which hath great recompence of reward.

For ye have need of patience, that, after ye have done the will of God, ye might receive the promise.

Hebrews 13:5

Let your conversation be without covetousness; and be content with such things as you have: **for He hath said, I will never leave thee, nor forsake thee.**

. . . for He [God] Himself has said, I will not in any way fail you nor give you up nor leave you without support. [I will] not, [I will] not, [I will] not in any degree leave you helpless nor forsake nor let [you] down (relax My hold on you)! [Assuredly not!] [AMP]

I Peter 1:6-9

Wherein ye greatly rejoice, though now for a season, if need be, ye are in heaviness through manifold temptations:

That the trial of your faith, being much more precious than of gold that perisheth, though it be tried with fire, might be found unto praise and honour and glory at the appearing of Jesus Christ:

Whom having not seen, ye love; in Whom, though now ye see Him not, yet believing, ye rejoice with joy unspeakable and full of glory:

Receiving the end of your faith, even the salvation of your souls.

I Peter 5:6-7

Humble yourselves therefore under the mighty hand of God, that He may exalt you in due time:

Casting all your care upon Him; for He careth for you.

I John 5:4

For whatsoever is born of God overcometh the world: and this is the **victory** that overcometh the world, **even our faith.**

Jude 20

But you, beloved, ***build yourselves up [founded] on your most holy faith [make progress, rise like an edifice higher and higher]****, praying in the Holy Spirit; [AMP]*

Revelation 3:7-8

. . . These things saith He that is holy, He that is true, He that hath the key of David, He that openeth, and no man shutteth; and shutteth, and no man openeth;

I know thy works: **behold, I have set before thee an open door, and no man can shut it:** for thou hast a little strength, and hast kept My word, and hast not denied My name.

Revelation 21:4

And God shall wipe away all tears from their eyes; and there shall be no more death, neither sorrow, nor crying, neither shall there be any more pain: for the former things are passed away.

Chapter 32

Righteous Thoughts & Meditations

Joshua 1:8

This book of the law shall not depart out of thy mouth; **but thou shalt meditate therein day and night, that thou mayest observe to do according to all that is written therein:** for then thou shalt make thy way prosperous, and then thou shalt have good success.

Psalm 1:1-3

Blessed is the man that walketh not in the counsel of the ungodly, nor standeth in the way of sinners, nor sitteth in the seat of the scornful.

But his delight is in the law of the Lord; and in His law doth he meditate day and night.

And he shall be like a tree planted by the rivers of water, that bringeth forth his fruit in his season; his leaf also shall not wither; and whatsoever he doeth shall prosper.

Psalm 4:4

Stand in awe, and sin not: **commune with your own heart upon your bed,** and be still.

Psalm 19:14

Let the words of my mouth, and the meditation of my heart, be acceptable in Thy sight, O Lord, my Strength, and my Redeemer.

Psalm 37:5

Commit thy way unto the Lord; trust also in Him; and He shall bring it to pass.

Commit your way to the Lord [roll and repose each care of your load on Him]; *trust (lean on, rely on, and be confident) also in Him and He will bring it to pass. [AMP]*

Psalm 63:6

When I remember Thee upon my bed, **and meditate on Thee in the night watches.**

Psalm 104:34

My meditation of Him shall be sweet: I will be glad in the Lord.

Psalm 119:15

I will meditate in Thy precepts, and have respect unto Thy ways.

Psalm 119:97-100

O how love I Thy law! **it is my meditation all the day.**

Thou through Thy commandments hast made me **wiser than mine enemies**: for they are ever with me.

I have more understanding than all my teachers: for Thy testimonies are my meditation.

I understand more than the ancients, because I keep Thy precepts.

Psalm 119:148

Mine eyes prevent the night watches, that I might meditate in Thy word.

Psalm 143:5

I remember the days of old; **I meditate on all Thy works;** I muse on the work of Thy hands.

Proverbs 12:5

The thoughts of the righteous are right: but the counsels of the wicked are deceit.

Proverbs 15:26

The thoughts of the wicked are an abomination to the Lord: but the words of the pure are pleasant words.

Proverbs 16:3

Commit thy works unto the Lord, and thy thoughts shall be established.

Proverbs 23:7

For as he thinketh in his heart, so is he: . . .

Proverbs 24:9

The thought of foolishness is sin: and the scorner is an abomination to men.

Isaiah 26:3

Thou wilt keep him in perfect peace, whose mind is stayed on Thee: because he trusteth in Thee.

You will guard him and keep him in perfect and constant peace whose mind [both its inclination and its character] is stayed on You, because he commits himself to You, leans on You, and hopes confidently in You. [AMP]

Isaiah 55:8-9

For My thoughts are not your thoughts, neither are your ways My ways, saith the Lord.

For as the heavens are higher than the earth, so are My ways higher than your ways, and My thoughts than your thoughts.

Matthew 6:25

Therefore I say unto you, **Take no thought for your life,** what ye shall eat, or what ye shall drink; nor yet for your body, what ye shall put on. Is not the life more than meat, and the body than raiment?

Matthew 6:31-33

Therefore take no thought, saying, What shall we eat? or, What shall we drink? or, Wherewithal shall we be clothed?

(For after all these things do the Gentiles seek:) for your heavenly Father knoweth that ye have need of all these things.

But seek ye first the kingdom of God, and His righteousness; and all these things shall be added unto you.

Mark 13:11

But when they shall lead you, and deliver you up, **take no thought beforehand what ye shall speak, neither do ye premeditate:** but whatsoever shall be given you in that hour, that speak ye: for it is not ye that speak, but the Holy Ghost.

Luke 12:22

And He said unto His disciples, Therefore I say unto you, **Take no thought for your life**, what ye shall eat; neither for the body, what ye shall put on.

Romans 1:21

Because that, when they knew God, they glorified Him not as God, neither were thankful; **but became vain in their imaginations,** and their foolish heart was darkened.

Romans 1:28

And even as they did not like to retain God in their knowledge, God gave them over to a reprobate mind, to do those things which are not convenient;

Romans 8:6

For to be carnally minded is death; **but to be spiritually minded is life and peace.**

Romans 12:2-3

And be not conformed to this world: **but be ye transformed by the renewing of your mind,** that ye may prove what is that good, and acceptable, and perfect, will of God.

For I say, through the grace given unto me, to every man that is among you, **not to think of himself more highly than he ought to think; but to think soberly,** according as God hath dealt to every man the measure of faith.

I Corinthians 2:16

. . . But we have the mind of Christ.

II Corinthians 10:5

Casting down imaginations, and every high thing that exalteth itself against the knowledge of God, and bringing into captivity every thought to the obedience of Christ;

Ephesians 4:17

This I say therefore, and testify in the Lord, **that ye henceforth walk not as other Gentiles walk, in the vanity of their mind,**

Philippians 2:5

Let this mind be in you, which was also in Christ Jesus:

Philippians 4:6-8

Be careful for nothing; but in everything by prayer and supplication with thanksgiving let your requests be made known unto God.

And the peace of God, which passeth all understanding, shall keep your hearts and minds through Christ Jesus.

Finally, brethren, whatsoever things are **true**, whatsoever things are **honest**, whatsoever things are **just**, whatsoever things are **pure**, whatsoever things are **lovely**, whatsoever things are **of good report**; if there be **any virtue**, and if there be **any praise**, **think on these things.**

Colossians 3:2

Set your affection on things above, not on things on the earth.

I Timothy 4:15

Meditate upon these things; give thyself wholly to them; that thy profiting may appear to all.

II Timothy 1:7

For God hath not given us the spirit of fear; but of power, and of love, **and of a sound mind.**

For God did not give us a spirit of timidity (of cowardice, of craven and cringing and fawning fear), but [He has given us a spirit] of power and of love ***and of calm and well-balanced mind and discipline and self-control. [AMP]***

Titus 1:15

Unto the pure all things are pure: but unto them that are defiled and unbelieving is nothing pure; but even their mind and conscience is defiled.

Titus 2:6

Young men likewise exhort to be sober minded.

Hebrews 12:3

For consider Him that endured such contradiction of sinners against Himself, **lest ye be wearied and faint in your minds.**

I Peter 5:7

Casting all your care upon Him; for He careth for you.

***Casting the whole of your care [all your anxieties, all your worries, all your concerns, once and for all] on Him**, for He cares for you affectionately and cares about you watchfully. [AMP]*

Chapter 33

Controlling the Tongue

Proverbs 18:21

Death and life are in the power of the tongue: . . .

A. Righteous Speech

Deuteronomy 6:7

And thou shalt teach them *(God's word)* diligently unto thy children, and **shalt talk of them** when thou sittest in thine house, and when thou walkest by the way, and when thou liest down, and when thou risest up.

I Kings 22:16

And the king said unto him, **How many times shall I adjure thee that thou tell me nothing but that which is true in the name of the Lord?**

Job 6:25

How forcible are right words! . . .

Psalm 39:1

I said, I will take heed to my ways, that I sin not with my tongue: I will keep my mouth with a bridle, while the wicked is before me.

Proverbs 10:11

The mouth of a righteous man is a well of life: but violence covereth the mouth of the wicked.

Proverbs 10:13-14

In the lips of him that hath understanding wisdom is found: but a rod is for the back of him that is void of understanding.

Wise men lay up knowledge: but the mouth of the foolish is near destruction.

Proverbs 10:19-21

In the multitude of words there wanteth not sin: **but he that refraineth his lips is wise.**

The tongue of the just is as choice silver: the heart of the wicked is little worth.

The lips of the righteous feed many: but fools die for want of wisdom.

Proverbs 10:31-32

The mouths of the righteous (those harmonious with God) bring forth skillful and godly Wisdom, *but the perverse tongue shall be cut down [like a barren and rotten tree].*

The lips of the [uncompromisingly] righteous know [and therefore utter] what is acceptable, *but the mouth of the wicked knows [and therefore speaks only] what is obstinately willful and contrary. [AMP]*

Proverbs 12:14

From ***the fruit of his words*** *a man shall be satisfied with good, . . .*

Proverbs 12:18-19

There are those who speak rashly, like the piercing of a sword, ***but the tongue of the wise brings healing.***

Truthful lips shall be established forever, *but a lying tongue is [credited] but for a moment. [AMP]*

Proverbs 13:2-3

A man shall eat good by the fruit of his mouth: . . .

He that keepeth his mouth keepeth his life: but he that openeth wide his lips shall have destruction.

Proverbs 15:1-2

A soft answer turneth away wrath: but grievous words stir up anger.

The tongue of the wise useth knowledge aright: but the mouth of fools poureth out foolishness.

Proverbs 15:23

A man hath joy by the answer of his mouth: and a word spoken in due season, how good is it!

Proverbs 16:24

Pleasant words are as an honeycomb, sweet to the soul, and health to the bones.

Proverbs 18:4

The words of a man's mouth are as deep waters, . . .

Proverbs 25:11

A word fitly spoken and in due season is like apples of gold in settings of silver. [AMP]

Proverbs 25:15

By long forbearing is a prince persuaded, **and a soft tongue breaketh the bone.**

Proverbs 27:21

As the refining pot for silver and the furnace for gold [bring forth all the impurities of the metal], so let a man be in his trial of praise [ridding himself of all that is base or insincere; for a man is judged by what he praises and of what he boasts]. [AMP]

Proverbs 31:8-9

Open your mouth for the dumb [those unable to speak for themselves], for the rights of all who are left desolate and defenseless;

Open your mouth, judge righteously, and administer justice for the poor and needy. [AMP]

Proverbs 31:26

She opens her mouth in skillful and godly Wisdom, and on her tongue is the law of kindness [giving counsel and instruction]. [AMP]

Ecclesiastes 9:17

The **words of wise men** are heard in quiet more than the cry of him that ruleth among fools.

Ecclesiastes 12:11

The words of the wise are like prodding goads, and firmly fixed [in the mind] like nails are the collected sayings which are given [as proceeding] from one Shepherd. [AMP]

Isaiah 50:4

The Lord God hath given Me the tongue of the learned, that I should know how to speak a word in season to him that is weary: He wakeneth morning by morning, He wakeneth Mine ear to hear as the learned.

Zechariah 8:16

These are the things that ye shall do; **Speak ye every man the truth to his neighbour;** execute the judgment of truth and peace in your gates:

Malachi 2:6 (Levi)

The law of truth was in his mouth, and iniquity was not found in his lips: he walked with Me in peace and equity, and did turn many away from iniquity.

Malachi 3:16

Then they that feared the Lord spake often one to another: and the Lord hearkened, and heard it, and a book of remembrance was written before Him for them that feared the

Lord, and that thought upon His name.

<u>**Matthew 12:34-37**</u>

O generation of vipers, how can ye, being evil, speak good things? **for out of the abundance of the heart the mouth speaketh.**

A good man out of the good treasure of the heart bringeth forth good things: and an evil man out of the evil treasure bringeth forth evil things.

But I say unto you, That every idle word that men shall speak, they shall give account thereof in the day of judgment.

For by thy words thou shalt be justified, and by thy words thou shalt be condemned.

<u>**Luke 21:14-15**</u>

Settle it therefore in your hearts, not to meditate before what ye shall answer:

For I will give you a mouth and wisdom, which all your adversaries shall not be able to gainsay nor resist.

<u>**Acts 4:13**</u>

Now when they saw the boldness of Peter and John, and perceived that they were unlearned and ignorant men, they marvelled; and they took knowledge of them, **that they had been with Jesus.**

<u>**Romans 10:8**</u>

. . . The word is nigh thee, even in thy mouth, and in thy heart: that is, the word of faith,...

<u>**Ephesians 5:19**</u>

Speaking to yourselves in psalms and hymns and spiritual songs, singing and making melody in your heart to the Lord;

<u>**I Thessalonians 2:4-5**</u>

But as we were allowed of God to be put in trust with the Gospel, **even so we speak; not as pleasing men, but God, Which trieth our hearts.**

For neither at any time used we flattering words, as ye know, . . .

<u>**Revelations 14:5 (the 144,000)**</u>

And in their mouth was found no guile: for they are without fault before the throne of God.

B. Restraining the Tongue

<u>**Job 6:24**</u>

Teach me, and I will hold my tongue: and cause me to understand wherein I have erred.

Psalm 34:12-13

What man is he that desireth life, and loveth many days, that he may see good?
Keep thy tongue from evil, and thy lips from speaking guile.

Proverbs 13:3

He that keepeth his mouth keepeth his life: but he that openeth wide his lips shall have destruction.

Proverbs 17:27-28

He that hath knowledge spareth his words: and a man of understanding is of an excellent spirit.
Even a fool, when he holdeth his peace, is counted wise: and he that shutteth his lips is esteemed a man of understanding.

Proverbs 21:23

Whoso keepeth his mouth and his tongue keepeth his soul from troubles.

Ecclesiastes 3:7

A time to rend, and a time to sew; **a time to keep silence,** and a time to speak;

James 1:19

Wherefore, my beloved brethren, let every man be swift to hear, **slow to speak**, slow to wrath:

James 1:26

If any man among you seem to be religious, and **bridleth not his tongue**, but deceiveth his own heart, this man's religion is vain.

I Peter 3:10

For he that will love life, and see good days, **let him refrain his tongue from evil, and his lips that they speak no guile:**

C. Foolish Speaking

Proverbs 6:2

Thou art snared with the words of thy mouth, thou art taken with the words of thy mouth.

Proverbs 10:19

In the multitude of words there wanteth not sin: but he that refraineth his lips is wise.

Proverbs 18:2

A [self-confident] fool has no delight in understanding but only in revealing his personal opinions and himself. [AMP]

Proverbs 18:6-7

A [self-confident] fool's lips bring contention, and his mouth invites a beating.
A [self-confident] fool's mouth is his ruin, and his lips are a snare to himself. [AMP]

Proverbs 29:11

A fool uttereth all his mind: but a wise man keepeth it in till afterwards.

Proverbs 29:20

Seest thou a man that is hasty in his words? there is more hope of a fool than of him.

Ecclesiastes 10:12-14

The words of a wise man's mouth are gracious and win him favor, ***but the lips of a fool consume him.***

The beginning of the words of his mouth is foolishness, and the end of his talk is wicked madness.

A fool also multiplies words, *. . . [AMP]*

Titus 2:9

Exhort servants to be obedient unto their own masters, and to please them well in all things; **not answering again;**

James 3:2

For in many things we offend all. **If any man offend not in word, the same is a perfect man, and able also to bridle the whole body.**

D. Evil Speaking

Psalm 12:2-4

They speak vanity every one with his neighbour: with flattering lips and with a double heart do they speak.
The Lord shall cut off all flattering lips, and the tongue that speaketh proud things:
Who have said, With our tongue will we prevail; our lips are our own: who is lord over us?

Psalm 34:13

Keep thy tongue from evil, and thy lips from speaking guile.

Psalm 50:19

Thou givest thy mouth to evil, and thy tongue frameth deceit.

Psalm 52:2-4

Thy tongue deviseth mischiefs; like a sharp razor, working deceitfully.
Thou lovest evil more than good; and lying rather than to speak righteousness. Selah.
Thou lovest all devouring words, **O thou deceitful tongue.**

Psalm 59:12

For the sin of their mouth and the words of their lips let them even be taken in their pride: and for cursing and lying which they speak.

Proverbs 11:9

An hypocrite with his mouth destroyeth his neighbour: but through knowledge shall the just be delivered.

Proverbs 12:13

The wicked is [dangerously] snared by the transgression of his lips, *but the [uncompromisingly] righteous shall come out of trouble. [AMP]*

Proverbs 12:18

There are those who speak rashly, like the piercing of a sword, *but the tongue of the wise brings healing. [AMP]*

Proverbs 26:23-26

Burning lips [uttering insincere words of love] and a wicked heart are like an earthen vessel covered with the scum thrown off from molten silver [making it appear to be solid silver].

He who hates pretends with his lips*, but stores up deceit within himself.*

When he speaks kindly, do not trust him, for seven abominations are in his heart.

Though his hatred covers itself with guile, his wickedness shall be shown openly before the assembly. [AMP]

Matthew 7:1

Do not judge and criticize and condemn others, so that you may not be judged and criticized and condemned yourselves. [AMP]

Matthew 12:34-37

. . . for out of the abundance of the heart the mouth speaketh.

A good man out of the good treasure of the heart bringeth forth good things: **and an evil man out of the evil treasure bringeth forth evil things.**

But I say unto you, That every idle word that men shall speak, they shall give account thereof in the day of judgment.

For by thy words thou shalt be justified, and by thy words thou shalt be condemned.

Ephesians 4:31

Let all bitterness, and wrath, and anger, and clamour, and **evil speaking**, be put away from you, with all malice:

Titus 3:1-2

Put them in mind to be subject to principalities and powers, to obey magistrates, to be ready to every good work,

To speak evil of no man, to be no brawlers, but gentle, shewing all meekness unto all men.

James 3:6, 8-12

And the tongue is a fire, a world of iniquity: so is the tongue among our members, that it defileth the whole body, and setteth on fire the course of nature; and it is set on fire of hell.

But the tongue can no man tame; it is an unruly evil, full of deadly poison.

Therewith bless we God, even the Father; and therewith curse we men, which are made after the similitude of God.

Out of the same mouth proceedeth blessing and cursing. My brethren, these things ought not so to be.

Doth a fountain send forth at the same place sweet water and bitter?

Can the fig tree, my brethren, bear olive berries? either a vine, figs? so can no fountain both yield salt water and fresh.

James 4:11

Speak not evil one of another, brethren. He that speaketh evil of his brother, and judgeth his brother, speaketh evil of the law, and judgeth the law: but if thou judge the law, thou art not a doer of the law, but a judge.

I Peter 2:1

Wherefore laying aside all malice, and all guile, and hypocrisies, and envies, and **all evil speakings,**

I Peter 2:21-23

For even hereunto were ye called: because Christ also suffered for us, leaving us an example, that ye should follow His steps:

Who did no sin, **neither was guile found in His mouth**:

Who, **when He was reviled, reviled not again**; when He suffered, He threatened not; but committed Himself to Him that judgeth righteously:

I Peter 3:9-10

Not rendering evil for evil, or railing for railing: but contrariwise blessing; knowing that ye are thereunto called, that ye should inherit a blessing.

For he that will love life, and see good days, **let him refrain his tongue from evil, and his lips that they speak no guile:**

Never return evil for evil or insult for insult (scolding, tongue-lashing, berating)*, but on the contrary blessing [praying for their welfare, happiness, and protection, and truly pitying and loving them]. For know that to this you have been called, that you may yourselves inherit a blessing [from God - that you may obtain a blessing as heirs, bringing welfare and happiness and protection].*

For let him who wants to enjoy life and see good days [good - whether apparent or not] ***keep his tongue free from evil and his lips from guile (treachery, deceit).*** *[AMP]*

E. Lying

Exodus 23:1

Thou shalt not raise a false report: put not thine hand with the wicked to be an unrighteous witness.

Leviticus 19:11-12

Ye shall not steal, neither deal falsely, **neither lie one to another.**

And ye shall not swear by My name falsely, neither shalt thou profane the name of thy God: I am the Lord.

Psalm 31:18

Let lying lips be put to silence; which speak grievous things proudly and contemptuously against the righteous.

Psalm 52:2-4

Thy tongue deviseth mischiefs; like a sharp razor, working deceitfully.
Thou lovest evil more than good; and **lying rather than to speak righteousness.** Selah.
Thou lovest all devouring words, O thou deceitful tongue.

Psalm 59:12

For the sin of their mouth and the words of their lips let them even be taken in their pride: **and for cursing and lying which they speak.**

Proverbs 6:16-19

These six things doth the Lord hate: yea, seven are an abomination unto Him:
A proud look, **a lying tongue,** and hands that shed innocent blood,
An heart that deviseth wicked imaginations, feet that be swift in running to mischief,
A false witness that speaketh lies, and he that soweth discord among brethren.

Proverbs 10:18

He that hideth hatred with lying lips, and he that uttereth a slander, is a fool.

Proverbs 12:19

Truthful lips shall be established forever, ***but a lying tongue is [credited] but for a moment.*** *[AMP]*

Proverbs 12:22

Lying lips are abomination to the Lord: but they that deal truly are His delight.

Proverbs 14:5

A faithful witness will not lie: **but a false witness will utter lies.**

Proverbs 19:5

A false witness shall not be unpunished, and **he that speaketh lies shall not escape.**

Proverbs 19:9

A false witness shall not be unpunished, and **he that speaketh lies shall perish.**

Proverbs 24:28

Be not a witness against thy neighbour without cause; and **deceive not with thy lips.**

Proverbs 26:28

A lying tongue hates those it wounds and crushes*, and a flattering mouth works ruin. [AMP]*

Proverbs 28:23

He that rebuketh a man afterwards shall find more favour **than he that flattereth with the tongue.**

Jeremiah 9:3

And they bend their tongues like their bow for lies: but they are not valiant for the truth upon the earth; for they proceed from evil to evil, and they know not Me, saith the Lord.

Jeremiah 14:14

Then the Lord said unto me, **The prophets prophesy lies in My name: I sent them not, neither have I commanded them, neither spake unto them:** they prophesy unto you a false vision and divination, and a thing of nought, and the deceit of their heart.

Lamentations 3:37-38

Who is he that saith, and it cometh to pass, when the Lord commandeth it not?
Out of the mouth of the most High proceedeth not evil and good?

Zechariah 8:17

And let none of you imagine evil in your hearts against his neighbour; and **love no false oath**: for all these are things that I hate, saith the Lord.

John 8:44

Ye are of your father **the devil,** and the lusts of your father ye will do. He was a murderer from the beginning, and abode not in the truth, because there is no truth in him. **When he speaketh a lie, he speaketh of his own: for he is a liar, and the father of it.**

Romans 1:25

Who changed the truth of God into a lie, and worshipped and served the creature more than the Creator, . . .

Colossians 3:9-10

Lie not one to another, seeing that ye have put off the old man with his deeds;

And have put on the new man, which is renewed in knowledge after the image of Him that created him:

James 3:14

But if ye have bitter envying and strife in your hearts, glory not, and lie not against the truth.

Revelations 21:7-8

He that overcometh shall inherit all things; and I will be his God, and he shall be My son.

But the fearful, and unbelieving, and the abominable, and murderers, and whoremongers, and sorcerers, and idolaters, and **all liars,** shall have their part in the lake which burneth with fire and brimstone: which is the second death.

Revelations 21:27 *(the new Jerusalem)*

And there shall in no wise enter into it any thing that defileth, neither whatsoever worketh abomination, **or maketh a lie:** but they which are written in the Lamb's Book of Life.

F. Gossip

Leviticus 19:16

You shall not go up and down as a dispenser of gossip and scandal among your people, *nor shall you [secure yourself by false testimony or by silence and] endanger the life of your neighbor. I am the Lord. [AMP]*

Psalm 52:2-4

Thy tongue deviseth mischiefs; like a sharp razor, working deceitfully.

Thou lovest evil more than good; and lying rather than to speak righteousness. Selah.

Thou lovest all devouring words, O thou deceitful tongue.

Proverbs 11:9

An hypocrite with his mouth destroyeth his neighbour: but through knowledge shall the just be delivered.

Proverbs 11:13

A talebearer revealeth secrets: but he that is of a faithful spirit concealeth the matter.

Proverbs 16:28

A froward man soweth strife: and a whisperer separated chief friends.

Proverbs 17:9

He that covereth a transgression seeketh love; **but he that repeateth a matter separateth very friends.**

Proverbs 18:8

The words of a whisperer or talebearer are as dainty morsels*; they go down into the innermost parts of the body. [AMP]*

Proverbs 20:19

He who goes about as a talebearer reveals secrets; therefore associate not with him who talks too freely. [AMP]

Proverbs 25:9-10

Argue your cause with your neighbor himself; ***discover not and disclose not another's secret,***

Lest he who hears you revile you and bring shame upon you and your ill repute have no end. [AMP]

Proverbs 25:23

The north wind brings forth rain; ***so does a backbiting tongue bring forth an angry countenance.*** *[AMP]*

Proverbs 26:20-21

Where no wood is, there the fire goeth out: **so where there is no talebearer, the strife ceaseth.**

As coals are to burning coals, and wood to fire; so is a contentious man to kindle strife.

Proverbs 26:22

The words of a whisperer or slanderer are like dainty morsels or words of sport *[to some, but to others are like deadly wounds]; and they go down into the innermost parts of the body [or of the victim's nature]. [AMP]*

II Thessalonians 3:11-12

For we hear that there are some which walk among you disorderly, working not at all, **but are busybodies.**

Now them that are such we command and exhort by our Lord Jesus Christ, that **with quietness they work,** and eat their own bread.

I Timothy 5:13

And withal they learn to be idle, wandering about from house to house; and not only idle, **but tattlers also and busybodies, speaking things which they ought not.**

I Peter 4:15

But let none of you suffer as a murderer, or as a thief, or as an evildoer, **or as a busybody in other men's matters.**

G. Slander

<u>**Psalm 31:13**</u>

For I have heard the slander of many: fear was on every side: while they took counsel together against me, they devised to take away my life.

<u>**Psalm 50:20**</u>

Thou sittest and speakest against thy brother; **thou slanderest thine own mother's son.**

<u>**Psalm 52:2-4**</u>

Thy tongue deviseth mischiefs; like a sharp razor, working deceitfully.
Thou lovest evil more than good; and lying rather than to speak righteousness. Selah.
Thou lovest all devouring words, O thou deceitful tongue.

<u>**Psalm 101:5**</u>

Whoso privily slandereth his neighbour, him will I cut off: . . .

<u>**Proverbs 10:18**</u>

He that hideth hatred with lying lips, and **he that uttereth a slander, is a fool.**

<u>**Proverbs 11:9**</u>

An hypocrite with his mouth destroyeth his neighbour: but through knowledge shall the just be delivered.

<u>**Proverbs 25:9-10**</u>

Argue your cause with your neighbor himself; *discover not and disclose not another's secret,*
Lest he who hears you revile you and bring shame upon you and your ill repute have no end. [AMP]

<u>**Proverbs 25:23**</u>

The north wind brings forth rain; ***so does a backbiting tongue bring forth an angry countenance. [AMP]***

<u>**Proverbs 26:22**</u>

The words of a whisperer or slanderer are like dainty morsels or words of sport [to some, but to others are like deadly wounds]; *and they go down into the innermost parts of the body [or of the victim's nature]. [AMP]*

<u>**Ecclesiastes 10:11**</u>

If the serpent bites before it is charmed, then it is no use to call a charmer ***[and the slanderer is no better than the uncharmed snake].*** *[AMP]*

Isaiah 57:20

But the wicked are like the troubled sea, when it cannot rest, whose waters cast up mire and dirt.

Matthew 7:1

Do not judge and criticize and condemn others, so that you may not be judged and criticized and condemned yourselves. [AMP]

Luke 7:33-34

For John the Baptist came neither eating bread nor drinking wine; and ye say, He hath a devil.

The Son of man is come eating and drinking; and ye say, Behold a gluttonous man, and a winebibber, a friend of publicans and sinners!

Revelations 21:7-8

He that overcometh shall inherit all things; and I will be his God, and he shall be My son.

But the fearful, and unbelieving, and the abominable, and **murderers**, and whoremongers, and sorcerers, and idolaters, and all liars, shall have their part in the lake which burneth with fire and brimstone: which is the second death.

Chapter 34

Walking in Righteous Obedience

A. Obedience to God & His Word

Exodus 19:5
Now therefore, **if ye will obey My voice indeed, and keep My covenant, then ye shall be a peculiar treasure unto Me above all people:** for all the earth is Mine:

Deuteronomy 5:1
And Moses called all Israel, and said unto them, Hear, O Israel, the statutes and judgments which I speak in your ears this day, that ye may learn them, and keep, and do them.

Deuteronomy 5:29
O that there were such an heart in them, **that they would fear Me, and keep all My commandments always,** that it might be well with them, and with their children for ever!

Deuteronomy 5:32-33
Ye shall observe to do therefore as the Lord your God hath commanded you: ye shall not turn aside to the right hand or to the left.

Ye shall walk in all the ways which the Lord your God hath commanded you, that ye may live, and that it may be well with you, and that ye may prolong your days in the land which ye shall possess.

Deuteronomy 6:3
Hear, therefore, O Israel, and observe to do it; that it may be well with thee, and that ye may increase mightily, as the Lord God of thy fathers hath promised thee, in the land that floweth with milk and honey.

Deuteronomy 6:18

And thou shalt do that which is right and good in the sight of the Lord: that it may be well with thee, and that thou mayest go in and possess the good land which the Lord sware unto thy fathers,

Deuteronomy 7:12-14

Wherefore it shall come to pass, **if ye hearken to these judgments, and keep, and do them,** that the Lord thy God shall keep unto thee the covenant and the mercy which He sware unto thy fathers:

And He will love thee, and bless thee, and multiply thee: He will also bless the fruit of thy womb, and the fruit of thy land, thy corn, and thy wine, and thine oil, the increase of thy kine, and the flocks of thy sheep, in the land which He sware unto thy fathers to give thee.

Thou shalt be blessed above all people: . . .

Deuteronomy 11:22-28

For if ye shall diligently keep all these commandments which I command you, to do them, to love the Lord your God, to walk in all His ways, and to cleave unto Him;

Then will the Lord drive out all these nations from before you, and ye shall possess greater nations and mightier than yourselves.

Every place whereon the soles of your feet shall tread shall be your's: from the wilderness and Lebanon, from the river, the river Euphrates, even unto the uttermost sea shall your coast be.

There shall no man be able to stand before you: for the Lord your God shall lay the fear of you and the dread of you upon all the land that ye shall tread upon, as He hath said unto you.

Behold, I set before you this day a blessing and a curse;

A blessing, if ye obey the commandments of the Lord your God, which I command you this day:

And a curse, if ye will not obey the commandments of the Lord your God, but turn aside out of the way which I command you this day, to go after other gods, which ye have not known.

Deuteronomy 13:4

Ye shall walk after the Lord your God, and fear Him, **and keep His commandments, and obey His voice,** and ye shall serve Him, and cleave unto Him.

Deuteronomy 29:9

Keep therefore the words of this covenant, and do them, that ye may prosper in all that ye do.

Deuteronomy 30:15-16

See, I have set before thee this day life and good, and death and evil;

In that I command thee this day to love the Lord thy God, to walk in His ways, and to keep His commandments and His statutes and His judgments, that thou mayest live and multiply: and the Lord thy God shall bless thee in the land whither thou goest to possess it.

<u>**I Samuel 12:14**</u>

If ye will fear the Lord, and serve Him, and **obey His voice, and not rebel against the commandment of the Lord,** then shall both ye and also the king that reigneth over you continue following the Lord your God:

<u>**I Samuel 15:22**</u>

And Samuel said, Hath the Lord as great delight in burnt offerings and sacrifices, as in obeying the voice of the Lord? **Behold, to obey is better than sacrifice, and to hearken than the fat of rams.**

<u>**I Kings 3:14**</u>

And if thou wilt walk in My ways, to keep My statutes and My commandments, as thy father David did walk, **then I will lengthen thy days.**

<u>**Job 36:11-12**</u>

If they obey and serve Him, they shall spend their days in prosperity, and their years in pleasures.

But if they obey not, they shall perish by the sword, and they shall die without knowledge.

<u>**Psalm 106:3**</u>

Blessed are they that keep judgment, and he that doeth righteousness at all times.

<u>**Psalm 143:10**</u>

Teach me to do Thy will; for Thou art my God: Thy spirit is good; lead me into the land of uprightness.

<u>**Isaiah 1:19**</u>

If ye be willing and obedient, ye shall eat the good of the land:

<u>**Isaiah 48:18**</u>

O that thou hadst hearkened to My commandments! then had thy peace been as a river, and thy righteousness as the waves of the sea:

<u>**Jeremiah 7:23**</u>

But this thing commanded I them, saying, **Obey My voice, and I will be your God, and ye shall be My people:** and walk ye in all the ways that I have commanded you, that it may be well unto you.

<u>**Matthew 5:19**</u>

Whosoever therefore shall break one of these least commandments, and shall teach men so, he shall be called the least in the kingdom of heaven: **but whosoever shall do and teach them, the same shall be called great in the kingdom of heaven.**

<u>**Matthew 7:21**</u>

Not every one that saith unto Me, Lord, Lord, shall enter into the kingdom of heaven; **but**

he that doeth the will of My Father Which is in heaven.

Matthew 7:24-25

Therefore whosoever heareth these sayings of Mine, and doeth them, I will liken him unto a wise man, which built his house upon a rock:

And the rain descended, and the floods came, and the winds blew, and beat upon that house; and **it fell not**: for it was founded upon a rock.

Matthew 12:50

For whosoever shall do the will of My Father Which is in heaven, the same is My brother, and sister, and mother.

John 4:34

Jesus saith unto them, **My meat is to do the will of Him that sent Me, and to finish His work.**

John 6:38

For I came down from heaven, not to do Mine own will, but the will of Him that sent Me.

John 13:17

If ye know these things, happy are ye if ye do them.

John 14:21

He that hath My commandments, and keepeth them, he it is that loveth Me: and he that loveth Me shall be loved of My Father, and I will love him, and will manifest Myself to him.

John 15:10

If ye keep My commandments, ye shall abide in My love; even as I have kept My Father's commandments, and abide in His love.

Acts 5:29

Then Peter and the other apostles answered and said, We ought to obey God rather than men.

Acts 5:32

And we are His witnesses of these things; and so is also the Holy Ghost, **Whom God hath given to them that obey Him.**

Acts 24:16

And herein do I exercise myself, to have always a conscience void of offence toward God, and toward men.

Romans 2:13

(For not the hearers of the law are just before God, **but the doers of the law shall be justified.**

Romans 5:19

For as by one man's disobedience many were made sinners, **so by the obedience of One shall many be made righteous.**

Romans 6:16

Know ye not, that to whom ye yield yourselves servants to obey, his servants ye are to whom ye obey; whether of sin unto death, or of obedience unto righteousness?

II Corinthians 10:5

Casting down imaginations, and every high thing that exalteth itself against the knowledge of God, **and bringing into captivity every thought to the obedience of Christ;**

Hebrews 5:8-9

Though He were a Son, yet learned He obedience by the things which He suffered;

And being made perfect, He became the author of eternal salvation unto all them that obey Him;

Hebrews 10:9

Then said He, **Lo, I come to do Thy will, O God.** He taketh away the first, that He may establish the second.

Hebrews 11:8

By faith Abraham, when he was called to go out into a place which he should after receive for an inheritance, **obeyed;** and he went out, not knowing whither he went.

James 1:25

But whoso looketh into the perfect law of liberty, and continueth therein, **he being not a forgetful hearer, but a doer of the work,** this man shall be blessed in his deed.

I John 2:3-6

And hereby we do know that we know Him, if we keep His commandments.

He that saith, I know Him, and keepeth not His commandments, is a liar, and the truth is not in him.

But whoso keepeth His word, in him verily is the love of God perfected: hereby know we that we are in Him.

He that saith he abideth in Him ought himself also so to walk, even as He walked.

I John 2:15-17

Love not the world, neither the things that are in the world. If any man love the world, the love of the Father is not in him.

For all that is in the world, the lust of the flesh, and the lust of the eyes, and the pride of life, is not of the Father, but is of the world.

And the world passeth away, and the lust thereof: **but he that doeth the will of God abideth for ever.**

I John 3:22

And whatsoever we ask, we receive of Him, because we keep His commandments, and do those things that are pleasing in His sight.

B. Obedience to Natural Authorities

Acts 24:16

And herein do I exercise myself, to have always a conscience void of offence toward God, and toward men.

Romans 13:1

Let every soul be subject unto the higher powers. For there is no power but of God: the powers that be are ordained of God.

Ephesians 6:1-3

Children, **obey your parents in the Lord:** for this is right.

Honour thy father and mother; which is the first commandment with promise;

That it may be well with thee, and thou mayest live long on the earth.

Ephesians 6:5-8

Servants, **be obedient to them that are your masters according to the flesh,** with fear and trembling, in singleness of your heart, **as unto Christ;**

Not with eyeservice, as menpleasers; **but as the servants of Christ,** doing the will of God from the heart;

With good will doing service, as to the Lord, and not to men:

Knowing that whatsoever good thing any man doeth, the same shall he receive of the Lord, whether he be bond or free.

Philippians 4:9

Those things, which ye have both learned, and received, and heard, and seen in me, **do:** and the God of peace shall be with you.

Colossians 3:20

Children, **obey your parents in all things:** for this is well pleasing unto the Lord.

Colossians 3:22-24

Servants, obey in all things your masters according to the flesh; not with eyeservice, as menpleasers; but in singleness of heart, fearing God:

And whatsoever ye do, do it heartily, as to the Lord, and not unto men;

Knowing that of the Lord ye shall receive the reward of the inheritance: for ye serve the Lord Christ.

Hebrews 13:7

Remember them which have the rule over you, who have spoken unto you the word of God: whose faith follow, considering the end of their conversation.

Obey your spiritual leaders and submit to them [continually recognizing their authority over you], for they are constantly keeping watch over your souls and guarding your spiritual welfare, as men who will have to render an account [of their trust]. [Do your part to] let them do this with gladness and not with sighing and groaning, for that would not be profitable to you [either]. [AMP]

I Peter 2:13-14

Submit yourselves to every ordinance of man for the Lord's sake: whether it be to the king, as supreme;

Or unto governors, as unto them that are sent by Him for the punishment of evildoers, and for the praise of them that do well.

I Peter 2:17-18

Honour all men. Love the brotherhood. Fear God. Honour the king.

Servants, be subject to your masters with all fear; not only to the good and gentle, but also to the froward.

I Peter 5:5

Likewise, you who are younger and of lesser rank, be subject to the elders (the ministers and spiritual guides of the church) - [giving them due respect and yielding to their counsel]. *Clothe (apron) yourselves, all of you, with humility [as the garb of a servant, so that its covering cannot possibly be stripped from you, with freedom from pride and arrogance] toward one another. For God sets Himself against the proud (the insolent, the overbearing, the disdainful, the presumptuous, the boastful) - [and He opposes, frustrates, and defeats them], but gives grace (favor, blessing) to the humble. [AMP]*

Chapter 35

Benefits of Fasting

A. General References to Fasting

<u>Deuteronomy 8:3</u>

. . . man doth not live by bread only, but by every word that proceedeth out of the mouth of the Lord doth man live.

<u>Job 23:12</u>

. . . I have esteemed the words of His mouth more than my necessary food.

<u>Psalm 35:11-14</u>

False witnesses did rise up; they laid to my charge things that I knew not.

They rewarded me evil for good to the spoiling of my soul.

But as for me, when they were sick, my clothing was sackcloth: **I humbled my soul with fasting;** and my prayer returned into mine own bosom.

I behaved myself as though he had been my friend or brother: I bowed down heavily, as one that mourneth for his mother.

<u>Psalm 69:10</u>

When I wept, **and chastened my soul with fasting, . . .**

<u>Isaiah 58:6-12</u>

Is not this the fast that I have chosen? to loose the bands of wickedness, to undo the heavy burdens, and to let the oppressed go free, and that ye break every yoke?

Is it not to deal thy bread to the hungry, and that thou bring the poor that are cast out to thy house? when thou seest the naked, that thou cover him; and that thou hide not thyself from thine own flesh?

Then shall thy light break forth as the morning, and thine health shall spring forth speedily: and thy righteousness shall go before thee; the glory of the Lord shall be thy rereward.

Then shall thou call, and the Lord shall answer; thou shalt cry, and He shall say, Here I am. If thou take away from the midst of thee the yoke, the putting forth of the finger, and speaking vanity;

And if thou draw out thy soul to the hungry, and satisfy the afflicted soul; then shall thy light rise in obscurity, and thy darkness be as the noon day:

And the Lord shall guide thee continually, and satisfy thy soul in drought, and make fat thy bones: and thou shalt be like a watered garden, and like a spring of water, whose waters fail not.

And they that shall be of thee shall build the old waste places: thou shalt raise up the foundations of many generations; and thou shalt be called, The repairer of the breach, The restorer of paths to dwell in.

Jeremiah 15:16

Thy words were found, and I did eat them; and Thy word was unto me the joy and rejoicing of mine heart: for I am called by Thy name, O Lord God of hosts.

Joel 1:14

Sanctify ye a fast, call a solemn assembly, gather the elders and all the inhabitants of the land into the house of the Lord your God, and cry unto the Lord,

Joel 2:12-13

Therefore also now, saith the Lord, Turn ye even to Me with all your heart, **and with fasting,** and with weeping, and with mourning:

And rend your heart, and not your garments, and turn unto the Lord your God: for He is gracious and merciful, slow to anger, and of great kindness, and repenteth Him of the evil.

Matthew 4:4

. . . It is written, **Man shall not live by bread alone, but by every word that proceedeth out of the mouth of God.**

Matthew 6:16-18

Moreover when ye fast, be not, as the hypocrites, of a sad countenance: for they disfigure their faces, that they may appear unto men to fast. Verily I say unto you, They have their reward.

But thou, when thou fastest, anoint thine head, and wash thy face;

That thou appear not unto men to fast, but unto thy Father Which is in secret: and **thy Father, Which seeth in secret, shall reward thee openly.**

Matthew 11:28-30

Come unto Me, all ye that labour and are heavy laden, and I will give you rest.

Take My yoke upon you, and learn of Me; for I am meek and lowly in heart: and ye shall find rest unto your souls.

For My yoke is easy, and My burden is light.

<u>**Matthew 17:21**</u>
Howbeit this kind goeth not out but by prayer and fasting.

<u>**John 4:34**</u>
Jesus saith unto them, **My meat is to do the will of Him that sent Me, and to finish His work.**

<u>**Romans 14:17**</u>
For the kingdom of God is not meat and drink; but righteousness, and peace, and joy in the Holy Ghost.

<u>**James 4:8-10**</u>
Draw nigh to God, and He will draw nigh to you. Cleanse your hands, ye sinners; and purify your hearts, ye double minded.
Be afflicted, and mourn, and weep: let your laughter be turned to mourning, and your joy to heaviness.
Humble yourselves in the sight of the Lord, and He shall lift you up.

B. Examples of Fasting from Scripture

<u>**Exodus 34:28**</u> *(Moses)*
And he was there with the Lord forty days and forty nights; **he did neither eat bread, nor drink water.** And he wrote upon the tables the words of the covenant, the ten commandments.

<u>**I Samuel 1:8**</u> *(Hannah)*
Then said Elkanah her husband to her, Hannah, why weepest thou? and why eatest thou not? and why is thy heart grieved? am not I better to thee than ten sons?

<u>**I Kings 19:8**</u> *(Elijah)*
And he arose, and did eat and drink, and went in the strength of that meat forty days and forty nights unto Horeb the mount of God.

<u>**Ezra 10:6**</u> *(Ezra)*
Then Ezra rose up from before the house of God, and went into the chamber of Johanan the son of Eliashib: and when he came thither, **he did eat no bread, nor drink water:** for he mourned because of the transgression of them that had been carried away.

<u>**Esther 4:16**</u> *(Esther)*
*Go, gather together all the Jews that are present in Shushan, **and fast for me; and neither eat nor drink for three days, night or day. I also and my maids will fast as you do.** Then I*

will go to the king, though it is against the law; and if I perish, I perish. [AMP]

<u>**Psalm 102:4**</u> *(David)*

My heart is smitten, and withered like grass; so that I forget to eat my bread.

<u>**Daniel 10:3**</u> *(Daniel)*

I ate no pleasant bread, neither came flesh nor wine in my mouth, neither did I anoint myself at all, **till three whole weeks were fulfilled.**

<u>**Luke 2:37**</u> *(Anna the prophetess)*

And she was a widow of about fourscore and four years, which departed not from the temple, **but served God with fastings and prayers night and day.**

<u>**Luke 4:1-2,14**</u> *(Jesus)*

And Jesus being full of the Holy Ghost returned from Jordan, and was led by the Spirit into the wilderness,

Being forty days tempted of the devil. **And in those days he did eat nothing: and when they were ended, he afterward hungered.**

And Jesus returned in the power of the Spirit into Galilee: . . .

<u>**Acts 9:9**</u> *(Saul)*

And he was three days without sight, **and neither did eat nor drink.**

<u>**Acts 10:30**</u> *(Cornelius)*

And Cornelius said, **Four days ago I was fasting until this hour;** and at the ninth hour I prayed in my house, and, behold, a man stood before me in bright clothing,

<u>**Acts 13:2-3**</u> *(The church at Antioch)*

As they ministered to the Lord, and fasted, the Holy Ghost said, Separate Me Barnabas and Saul for the work whereunto I have called them.

And when they had fasted and prayed, and laid their hands on them, they sent them away.

<u>**Acts 14:23**</u> *(Paul & Barnabas)*

And when they had ordained them elders in every church, **and had prayed with fasting,** they commended them to the Lord, on Whom they believed.

Chapter 36

Being a Witness to the Unsaved

A. Sharing the Light to a Dying World

Isaiah 52:7

How beautiful upon the mountains are the feet of him that bringeth good tidings, that publisheth peace; that bringeth good tidings of good, that publisheth salvation; that saith unto Zion, Thy God reigneth!

Matthew 5:14-16

Ye are the light of the world. A city that is set on an hill cannot be hid.

Neither do men light a candle, and put it under a bushel, but on a candlestick; and it giveth light unto all that are in the house.

Let your light so shine before men, that they may see your good works, and glorify your Father Which is in heaven.

Matthew 22:9

Go ye therefore into the highways, and as many as ye shall find, **bid to the marriage.**

Matthew 28:18-20

And Jesus came and spake unto them, saying, **All power is given unto Me in heaven and in earth.**

Go ye therefore, and teach all nations, baptizing them in the name of the Father, and of the Son, and of the Holy Ghost:

Teaching them to observe all things whatsoever I have commanded you: and, lo, I am with you alway, even unto the end of the world. Amen.

<u>Mark 1:17</u>

And Jesus said unto them, **Come ye after Me, and I will make you to become fishers of men.**

<u>Mark 16:15-16</u>

. . . **Go ye into all the world, and preach the Gospel to every creature.**

He that believeth and is baptized shall be saved; but he that believeth not shall be damned.

<u>Acts 1:8</u>

But ye shall receive power, after that the Holy Ghost is come upon you: **and ye shall be witnesses unto Me both in Jerusalem, and in all Judea, and in Samaria, and unto the uttermost part of the earth.**

<u>Acts 4:13</u>

Now when they saw the boldness of Peter and John, and perceived that they were unlearned and ignorant men, they marvelled; and they took knowledge of them, **that they had been with Jesus.**

<u>Romans 1:16</u>

For I am not ashamed of the Gospel of Christ: **for it is the power of God unto salvation to every one that believeth;** to the Jew first, and also to the Greek.

For I am not ashamed of the Gospel (good news) of Christ, for it is God's power working unto salvation [for deliverance from eternal death] to everyone who believes with a personal trust and a confident surrender and firm reliance, to the Jew first and also to the Greek, [AMP]

<u>Romans 10:13-15</u>

For whosoever shall call upon the name of the Lord shall be saved.

How then shall they call on Him in Whom they have not believed? and how shall they believe in Him of Whom they have not heard? and how shall they hear without a preacher?

And how shall they preach, except they be sent? as it is written, **How beautiful are the feet of them that preach the Gospel of peace, and bring glad tidings of good things!**

<u>II Corinthians 9:13</u>

Because of the service by which you have proved yourselves, ***men will praise God for the obedience that accompanies your confession of the Gospel of Christ,*** *and for your generosity in sharing with them and with everyone else. [NIV]*

<u>II Timothy 4:5</u>

. . . **do the work of an evangelist,** make full proof of thy ministry.

<u>I Peter 3:15</u>

But sanctify the Lord God in your hearts: **and be ready always to give an answer to every man that asketh you a reason of the hope that is in you** with meekness and fear:

B. Scriptures to Share with Non-Believers

Matthew 10:32

Whosoever therefore shall confess Me before men, him will I confess also before My Father Which is in heaven.

John 1:12

But as many as received Him, to them gave He power to become the sons of God, even to them that believe on His name:

John 3:16-17

For God so loved the world, that He gave His only begotten Son, that whosoever believeth in Him should not perish, but have everlasting life.

For God sent not His Son into the world to condemn the world; but that the world through Him might be saved.

John 3:36

He that believeth on the Son hath everlasting life: and he that believeth not the Son shall not see life; but the wrath of God abideth on him.

John 14:6

Jesus saith unto him, I am the Way, the Truth, and the Life: no man cometh unto the Father, but by Me.

Acts 3:19

Repent ye therefore, and be converted, that your sins may be blotted out, when the times of refreshing shall come from the presence of the Lord;

Acts 4:12

Neither is there salvation in any other: **for there is none other name under heaven given among men, whereby we must be saved.**

Acts 16:31

And they said, **Believe on the Lord Jesus Christ, and thou shalt be saved, and thy house.**

Romans 3:10

As it is written, **There is none righteous, no, not one:**

Romans 3:23

For all have sinned, and come short of the glory of God;

Romans 5:8

But God commendeth His love toward us, in that, **while we were yet sinners, Christ**

died for us.

<u>**Romans 5:12**</u>

Wherefore, as by one man sin entered into the world, and death by sin; and **so death passed upon all men, for that all have sinned:**

<u>**Romans 6:23**</u>

For the wages of sin is death; but the gift of God is eternal life through Jesus Christ our Lord.

<u>**Romans 10:8-10**</u>

But what saith it? The word is nigh thee, even in thy mouth, and in thy heart: that is, the word of faith, which we preach;

That if thou shalt confess with thy mouth the Lord Jesus, and shalt believe in thine heart that God raised Him from the dead, thou shalt be saved.

For with the heart man believeth unto righteousness; and with the mouth confession is made unto salvation.

<u>**Romans 10:13**</u>

For whosoever shall call upon the name of the Lord shall be saved.

<u>**I Corinthians 15:1-4**</u>

Moreover, brethren, I declare unto you the Gospel which I preached unto you, which also ye have received, and wherein ye stand;

By which also ye are saved, if ye keep in memory what I preached unto you, unless ye have believed in vain.

For I delivered unto you first of all that which I also received, **how that Christ died for our sins according to the scriptures;**

And that He was buried, and that He rose again the third day according to the scriptures:

<u>**II Corinthians 5:17**</u>

Therefore if any man be in Christ, he is a new creature: old things are passed away; behold, all things are become new.

<u>**Galatians 2:16**</u>

Knowing that a man is not justified by the works of the law, but by the faith of Jesus Christ, even we have believed in Jesus Christ, that we might be justified by the faith of Christ, and not by the works of the law: **for by the works of the law shall no flesh be justified.**

<u>**Ephesians 2:8-9**</u>

For by grace are ye saved through faith; and that not of yourselves: it is the gift of God:

Not of works, lest any man should boast.

I Thessalonians 5:9-10

For God hath not appointed us to wrath, but to obtain salvation by our Lord Jesus Christ,

Who died for us, that, whether we wake or sleep, we should live together with Him.

I Timothy 2:4-6

Who will have all men to be saved, and to come unto the knowledge of the truth.

For there is one God, and one Mediator between God and men, the Man Christ Jesus;

Who gave Himself a ransom for all, to be testified in due time.

II Peter 3:9

The Lord is not slack concerning His promise, as some men count slackness; but is long-suffering to us-ward, not willing that any should perish, but that all should come to repentance.

I John 1:8-9

If we say that we have no sin, we deceive ourselves, and the truth is not in us.

If we confess our sins, He is faithful and just to forgive us our sins, and to cleanse us from all unrighteousness.

I John 5:11-13

And this is the record, **that God hath given to us eternal life, and this life is in His Son.**

He that hath the Son hath life; and he that hath not the Son of God hath not life.

These things have I written unto you that believe on the name of the Son of God; **that ye may know that ye have eternal life, and that ye may believe on the name of the Son of God.**

Revelations 3:20

Behold, I stand at the door, and knock: **if any man hear My voice, and open the door,** I will come in to him, and will sup with him, and he with Me.

Printed in the United States
78953LV00006BB/64